175 NOT OU

Nigel Jepson

175 Not Out!

Nigel Jepson

YOUCAXTON
PUBLICATIONS

ISBN 978-1-914424-59-5
Published by YouCaxton Publications 2022
YCBN: 01

YouCaxton Publications
www.youcaxton.co.uk

This book has been written as a celebration of the contributions and achievements of all who have played a part in the story of Ramsbottom Cricket Club, in whatever capacity, from its founding in 1845 onwards.

Please note: proceeds from sales of this book (allowing for an initial print-run of 200 copies) will transfer directly into R.C.C. funds, enabling the club to put the raised sum of money to use as it should so wish.

Contents

Photographs

Front Cover: Ramsbottom C.C. Pavilion with View of Peel Tower.

Selection 1: Between Chapters 4 & 5

1. Ramsbottom C.C. 1885
2. W. Fenwick: Player
3. W. Fenwick: Administrator
4. Jerry Ellis and Joe Leach 1903
5. Jack Redfern
6. Emmott Robinson
7. Fred Duerr
8. Bill Hickmott
9. Lancashire League Champions: 1921
10. Lancashire League Champions: 1925
11. New Ground 'Mechanical Appliance': 1926
12. Worsley Cup Winners: 1939
13. Syd Hird
14. Billy Whitworth
15. Worsley Cup Winners: 1957

Selection 2: Between Chapters 9 & 10

16. Peter Philpott
17. Seymour Nurse
18. Lancashire League Champions: 1974
19. 1974 Cup Presentation L. to R. – Duncan Brooks, Ronnie Greaves, Maurice Haslam, Ray Bright, Jim Cropper.
20. Sergeant Everett Wears Helmet; with 3-year-old daughter Zoe.
21. Murray Bennett Wears Shades
22. 2nd XI Cup Winning Team 1987
23. Ramsbottom 'Cricketing Ladies Committee'
24. Ian Chappell Pays a Return Visit to Acre Bottom 1989
25. Lancashire League Centenary Champions: 1992
26. Jack Simpson: Pincers Action at Church with Nick Riley

Sources and Acknowledgements

Chapters One to Four: 1845 to 1945.

A very important source in relation to the early years of the club was the 'History of Ramsbottom Cricket Club - 1845 to 1935': written by James Spencer, club secretary from 1935 to 1946. This 12-page history was incorporated into a *Souvenir Handbook* which came out in 1936 (priced one shilling), in aid of a *Floral Bazaar*, encompassing different fund-raising activities carried out that year at the club. Thanks to Maurice Haslam for providing this valuable resource.

Dave Edmundson's *See the Conquering Hero - the story of the Lancashire League: 1892 to 1992'* proved useful in respect of the whole of the period covered by the book, but particularly so in terms of describing how the Lancashire League came into being and Ramsbottom's involvement from those early years onwards. As with a lot of other book sources that usefully came my way, thanks to Peter Spencer.

Maurice Haslam and Ian Bell, joint 'custodians' of the heritage domain within the cricket club, have between them helped furnish a lot of relevant documents, for example '100 Not Out' - a souvenir programme brought out in 2004 - which celebrated the 100-year existence of the Pavilion. It not only provided interesting details relating to its construction back in 1904 but also a detailed account of the celebrated batting feats of pro Jerry Ellis and his opening batting partner at that time, Joe Leach. Further thanks to Maurice for providing me with access to a fascinating artefact – tiny in size but precious in content - namely, *The Ramsbottom Cricket Club Handbook for Season 1883*.

Chris Aspin, who has written a book on the history of Haslingden Cricket Club as well as many others on a range of different topics, is thanked for helping me track down the autobiography written by esteemed Lancashire cricketer, Richard Gorton Barlow (1851-1919), entitled *Forty Years of First-Class Cricket*. It was also through Chris that I came across the poem: *At Lord's* by Francis Thompson, nostalgically recalling his memory of seeing Lancashire's opening batsmen playing in a match (likely to have taken place in 1878), containing the line: 'O my Hornby and my Barlow long ago!'

Local historians Andrew Todd and John Simpson helped by advising on certain relevant newspaper source material, mostly in relation to the period up to the end of the First World War.

A source of major importance, in the broader context of this study, has been *Ramsbottom Cricket Club - 1845 to 1995 - A Sesquicentenary Celebration*, compiled and edited by Jim Rushton in 1995. With 'narrative contents' and a wealth of illustrations, including 'photographs and reproductions', it casts a highly informed eye over many different aspects of the history of the club up until virtually the end of the 20th century.

Ramsbottom Cricket Club is blessed in having a wide-ranging archive base, curated by Maurice and Ian, plus the bonus that so much of it is readily available for visitors to view on site. Further than this, behind the scenes, records exist on a year-by-year basis from the 1890s onwards with a range of different items stored, for example scorebooks and newspaper cuttings. Whilst it has to be said that the Lancashire League website is admirable for the sheer weight of information it contains going back to 1892, the opportunity to access primary source materials on the actual club ground gave a special feel to the research process.

It was this same aspect that attracted Nigel French to become a life-long fan of Rammy Cricket Club. On a tour of cricket grounds he had embarked on in the mid-1990s, he visited Acre Bottom, encountering the then club history 'curator', Alan Morris. Nigel's recall of Alan as an 'engaging, welcoming character who sold the club to me' provided interesting testimony from someone who, despite having to travel from Crosby, was so taken by the experience that he became a regular visitor and supporter, 'falling in love with the club and the town'. Thanks to Nigel for sharing his memories.

In relation to Emmott Robinson (pro at the club from 1908 to the end of 1913), the author has gratefully drawn on the various works of famous Manchester Guardian cricket writer, Neville Cardus, notably his inimitable descriptions of Robinson when he went on to play for Yorkshire in the early inter-war years. No doubt, as it was said at the time, Emmott picked up everything he knew from the time he spent playing at Rammy!

ooooo

With respect to the photos presented between Chapters 4 and 5, acknowledgement is gratefully made that quite a few of them were shown in the 'Sesquicentenary Celebration' booklet brought out in 1995.

ooooo

Chapters Five to Eight: 1946 to 1987.

Thanks to John Heys, Andrew Rothwell and Maureen Smith for sharing various memories and photographic material from the earlier years of this period. For example, Maureen's photos showing her as a teenager taking part in athletic events held at the club connect up interestingly with the fact that she was presented her prize by Harry Lambert (pro – 1949/50). Incidentally, another link Maureen had with the club was that her husband Ronnie served as Club secretary from 1973 to 1978.

Andrew Rothwell is related to Fred Rothwell, who apart from many other associations with the club such as 'Poets' Corner', was club scorer and appeared on a photo of the Worsley Cup winning side of 1957. As mentioned in the text, John's father Frank Heys was Club Treasurer from 1957 to 1962 and was later to become a greatly respected Chairman from 1964 to 1980.

The highly respected Australian cricketer, Peter Philpott (club pro: 1955 and 1959/60), sadly recently-deceased, contributed much to the story of Rammy's post-World War II years in his memoir: *Forty Years and Ramsbottom*. Peter's descriptions of notable characters he played with, such as Harold Monkhouse, and played against, for example Roy Gilchrist, are graphically well-drawn. In addition, the author is grateful to have been able to call upon and quote from his autobiography - *Two Times Thirty-Five* - kindly loaned by Maurice Haslam.

It is indeed from Peter Philpott's two spells as pro (1955 and 1959/60) that first-hand memories started to emerge from those who had benefitted from Peter coaching them as pupils at Peel Brow School in the late 50s. In this respect, the author's thanks to the Philpott-inspired intake of Henry Hall, Dally Brooks (communicating from Spain), Maurice Haslam, John Ashworth (from Australia) and Brian Fielding who, in the process of discussing their involvement at the club as a whole, all paid tribute to the exemplary role Peter Philpott played as mentor to them in their formative years. Incidentally, the above players are thanked also for sharing details of their subsequent on-going involvement with the club, particularly with respect to Maurice and Brian whose service to the club has been continuous in many different ways.

Meanwhile Brian Quinton, currently in his late 80s, and occupying 'senior position' as a source, is thanked for providing an account of his memories in association with the successful 1957 Worsley Cup winning campaign. Thanks also to his close contemporaries, Derek Webster and John Cardwell, for their recollections from these times.

In relation to the years Seymour Nurse spent as pro at the club (1961/2, 1964), John Steele's anecdotes proved both detailed and finely described, as one might expect from an English teacher, about the popular West Indian pro. Also, both he and John Ashworth provided defining accounts of the perils of facing up to the menacing West Indian speed merchant, Charlie Griffith.

Dally Brooks and Ray Bright memorably recalled the championship-winning season of 1974 as if it were yesterday! As did Maurice Haslam whose pen-portraits successfully evoke the character and abilities of colleagues from that campaign.

Mick Everett proved a mine of useful and interesting information regarding his involvement at the club, from the time he first started playing in 1977 onwards, featuring his memorable encounter with 'Whispering Death' Michael Holding in that famous match at Rishton (well-documented also in the national press), at the start of the 1981 season.

Apart from his assistance with resources, Ian Bell also was very informative in sharing memories and highlights of his long career as a batsman at the club.

Graham Ratcliffe is thanked for providing his witty description regarding when he acted as a runner for the injured Henry Hall in a second round Worsley Cup tie in 1983.

The greatly-respected Australian pro, Murray Bennett, responded fully and entertainingly to a request to re-kindle memories of what it was like coming over from Australia to be club pro in 1984.

Acknowledgement is owed to Tim Heald (now sadly deceased) for references from his 1986 book *The Character of Cricket*. Vividly, he described coming to the ground and meeting then-secretary, Peter Spencer (who kindly loaned me this book), and also Harry Williams, who happened to be serving behind the bar and at the same time marking the author's card as to be on his best behaviour!

In telling their own distinctive tales, Mark Price and Steve Monkhouse had in common that, in addition to playing for the Rams, they also spent considerable periods of time elsewhere as pros, including playing county cricket.

ooooo

With respect to the photos presented between Chapters 9 and 10, the author benefitted hugely from Maurice Haslam's very special 'collection', as both photographer in his own right but in addition as collator of other suitable photographic material that he rendered available for the book.

ooooo

Chapters Nine to Thirteen: 1988 to 2020/21

Jon Fielding, like his father Brian, had also found himself drawn into playing pro cricket beyond Rammy. In his own case, this came about following being part of the championship-winning team of 1992.

Although later returning to the club from 2010 onwards, appreciation goes out to him for the description he gave of the critical home match that took place against Haslingden during the course of the 1992 campaign in addition to observations concerning the further championship-winning 2010 season.

Jack Simpson (now living in Spain) is thanked for providing a detailed account of his highly successful time at the club from 1987 to 1996.

The author was grateful to be able to draw on various quotations from the autobiography of record-breaking New Zealand pro, Chris Harris, entitled *Harry: The Chris Harris Story*, including reference to first impressions, back in 1995, of encountering then Chairman Brian Fielding and Manager Mick Everett.

Various programmes from Worsley Cup finals were kindly loaned the author by Peter Spencer, starting with that against Bacup in 1996. Thanks also to Ben Dack for his memories from that match, as well as those provided by Steve Dearden.

A particular publication of interest which Maurice Haslam and Ian Bell brought to my notice was *Beyond the Boundary: A Celebration of the Lancashire Cricket League* (1998). Interestingly, it contained highlights of the history of each of the fourteen clubs. As was mentioned in the text, each of the clubs was required to name the one special player considered to be their greatest pro of all times. The Rams had selected Chris Harris.

Duncan Hamilton's book *Last English Summer* (2010) provided an extremely useful source, particularly the chapter entitled *See the Conquering Hero Comes* which described a visit to Acre Bottom. As well as watching the match against Accrington on the day, Hamilton discussed with then Chairman Rod Hamer the challenge of clubs like Rammy remaining solvent. The answer was that, to do so, the club was dependent on having an army of volunteers helping out, plus money taken from hiring out social facilities.

Picking up on this particular theme, gratitude is expressed for the willingness of all the following to discuss the role they had played at the club from 2009 onwards (and in many instances before that time) in terms of service on the Club's committee: Rod Hamer, Peter Spencer (about to reach his 50th year serving in a variety of roles on the committee), John Fox (current Chairman), Jon Fielding (current Vice-Chairman), Ben

Dack (Treasurer), Sheila McQueeney (Club Secretary), Carol Rothwell (Membership Secretary), Rob Read (Sponsorship Secretary) and Andy Dalby (League Representative).

In particular, my thanks to John Fox, not only for entering into informative detail about his different levels of involvement up to the present time but also for facilitating opportunities for me to speak with committee members and other people whom, in his role as Chairman, he has responsibility for oversight of their work.

In relation to conversation with Andy Dalby, apart from the aspect of his job as 'League Representative', I was grateful to have chance to discuss with him his experience as Director of Cricket since 2009 during which period of time the club has enjoyed such notable success on different competitive fronts.

Grateful thanks also for the chance to have had time to talk with current Committee members such as Harry Williams, Andrew Rothwell and Phil Croft, as well as valued Life Members of the club, Derek Read and Jack Wolfenden, both of whom, as with Harry, have served on both cricketing and footballing fronts across the Acre Bottom site as a whole.

Speaking with Phil Croft helped get to grips with all the latest developments - as described in the Introduction and Postscript - that are taking shape both in the women's section and also in younger girl and boy age-groups. Likewise, meeting Iain Round helped the author become better informed, particularly covering ins and outs of cricketing life over recent years at 2nd and 3rd XI levels.

In addition, the opportunity to hold conversations with groundsmen Roger Davies and Phil Heaton was greatly appreciated. Also with bar manager Sophie Fletcher and 'man-on-the-gate' Scott Heywood both of whom, incidentally, were already known to me from when I was researching the book on Rammy United: *Come On You Rams* (2020).

With specific regard to Harry Williams, the author was in a similar way well-acquainted with his pivotal role in establishing the football club on the Acre Bottom site from 1980 onwards. He too in his early youth had been part of Peter Philpott's 'class' at Peel Brow School only to end up channelling his sporting energies subsequently towards football management. Whilst at the same time having continued to serve for so long on the Rammy Cricket Club committee, Harry's role has been highly influential in helping the two 'operations' on site link up so well from 1980 right up until the present time.

Reference has already been made to the splendid Lancashire League website. For the purposes of this study, it has proved a magnificent tool in terms of getting to grips with the statistical side of things, e.g. scorecards, player details, league tables, reviews of seasons, details of club presentation evenings etc. Apart from acknowledging the wealth of data that it was possible to draw upon, credit needs giving to website co-ordinator Nigel Stockley for being approachable, friendly and highly efficient in handling any collateral inquiries/questions put his way.

As well as all the different databases on the Lancashire League's website, it helped that there were further additional outlets to tap into. A very interesting one was *Features - Match of a Lifetime: My Favourite Game*. Under this heading, for example, the chance arose to gain further insights into the magnificent triple Cup-winning year of 2010 - courtesy of a four-part section entitled: *Ramsbottom finds the Missing Link*. In tandem with reviews of individual matches Rammy had played in that year, an attached personal commentary from skipper Jon Fielding provided an engrossing 'running diary' as to how he saw matters progressing at different critical stages during that particular season.

2010 marked the start of an intensely successful period of time in the club's history. Acknowledgement is duly given here to the contributions made by a host of 'millennial' players taking part in the project by discussing with the author their involvement in this more recent 'era', notably Mick Haslam, Simon Read, Mark Dentith, David Bell (made contact with in Denmark), Alex Bell, Rob Read and Chris Wood. Following on from this, a very thorough and interesting telephone conversation took place with Tom Parton (currently based in Australia). In addition, thanks to Daryn Smit for talking through his considerable and massively successful involvement with the club as pro.

Special thanks to Jon Fielding, who as well as being willing to relate and share accounts of matches, also provided a variety of interesting memorabilia, all of which gave great 'added-value' to the project, including photos, letters and newspaper clippings.

Another book, more recently written about cricket in general – but which carried a most useful section in it on Ramsbottom - is Michael Henderson's *That Will Be England Gone: The Last Summer of Cricket* (2020). Briefly having chance to talk with the author at the ground, when he was visiting to watch a game, thanks also to Michael for his lending encouragement towards the writing of this book.

Mention has been made of the Lancashire League website. Despite naturally being more limited in scope, credit needs also to be paid to Ramsbottom Cricket Club's own website, ably co-ordinated by Graham Ratcliffe. Further acknowledgement is owed on the basis that virtually all the statistical data, incorporated into the 'Appendices' item of this book, stems from the 'Hall of Fame' section on the Rammy club website.

Most tellingly of all, this book could not have been written without Maurice Haslam's personal assistance and support. His understanding of cricket is vast in overall terms but his knowledge surrounding club and league matters has proved utterly invaluable to the author on so many different fronts. No-one could have been more patient and reliable. He has such a healthy, innate respect for club traditions that fitted in superbly with the original concept that this book would be put together in the way of celebrating 175 years of proud Ramsbottom Cricket Club history.

ooooo

Ending this section with reference more towards my own 'home front', I wish to pay credit to my wife Anna for her support in many different ways across the recent months it has taken to carry out the project. In the course of occasional conversation involving wives of club cricketers, I became aware of the term 'cricketing widow'. However, despite the fact I spent so many solitary hours and days hammering away on the word processor in an upstairs room of the house, Anna often though still found herself being called upon to bale out her husband, not least on technological grounds. Even though Anna's interest in cricket itself never raised itself much beyond Level One, her value in terms of providing I.T. back-up was always up there towards Level Ten.

Likewise, I would like to thank daughters Sarah and Kathryn, who, although having a similar level of (i.e. lack of) interest in the subject-matter, were always supportive in terms of listening to Dad going on about this latest book he was intent on writing.

Introduction

WRITING A HISTORY of Ramsbottom Cricket Club seemed a natural progression from having written a history of Ramsbottom Football Club in 2020. That's how it seemed to me but I felt a need to check what others may have thought on the matter..

Initially, I consulted Maurice Haslam and Mick Everett, two longstanding stalwarts of the Cricket Club. Now in their seventies - their illustrious playing days long over - the pair of them though had not only stayed good friends in the meantime but also both remained closely connected with the club in a number of different ways up to the present day.

I had first come across Maurice and Mick as a fellow-user of the leisure facilities of the Old Mill Hotel in Ramsbottom. They often went there, as part of a group, to take part in light physical exercise before using the spa facilities. From the banter that flowed amongst the members of this group - apart from regular mention of Mick's 'dodgy knees' - it was obvious they shared a common love of sport and of cricket in particular. Even though I didn't grasp it immediately, they all happened to have strong links with the local cricket club, including members of the Read family, Derek, son Simon and nephew Rob.

For my own part, despite having lived in Rammy since the mid-90s, I had only begun taking an interest in local cricket from 2010 onwards, the season when the Rams had famously lifted the Lancashire League championship trophy.

That I had not gone to watch before was remiss of me. Not least because the house I live in stands on a hillside directly overlooking the Acre Bottom cricket ground. For example, back in the 2002 season, when Michael Clarke was club pro, whilst out in the back garden, I had often heard his name announced on the PA system for having clocked up yet another half- or full century. Even so, I still hadn't got round to wandering down to the ground and witnessing first-hand the feats achieved by this talented young Aussie. My considerable loss! Between 2004 and 2015, Michael was to go on to play 115 Test matches for Australia, scoring 8,643 runs at an average of close to 50 per innings.

Later on, after beginning to watch more regularly from 2010 onwards, I grew interested in becoming a Club Member. I found I needed two existing members to back my application. Who else but Maurice and Mick? Chancing upon them at the ground one match-day, I interrupted their viewing to ask if they would kindly attach their signatures to the form I was filling in. Gladly, they obliged. It was Derek Read, sitting close by at the time, who said – 'You've got the best two names you could have there!'

Anyway, when I was later to put the question to them of writing a book about the club, they appeared to take to the idea. In fact, the timing was just right, they stated, because it would coincide with an upcoming landmark in the club's history – namely, celebrations surrounding the club's 175th year since having been founded in 1845.

How best to progress? Maurice set up a meeting with Club Chairman, John Fox, and Vice Chairman, Jon Fielding, who also seemed keen on the project moving forward. Having the chance to meet up in the club pavilion was a nice touch which added an extra sense of occasion. After all, it is well-known that the green and cream striped edifice is iconic in cricketing history from the time it had been constructed in 1904, invariably eliciting praise from visitors to the ground.

Originally from Shropshire, John Fox's family had moved to Heywood in the 1970s. John played at 2nd and 3rd XI Ramsbottom Cricket Club levels in the 1990s; subsequently devoting his time towards conducting his local business, SIPP Liberty. He has played a leading role in sponsoring both Ramsbottom cricketing and footballing establishments.

Regarding Vice Chair, Jon Fielding, his reputation as a 1st XI player at the club is truly legendary in every respect. Much of the latter half of this book covers his various exploits over the years.

After receiving formal go-ahead from John and Jon, Maurice Haslam offered to play the role of 'link contact', facilitating matters such as arranging meetings with ex-players and other relevant processes like gaining access to documentary evidence on the history of the club.

My first follow-up session with Maurice, to start the ball rolling, took place in the so-called 'Long Room' of Ramsbottom Cricket Club pavilion. First impression being that it was meticulously set out in a style reminiscent of Lords' itself. With a natural sense of pride, Maurice - together with fellow-curator of the 'shrine', Ian Bell - provided me with a mini- tour of the Long Room, for which I was very grateful. Ian, by the way, is another notable, former club-player.

The wall-space of the Long Room is crammed with a whole host of pictures and artefacts, which combine to tell the story of all the great 'legends' who have played for the club. One immediate impression was the sheer quality of the pros (the so-called 'paid men') who, from the 1930s onwards, had ventured from overseas to play at Rammy, including:

- Aussie cricketers of the stature of Syd Hird, Peter Philpott, Ray Bright, Ian Chappell, Keith Stackpole, Murray Bennett, David Hookes, Brad Hodge and Michael Clarke (he of the summer of 2002!) and Alex Doolan;
- South Africans of the calibre of Eddie Fuller, Clive Rice, Brian McMillan, Francois du Plessis, Pieter Malan, and more latterly Sen Muthusamy as well as the outstanding Daryn Smit;
- West Indians of the quality of Seymour Nurse and Keith Arthurton;
- Indian sub-continent players of the ilk of Bapu Nadkarni, Wasim Raja, Karson Ghavri, Kartik Murali and Sunil Joshi;
- New Zealander Kiwi Chris Z. Harris, with the stunning credential of being only one of four players in the entire history of the Lancashire League to have performed the 'double' of scoring a thousand runs and taking a hundred wickets in a season.

At the same time, it would be committing an injustice to suggest though that the club's 'legends' have been confined to international stars such as quoted above. Unquestionably, the club has been highly fortunate in having also been able to call upon the talents of an amazing array of cricketers, many of them celebrated too on the walls of the

Long Room, hailing from the local area in and around Ramsbottom itself.

ooooo

Founded in 1845, the game has been played on its present Acre Bottom site since 1864. A vital milestone in the history of Ramsbottom Cricket Club followed came about through connecting up to the newly-formed Lancashire League from 1892 onwards. Several great players, emerging from the local area, successfully represented the club from this time onwards.

For example, William Fenwick, who was to become a longstanding club administrator when his playing days finished, took a phenomenal 137 wickets in the season of 1900. Further on in time, Rammy's Fred Duerr and English pro Bill Hickmott, having formed a deadly bowling partnership, were to be pivotal in the club capturing its first two championship wins in 1921 and 1925.

With regard to both professional and amateur players, there have been many outstanding individuals whose achievements warrant recognition. However, the important lesson to be learnt over the years was that the most successful sides in the club's history, especially so in more recent times, depended upon operating as a unit and drawing out good team performances. This can be sensed just by glancing at any of the team photos on display in the Long Room and picking out the proud looks on the faces of the many different trophy-winning sides.

The club's 'Roll of Honour' - see in the Appendices - presents the full list of League trophies won over the years. For example, the championship title has been won six times to date. After the title wins of 1921 and 1925, the next season was 1974, followed by 1992 (the Lancashire League's centenary year), 2010 and 2016. The circumstances in which victory was achieved in each of these campaigns were very different and make for compelling reading, especially with ex-players, such as Maurice Hallam and Jon Fielding, providing personal insights into matches, players and various incidents of note.

Regarding the Worsley Cup, Rammy had only won it twice previously, in 1939 and 1957, before going on something of a spree between 1996 and 2011, winning it six times. These victories were all down to great team efforts.

Completing the 'big four' trophy roster, the Colne and 20/20 Cups are relatively recent additions. The Colne Cup, the curtain-raiser for each season in a similar manner to football's Charity Cup, was introduced in 1997. The Rams had the honour of lifting the trophy in this inaugural season, to be followed by further victories in 2006, 2010, 2011 and 2017.

The 20/20 competition is still more recent but the Rams took to the format very quickly and have picked up the trophy on four occasions already, in 2010, 2011, 2012, 2019. As can be seen from the above, there were two seasons – 2010 and 2011 – in which the club was to win three trophies, just falling short of the 'quadruple'.

The achievements of the 2nd and 3rd XI's are also taken account of, the notable stand-out years for the 2nds being when they pulled off a 'double double' of championship and cup title wins in 2006 and 2007.

ooooo

The principal aim of this project has been as much as possible to seek out first-hand accounts from individuals who have been actively involved with the club, either as players or in other relevant capacity. Of course, it has to be appreciated that Ramsbottom Cricket Club goes back all the way to 1845! In the event, the earliest 'living memories' it was possible to call upon in this study have been those of current octogenarian ex-players such as Brian Quinton, Derek Webster, John Cardwell, Henry Hall and John Steele, whose recollections stem back as far as the 1950s.

In relation to pursuit of evidence over the period of time prior to this, much useful detail was unearthed from the club's archive base plus that of the Lancashire League website, as well a rich variety of resource materials, all of which are itemised in the section under 'Sources and Acknowledgements'.

ooooo

Until very recently, the Lancashire League was able to boast something of an almost unique record in terms of continuity: namely, that its structure had remained unaltered since 1897, the year when Todmorden had joined as a fourteenth league-member. Any organisation's strength though is also shown by its ability to adapt to circumstances arising that bring about the need for change.

The precise ways in which the League's structure and membership have evolved in more recent times has also proved interesting to track. There is no doubt that, as with many other local leagues, the Lancashire League found itself having to face up to a serious challenge from the turn of the 21st century onwards, and not only just in financial terms, in order to remain a viable entity. The fact that the league has not only managed to survive but also become stronger can be attributed to having been willing to adopt an open-minded attitude whilst also sticking by the principle of involving local communities at grass-roots level.

Ramsbottom Cricket Club has unquestionably exemplified this spirit. From 1845 onwards, its success has come about through maintaining on-going ties between club and community. That is plainly evident in the commitment and loyalty that ex-players continue to demonstrate towards their club, for example through attendance at regular reunion events but in a host of other active ways besides.

Added to this, there is clear determination at the present time to broaden the basis of community involvement further. For example, as well as the traditional provision of three men's teams, major emphasis has been focussed in recent seasons on developing the women's section and also an accelerated programme of Academy involvement of both boys and girls. The 'All Stars' entry level participation programme for children aged five to eight, through from the 8 to 11 year-old 'Dynamos' programme, with qualified coaches at Level 2 or 3, provides support and tuition aimed at fostering a love of the sport.

All this bodes very well for the club's future success!

Nigel Jepson, November 30, 2021.

One: Ramsbottom Cricket Club is Founded

ALTHOUGH IT WAS in 1845 that Ramsbottom Cricket Club came into formal existence, the game of cricket was played in the local area on an informal basis well before this. With the industry and population of the town developing rapidly during the 1820s and 1830s, there was also a growing interest in playing sport. Even if long working hours in the new factories meant that leisure time was limited, there is certainly evidence to show that cricket had already become popular amongst a group of young men who were to prove influential in the club's formation in the mid-1840s.

One was George Goodrick, tenant landlord of the Grant Arms Hotel which stood at the 'Top o' th' Brow' in the Market Square. Noted for the quality of his underarm bowling, this was at a time when controversy raged across the country as to the respective merits of this delivery technique compared with the lately developed overarm version.

As landlord, Goodrick played an important role in organising what took place in the way of games and practices. Meanwhile, no doubt, the flow of alcohol would have served to fuel camaraderie in the same way that it has continued to do up to the present day!

In such circumstances, a group of players emerged during these years that would be at the heart of the decision taken in 1845 to form Ramsbottom Cricket Club. Chief among these 'founders' were three members of the local Stead family - Lawrence, Henry and Joseph Stead. The family was to gain a solid reputation as cotton manufacturers in the town, having learnt the business by working first at the Grant factory known as 'The Square'. In 1854, the firm of Messrs Lawrence Stead & Brother was formed and their business expanded so quickly that they

1

were soon employing up to a thousand workers. It is noted that all the Steads were of 'exceptionally fine physique, strong, genial-natured and sympathetic.'

The above is quoted from a *History of Ramsbottom Cricket Club - Its Rise and Progress - 1845 to 1935* which came to be written in 1936 by James Spencer, club secretary from 1935 to 1946. This twelve-page piece of work is an invaluable source by way of providing evidence about the period in question.

Meanwhile, other players from this time were William and Edward Ashton, members of another factory-owning family who, along with the Grants, owned a considerable amount of land and properties in and around Ramsbottom. It can be seen from the membership, as described so far, that the initial development of the sport of cricket in the town stemmed from the involvement of the well-heeled or, in the case of George Goodrick, well-placed.

The only other name of a player which can be traced back to these formative years is that of Edward Ashworth. Although living further down the Rossendale valley, he apparently stopped by on his journeys to trading markets in Manchester. He was known to be an excellent wicket-keeper.

Two impediments stood in the way of their evident passion to play the game. First of all, finding the time. Work ethos demanded a minimum of seventy hours a week. That is why practice sessions were often arranged to take place, light permitting, very early in the morning. No concessions by way of time-off would be afforded to any member of a factory-owning family. To the contrary, demands were likely to be greater, by way of needing to be seen to set an example to the broader work-force.

The second was finding somewhere to play. The first site used was on a newly-mown meadow at Dickfield, near Kibboth Crew. However, it was far from ideal. 'Kenyon's Field', close to the river side, was secured fairly soon after. In all, five temporary sites - none of them satisfactory - were used over a period of some twenty years before the club became established on its current Acre Bottom site in or about 1864.

Regarding matches played against teams from other towns, the first such recorded encounter is one against Accrington, although no exact date has been found as to when it took place. The match happened in curious circumstances. It appears that an Accrington side had been journeying to play a match in Bury but, owing to some mishap, it had never got going or else been abruptly terminated. Breaking off on their return journey in Ramsbottom, they had been invited to join in some kind of practice taking place.

The upshot of this was that a prospective match was arranged between the two sides. It was one which Accrington might have been expected to win but it was Ramsbottom who emerged victors. Although lacking any evidence such as a scorecard, the decisive factor in the game appeared to have been Goodrick's bowling.

However, the main aspect of the match to stick most strongly in the memory of those attending was the presence of a character called 'Owd Bassett', the so-called public bellman. As town-crier, his booming tones carried vast distances. 'A local inhabitant said that once when walking along the summit of Holcombe Hill he heard Bassett's voice from all the way down in Bridge Street crying out: "Cockles and mussels for sale" as clearly as if he had been ten yards away'.

For this particular match, Bassett seems to have set himself up as a one-man PA system and much more besides: 'He was attired in a coat of many colours, manufactured from a piece of carpeting, and wore a straw hat, his waistcoat and trousers also being of unusual material and appearance. He walked about the ground entertaining the visitors with gestures, stories and an exhibition of his vocal 'strength'.

Another well-remembered match from these earliest times was one arranged by John Hill, a Stubbins Mill manager, the visitors being a team from Manchester. 'The city men smiled at the underhand bowling of their opponents, but grew serious when they found themselves all out for 34. However, the smile returned when six of the Ramsbottom side fell without a run being scored. Then James Spencer (late Registrar of Births and Deaths) and Will Heap between them scored over 20, and in the end Ramsbottom had a decisive victory'.

The decision to move to the Acre Bottom site was not a straightforward one. It involved club members having to carry out a lot of work on the site, for example draining and filling in a 'lodge of water', the size of a small lake, and levelling out a large embankment. In the case of all of the grounds the club had played on to date, it had involved hiring the land off its owners. Acre Bottom was no different with the land being owned in the mid-1860s by William Grant junior who had inherited the Nuttall estate when his father John had died in 1855.

William Grant was to serve as the first President of the club from 1869 until 1874. It is not thought that William had played locally in his youth. He was the first member of the Grant family to have been educated within the public school system where playing cricket was not just a sport but a religion. However, the Grants were above all else businessmen and this did not preclude charging the club an annual rental sum, a practice which was to go on until the club eventually bought the land from Sir Peter Grant Lawson in 1947 at a cost of £1,000, courtesy of a 'house to house collection made by members to defray the cost.'

In 1879, the importance of ensuring the club had a playable wicket was underlined by the first professional appointment being made of 'Roberts of Accrington', who was engaged as groundsman and also played for the club for two seasons. The year Roberts arrived coincided with the unusual occurrence of a match played in the evening "by the aid of Electric Light". While it is not known for sure whether this event marked a world precedent by way of a night match, the experiment appears to have backfired, incurring financial loss into the bargain.

In 1881, the club took a bigger step in the direction of entering into the realm of professionalism with the signing of Arthur Thornton of Saltaire (close to Bradford) as full-time pro on a decent enough annual salary for the time of £54. It appears he was not only popular but an excellent player and coach. In the same year, a new pavilion was constructed at a cost of £150. With the club aware of the need to enlist financial support from its membership, a 'bazaar' was held which succeeded in raising £226, not only paying for the pavilion but also helping to reduce existing club debts.

A curious match took place on 5 August 1882 when all the players were dressed in the "old style" with tall hats and black trousers. Prestigiously, an All-England XI appeared at Acre Bottom in 1884 which included the following: Hornby, Barlow, Briggs, Nash and Robinson of Lancashire County, Ulyett, Bates, Peate, Hall and Hunter of Yorkshire County, also Lockwood of Surrey County. Such touring professional teams no doubt greatly helped strengthen the popularity of cricket in the various mill towns of Lancashire. In his autobiography, *Forty Seasons of First-Class Cricket*, one of the cricketers named above - Richard Gorton Barlow - described playing in a game at Ramsbottom where a batsman's shot struck the wooden leg of the umpire standing at square leg, causing him an unpleasant fall.

An indication of the type of teams Rammy more generally played against at this time is provided in the *Ramsbottom Cricket Club Handbook for Season 1883*. On page 60, it is interesting to view the fixture-list itemised for the year ahead. It can be seen that quite a lot of the matches were scheduled to take place against clubs that would, in the not-too-distant future, end up joining Rammy as founder-members of the Lancashire League from 1892 onwards.

The earliest surviving photograph of a team representing Ramsbottom Cricket Club is one taken in 1885, showing some of the players in the types of striped jackets and hooped caps that were, in sporting terms, making fashion statements typical of those late Victorian times. Although the structure of county cricket as we know it to-day did not develop until 1890, many matches were played before this time between representative county XIs. The spread of railways from the 1840s onwards greatly enhanced the scope for cricket teams to travel wider distances across the country.

Even if cricket had traditionally been seen as a 'gentleman's sport', it had soon been taken up by the industrial middle classes. Beyond this, cricket was also now beginning to become popular amongst the 'grass roots working-class population'. Towns in Lancashire were crying out for the development of sports and activities to give young men healthy recreation and also as an expression of civic pride.

The regimented Factory System had spread so rapidly across the East Lancashire region that even the mill-owner bosses recognised the need to do something to help provide their workers with some more positive way of spending their leisure-time beyond frequenting beer-houses to drown their sorrows from the drudgery of the workplace.

A whole host of clubs from different towns and areas across East Lancashire had sprung up at roughly the same time as Ramsbottom C.C. had. For example, Colne had originally started out as a club in 1830 but disbanded in 1854 before being revived in 1860. Burnley was founded in 1834 and Accrington a year later in 1846. Then Haslingden (1853), Church (1856), Enfield (1859), Bacup (1860), Lowerhouse (1864), East Lancashire (1864), Rishton (1865). Nelson had been formed in 1878 and Rawtenstall in 1886. What these particular clubs had in common was that they were destined to become founder members of the much-vaunted Lancashire League that would come into being in 1892.

In the meantime, until agreement was reached as to forming a centrally-regulated league, matches between East Lancashire clubs had continued to be organised on an 'ad hoc' basis with often riotous consequences, particularly in local derbies. For example, the Bacup Times of 1879 commented on crowd behaviour in matches between Bacup and Haslingden: 'A bitter spirit of rivalry exists between the two clubs, and whenever a match takes place, the game is attended with deplorable ill-spirit and ungovernable excitement on the part of spectators'.

The free spirit in which cricket had started out being played in the 1840s was now crying out for tighter organisation and governance if the sport was to prosper further. This much was clear after the representatives of thirteen cricket clubs – including Ramsbottom – signed up in 1890 to establishing the North-East Lancashire League. This was the short-lived forerunner to the Lancashire League proper which would come into being at the start of 1892. The thirteen founder members were later to accede to Todmorden joining the league in 1897 as a fourteenth member.

Significantly, the late 1880s and opening years of the 1890s were to witness a number of fledgling Cricket Leagues setting up in Lancashire. It is thought the Bolton Association, in 1888, was one of the first Cricket Leagues founded across the whole country. Only a few years after, in 1892, not only the Lancashire League came into being but also the Central Lancashire League and the Ribblesdale League.

ooooo

Only two years before Ramsbottom Cricket Club joined the Lancashire League in the year of 1892, one of the founding fathers of Ramsbottom Cricket Club, George Goodrick, landlord of the Grant

Arms to the end, died in his eighty-sixth year and was laid to rest with honour at St. Andrew's Church, Ramsbottom, on 31 January 1890.

It is hard to know for sure what he would have made of the town's commitment to becoming part of this new League structure. One suspects though, from the troubles he took to try and organise cricketing life in those early days back in the 1840s, that he would have welcomed the development with open arms, even if his favoured underarm style of delivery had long since passed into disuse.

Two: William Fenwick Takes 137 Wickets in a Season

WILLIAM FENWICK WAS a major force for Ramsbottom in the early Lancashire League years, winning fame for capturing the highest number of wickets in a season. He did so in the year 1900 and the record still holds to this day. His remarkable tally read:

Overs	Maidens	Runs	Wickets	Average
328.3	46	997	137	7.27

By way of trying to put the achievement into some sort of perspective, this marked the first time an amateur player had taken more than a hundred wickets in a season since the League had started in 1892. With the fourteen teams in the league competition playing each other home and away, making a total of 26 matches played, amassing 137 wickets represented a staggeringly high average of 5.27 wickets per innings. The term '5for' was not in currency at the time but Fenwick managed the feat virtually every match that season, achieving five hat-tricks along the way.

The tone for this season was set in the very first match, played at home on 14 April 1900 against East Lancashire. During the course of it, Ramsbottom created another record, still existing to this day, by dismissing an opposition team for the lowest score in League history, bowling out East Lancashire for a total of only 8 runs. Fenwick took 7 for 3 and professional Walter Taylor 2 for 5 with the other wicket being a run out. Ramsbottom themselves had scored a mere 45 runs and it might have been a much closer outcome had it not been for Joe Leach scoring over half of that total before being bowled out for a priceless 24 on the day.

Incidentally, Joe Leach proved an invaluable stalwart for the club in its early years. He had started playing in 1892 and would continue until 1920, accumulating 7,468 runs, making him third highest amateur run scorer in club history, headed only in later times by Billy Whitworth and Ian Bell. Taking account again of the statistics of the 1900 match against East Lancashire, Leach was certainly the exception to the rule operating at the time, that batsmen were mere cannon fodder for bowlers.

There is no doubt that in the early years of the League, ball ruled over bat to a stunning degree. The match, described above, against East Lancashire might be viewed as an extreme example of low innings totals. However, it was very common for sides to be bowled out for scores under three figures during the period running up to 1914. Pitches still played unreliably, enabling bowlers to assert the upper hand. Statistics show that even the professionals found it tough going making runs. And if a club pro wasn't able to make good runs, there was little hope further down the order.

This is not to detract though from the remarkable bowling record achieved by William Fenwick. Even if favoured by the prevailing state of pitches, it cannot be denied he succeeded in exploiting the situation to the full. Although the wonder year of 1900 represented the pinnacle for him, Fenwick was a consistently good performer over the years he played, taking 512 wickets in his career, making him the fifth leading wicket-taker in the club's history. However, he played in many fewer matches than those above him in the rank order. Tellingly, if the strike rate of balls bowled per wicket is taken into account, Fenwick is way ahead of the field at 19.01 compared to the next contender in this category, Fred Duerr standing at 25.94.

Fenwick's playing career came to an end in the early years of the century but he went on to serve the Club as Hon. Treasurer from 1919 to 1938 and as President from 1947 to 1950. He also was on the Committee of Lancashire County Cricket Club and was Chairman of the Ground Committee.

In his Annual Report in 1951, Jack Isherwood, Hon. Secretary of the Lancashire League, concluded his statement in respectful honour of the recently departed William Fenwick with the observation: 'His well-played innings of 87 will leave its mark for many years to come'.

ooooo

One particular requirement of the League, since its inception, was that clubs were to host professional players, the quota at first being two. It was determined at two per club - no more, no less - to make it a level playing-field for everyone. The practice of employing professionals was not of course new. In fact, by making it two per club, the League was setting out to regularise an existing situation which was often getting out of hand. For example, Haslingden had had as many as five pros on their pay-roll in the build-up to a needle match against Bacup in 1891.

From the start of the League onwards until the turn of the century, the pro pairings for Ramsbottom were:

1892/93/94 - Daff Whittaker and N. Jackson;

1895 - Daff Whittaker and Fred Hassall;

1896 - Ellis Town and A.E. Hatfield;

1897 - Ellis Town and Joshua Penny;

1898 - Frank Shacklock and A. White;

1899 - Ernest Creighton and H. Page

Not much is known about many of these players beyond the statistics they achieved on the field of play. More is known though about David (Daff) Whittaker, a left-handed batsman and left arm medium-pace bowler. He was 35 on first arriving at Ramsbottom and had played a few games for Lancashire but for the most part his previous experience was at club cricket level. Over the four years he was with Rammy, he fared well enough, scoring 1,578 runs at an average of 20.76 while taking 345 wickets at 8.98. In 1896, he moved to Rishton. It was reported in his obituary that, becoming despondent at a later time when he could no longer earn a living as a pro cricketer, he tragically took his own life in 1901.

In cricketing terms, N. Jackson and Fred Hassall achieved more with the bat than they did with the ball. Ellis Town, although not a prolific run-scorer, took 108 wickets in his two seasons at an average of 10.69. All other players listed above were also much more proficient as bowlers. While a few had had some experience at Minor Counties level, Frank Shacklock was more renowned for the fact that, though he was coming to the club at the age of 37, he had played regularly for both Nottinghamshire and Derbyshire at county level.

∞∞∞

It is hard to appreciate nowadays how differently the concept of professionalism was viewed at that time. Pros were seen as mercenaries and granted low social status, regarded as paid servants of club members and addressed by surname only. They needed to have broad shoulders in all kinds of ways, not having to be sensitive when ordered to perform menial tasks by those who saw themselves as superior within a class-ridden society that was prevalent then and arguably continued to remain so up until at least the end of the 1930s.

Pros were expected to do all the 'donkey work' during the week, including for example bowling on demand in the nets, maintaining and cleaning members' boots and kit, tending the wicket and carrying out all aspects of ground maintenance. Then, when it came to the weekends, they were naturally expected to bowl the opposition out cheaply whilst making a decent contribution with the bat.

Most conducted themselves with good enough grace. After all, their livelihood depended on doing so. However, there were instances recorded in Lancashire League documents of unacceptable behaviour on the part of pros, for example one being in a drunken state at the start of a game and another found guilty of match-fixing.

Choosing the 'right' kind of pro was very important. Clubs expected good all-round character but first and foremost placed value on prowess as a bowler. The advent of the leagues had proved a very useful source of employment for pros. The profile of many of them was that they were good enough to have been taken on at county level at an early stage of their career but then proved not quite good enough to be retained. By joining a league team, they were cutting their losses. There were certainly no internationals or world stars playing in the Lancashire League at this time.

Even though the wages paid were far from high, a year's position at a league club provided pros with greater security in financial terms compared with the haphazard existence of nominally being on the books of a county club but not a member of the first XI.

ooooo

The ruling that each club should have two pros was not to last long. With a lot of the less well-off clubs finding it hard to keep up with paying a double amount of wages, the dispensation was made in 1900 to reduce capacity to a single 'paid man' per club.

Despite those spectacular achievements of 1900, the Rams had ended the season only in 6th place. This broadly reflected placings the club had achieved from 1892 onwards with a best position to date of 3rd in 1895. Walter Taylor (pro from 1900 to 1902) had shown himself a useful all-rounder, scoring 1,411 runs at an average of 20.45 as well as taking 210 wickets at 12.85. When Taylor's three-year tenure finished at the end of the 1902 season, much was anticipated of the new pro signed up in his place, Jerry Ellis.

Born in Summerseat in 1866, he had been on the books of Lancashire County Cricket Club between 1892 and 1898 but did not get much of a chance to play in the first team. He managed only six appearances, although in one of these he had achieved figures of 8-21 against Leicestershire. His main success to date had been playing for Bolton and he was a well-respected professional player on the Lancashire circuit.

Aged 37 when he signed for Ramsbottom, the club was not to be disappointed in their new acquisition. In his first season, in 1903, Jerry achieved an impressive total of 837 runs (at an average of 41.85), the highest total in the Lancashire League and a Rammy record which was to remain unsurpassed for a further 33 years.

As an all-rounder, Ellis also took a season's tally of 75 wickets. Perhaps even more notably that year, he created a club and League record in the course of an opening partnership with Joe Leach which realised a total of 207 runs without loss. The circumstances in which this feat was achieved were no less remarkable.

The match took place at Acre Bottom on 20 June 1903. Lowerhouse went in first and declared on a commanding total of 205 for the loss of 5 wickets, though having occupied the crease for 3 hours and 10 minutes. In an age when sides weren't allocated equal numbers of overs to bat, it meant that the home team was left only one hour and fifty minutes playing-time to contest this number of runs before stumps were drawn.

The considered opinion on the day was that it was a forlorn hope to expect anything other than a draw. However, openers Ellis and Leach set out boldly. Launching an onslaught from the word go, 50 runs were clocked up in less than 25 minutes. In due course, 200 runs had been accumulated in just over 100 minutes when the umpire declared the last over was about to take place. With six runs needed, Jerry made the winning shot off the fourth ball. The atmosphere around the ground had been building up to fever pitch and now, with the tension released, the enthusiasm of the crowd knew no bounds and Jerry and Joe were shouldered off the pitch amidst ecstatic celebrations.

Jerry Ellis had scored 129* and Joe Leach 73*. As said above, it was a League record for a first wicket stand, although only remaining so until 1905 when Fletcher (pro) and Stapleton put on 220 for Rishton against another luckless Lowerhouse line-up. However, it stayed in the Rammy record book a lot longer, unsurpassed until 1940 when Billy Whitworth (133*) and Jack Pearson (97) put on 240 for the first wicket in an away match at Rawtenstall.

Talking of records, while Ellis' superlative knock of 129* against Lowerhouse fell five runs short of Leach's 134 against Bury in 1894 (one of two centuries he scored that season, the other being 103* at home against Bacup), Ellis managed in 1903 to capture the record with a score of 144* away at Enfield, also taking 5-32 in this same match.

Jerry Ellis was to remain the club's professional through 1903, 1904 and 1905. He scored 688 runs in 1904 (at an average of 32.76) but exceeded his previous season's bowling tally by taking 80 wickets. In his last season, he was unfortunately to drop lower on both counts with a total of 483 runs scored (at an average of 23.00) and 41 wickets taken.

Disappointingly again though, Rammy's overall position in the league championship in these years did not live up to the statistics achieved by certain individual players or in one-off games such as that against Lowerhouse. The club finished 7th in 1903, 10th in 1904, plummeting down to 13th by the end of 1904. With Arthur Sladen as pro the following two years, the club was to fare no better, ending again in 13th position in both 1906 and 1907. Sladen, a slow left arm bowler, had performed well enough himself, taking 137 wickets over the two seasons at an average of 12.01, with a best bowling performance of 9-28 at home against Colne in 1906. Even so, the total of 137 wickets was only the same tally as William Fenwick had achieved in the single season of 1900!

After his spell at Rammy, Jerry Ellis had played for Whalley and then Blackpool before spending his last four years captaining Barrow, retiring in 1925 aged 59. Ramsbottom Cricket Club contributed to his leaving gift and sent a representative to attend the presentation ceremony. Jerry lived in Billington (near Whalley) until his death, aged 77, in 1943.

ooooo

An important development associated with the time that Jerry had been pro at Rammy was the construction of a new pavilion. The old one had been built more than twenty years earlier, prior to the League's formation and was no longer seen as fit for purpose. A fund-raising campaign had been put in place culminating, in 1903, in a four-day money-raising bazaar. Overall, the sum of £740 was collected.

This new pavilion, standing a few feet further back than the demolished edifice it replaced, was built to the overall dimensions of 79 feet long (just over 24 metres) and 30 feet wide (just over 9 metres) , including a small veranda in front. There was an open hall in the centre, 30 ft. (just over 9 metres) by 20 ft. (just over 6 metres) and on each side facing the front were the players' dressing rooms. A ladies' grandstand was built, overlooking the cricket ground. It is evident though that 'ladies' did not just watch cricket but also played, as evidenced in a team photograph taken in 1912. At the north end, a room looking out on to the tennis lawn was provided for participants of that sport. It is interesting to note that the racket-game was also played on site at this time. At the south end, a tearoom was to be added on to the pavilion in 1912.

An official opening ceremony took place before the start of the first home match of the season against Enfield on Saturday, 16 April 1904. Thankfully, the weather was in 'excellent behaviour with quite a wealth of sunshine and balmy air when the proceedings were begun under the shadow of the old clock. The assembly was a large one and, up to the time of the pitching of wickets, it kept increasing'. Mr. William Barlow, Chairman of the Club (from 1895 to 1905) and Honorary Secretary of the League (from 1900 to 1935), was in charge of proceedings. Local dignitary Captain A.T. Porritt, 'a confirmed cricket enthusiast and distinguished figure within the community' was invited to conduct the ceremony.

It has been mentioned earlier how the club's development had involved many prominent people linked with the growth of industry in the town. Apart from the contributions of the Ashton and Stead families, there had been input as first President of the club (1869 to 1874) from William Grant, nephew of the famous factory-owner brothers William and Daniel, whose names had been immortalised as models for Charles Dickens' characters, the Cheeryble Brothers, in his novel *Nicholas Nickleby*.

Following the death of William Grant, the Rev. W. H. Corbould (vicar of St. Paul's since 1871), had taken on the role of President until 1893. His successor in the position was Richard M. Porritt, a member of the longstanding factory-owning Porritt family, who owned Stubbins Vale Mill together with a considerable amount of property in the wider local community. He was to serve as President of the Cricket Club until his death in 1906.

A.T. (Austin Townsend) Porritt, 29 years old on the occasion of opening the new pavilion in 1904, was the son of R.M.Porritt. Not only would he prove a generous benefactor to Ramsbottom Cricket Club for years to come - serving in his turn as President from 1922 through to 1946 - but he was also dedicated to making sporting and leisure facilities accessible to the public whenever he could. He was later to donate both Chatterton Park and Nuttall Park for the use and enjoyment of people in the local community.

ooooo

Despite finishing in lowly thirteenth position over three consecutive seasons from 1905 to 1907, an upswing in the fortunes of the Club was to come after the arrival of Emmott Robinson as pro. He was to remain at the club for six seasons.

Born in 1887 in Keighley, Emmott Robinson was a Yorkshireman head to toe. On this account, and also due to some of his more endearing mannerisms on the field of play, he was to become the focus of a lot of media attention and most notably the pen of the Manchester Guardian cricket correspondent, Neville Cardus. In fact, Robinson was destined to become a veritable cult figure in the sport. All this though would come about when, at the ripe age of 36, he was eventually to earn for himself a much-coveted place in the Yorkshire 1st XI, playing for the Tykes from 1919 to 1931, during which period they won the county championship six times.

The prospect of such celebrity status lying ahead of him had seemed highly improbable at the time though in 1908 when he first set foot in Ramsbottom as new pro. After playing only occasionally for the Yorkshire 2nd XI between 1904 and 1907, like many others before him, Emmott had decided to cut his losses and ply his trade in the Lancashire League, not only to help pay his way but also hopefully gain practical experience. From the start, he made an impact by scoring two centuries in his first season, 101 at home against East Lancashire and the other when he thrashed his way to 181* against Todmorden on 4 July 1908.

This mammoth total of 181* created a league record at the time. It was to last as such until surpassed by a total of 188* made in 1913 by Accrington's South African pro Charlie Llewellyn, incidentally the first test cricketer to be signed up as a pro in the Lancashire League. If five years does not seem very long for Robinson's league record to have lasted, it needs adding that, as a club record, it was to endure right up until the start of the 21st century.

As far as team performance went, the club ended up in 9th place in 1908, rising to 6th= in 1909 but dropping back to 11th= in 1910. The club was not unduly disheartened though by this apparent setback. It was felt that there was still a lot of untapped potential amongst a pool of players who very much enjoyed playing cricket with Robinson as pro. There was also a buoyancy around the club from having triumphed unbeaten in the Lancashire Junior Cricket League as 2nd XI championship winners in 1910, marking the club's first representative league honour.

Old warhorse Joe Leach was still going on grinding out the runs and would continue to do so for quite a few years longer. In 1909, he notched up the last of his three centuries - 100* at home against Bacup. Three times in his career, he was to have scored 500+ runs in a season: in 1894 (582), 1895 (538) and 1904 (575). Joe was to play 477 matches for the club from 1892 up to 1920, scoring 7,468 runs. His average of 18.17 is even more striking for the fact that he was playing at a time when largely unprepared pitches rendered it particularly difficult for batsmen.

ooooo

Across the six years that Emmott Robinson was pro with Rammy, he scored 3,607 runs (average 30.31) and as a medium-pace bowler took 325 wickets (average 15.47). However, over and above the statistical evidence, the powerful, motivating influence he had on the team was incalculable.

Emmott was a very popular and enthusiastic pro who always urged and persuaded his fellow team-mates to produce their best. Despite the earlier reference to pros being perceived as 'paid servants', it is clear that he came to win the whole-hearted respect of club members in a way that was highly uncommon at the time. Everyone seemed to appreciate and take note of what he said and did. For example, in his 1936 *History of the Club*, James Spencer referred back affectionately to the time when Emmott Robinson was pro, quoting sayings of his such as 'Allus goa for a run when it's on, t'other side's two to get then'.

The distinctive characteristics which the writer Neville Cardus later revelled in portraying to his readers would have already been well-known to spectators who watched him playing in his earlier days at Acre Bottom. For example, his obsessive protection of the shine on a new ball. In the words of Cardus, 'he cherished the new ball dearly; he would carry it between overs in person to the next bowler needing

17

it after himself; and he would contain it in the two palms of his hands like a sacred chalice'. If some fielder was rash enough to return it to the keeper on the bounce, a wail of 'Nay, nay!' could be heard from a wincing pro.

Emmott always appreciated he could not take on the opposition on his own. He needed to inspire the amateur players around him. He quickly appreciated Jack Redfern's strong potential to make good runs. The two of them came to enjoy a magical chemistry and understanding. Those, like James Spencer, who had seen them batting together, commented that their running between the wickets was a 'joy to behold'.

1909 had been notable for Ramsbottom's Fred Duerr being the most successful amateur bowler in the league that season, taking 69 wickets at an average of 8.24. Duerr would prove a valuable acquisition for the club, having previously spent six seasons at Bacup where he had already captured 334 wickets at an average cost of 11.71 before transferring to Acre Bottom. The motive behind doing so was in pursuit of his job livelihood as a colourist in the fabric industry which involved him transferring to go and work at a factory in Stubbins, near Ramsbottom, owned by Messrs. Turnbull and Stockdale.

Back to the batting line-up though, Redfern's run contribution was immense, scoring only marginally fewer runs than Robinson did as pro, with a particularly successful season in 1911. That year, he scored 815 runs, an amateur player record for the club at the time.

ooooo

1911 proved the club's most successful season to date since the Lancashire League had started. First, they won what was called the Maden Cup, a competition involving Rossendale Valley clubs. The trophy was lifted following a controversial match against Haslingden at Bentgate on 22 June. Due to extremely windy conditions, the teams agreed to play without bails. This decision was taken when the home team's score stood at 32-3. Haslingden duly completed their innings, totalling 138 all out with Fred Duerr taking 8-62.

At the start of the Rams' innings, Hassy's pro, Albert Nash brought out a new set of stumps with deep set grooves. Ramsbottom objected and

Haslingden agreed to continue without bails. However, Nash refused to bowl. For a bowler who was to take 76 wickets that season, his lack of participation came as something of a bonus to the visitors. Robinson and Redfern proceeded to put on 86 for the first wicket. After both were dismissed on this same total, Joe Leach came in at no. 4 to steady the ship and was 28* when the Rams reached 141-3 to capture the trophy.

Incidentally, for his refusal to bowl, Haslingden C.C. initially took the decision to sack Albert Nash although later re-instating him until the end of the season. However, he was to leave the club at the end of the season halfway through a two-year contract. Meanwhile, as the season progressed, a still more prized prospect lay within Rammy's grasp as they vied neck-and-neck with close rivals Nelson in the race to win the league title.

In the end, Ramsbottom and Nelson tied for top spot with 35 points each. Under the rules, a play-off match was necessary, this to be of two innings each side and on a neutral ground. For days ahead, the potential outcome of this match was the sole conversation in town. The club committee did everything in its power to support the team's preparations. For example, they agreed to bring in Robinson's fellow Yorkshireman, the renowned Schofield Haigh, who had played for Yorkshire since 1895 and also for England, to coach the players.

Amidst ever mounting tension, the decisive encounter took place at Accrington. Taking first knock, Ramsbottom's openers Robinson and Redfern made a steady start, scoring 25 runs before Redfern was out for 10. Robinson went on to top-score with 42 in what seemed a modest first innings total of 146. However, it looked more promising after Harold Oldroyd had ripped into the opposition, achieving figures of 6 for 39 with Fred Duerr taking 3 for 32 and Nelson bowled out for 90.

With Rammy's hopes running high at this stage, Robinson and Redfern took to the wicket again. Unfortunately this time round, the pro was out for a duck. Although Redfern held out heroically, he ran out of partners down the order. Despite carrying his bat, 26 runs not out, the Rams' second innings was a sad affair, being skittled out for a paltry 55. Nelson were still required to score 112 though. In the event, they duly knocked off the runs required, reaching 112 for 3 and thereby gaining victory by a comfortable-looking seven-wicket margin.

Although both Emmott Robinson and Jack Redfern must both have rued this missed opportunity in the play-off match, their overall contribution to the success of the club during these years cannot be under-estimated. For example, together with the two centuries notched up in the first season Robinson was at the club in 1908, he was to score three more, one in 1911 of 102* against Rishton and then two in 1912: 117* at home against Burnley and 103* against East Lancashire, also at Acre Bottom.

Meanwhile, Jack Redfern, allowing for his longer span of service at the club, managed to score four centuries, the first going back to 1902: 110* away at Church; then in 1911: 100* away at Lowerhouse; next in 1912: 113* away at East Lancashire and lastly in 1913: 103* away at Nelson. Although he would go on playing for the club until the end of the 1921 season, his halcyon years occurred pre-war, notching up three 500+ run-scoring seasons in 1902 (545), 1911 (815) and 1913 (565). In the 251 matches he was to play for the club between 1902 and 1921, he scored 5,350 runs at an extremely competitive average of 25.97. He also proved himself a very able captain during these years.

After the huge excitement generated in 1911 though, the following season had been an anti-climax with the club ending 10th. One reason for this was the consistently bad weather which caused ten matches to have to be abandoned. 1913, Robinson's last season, was a better one again with the club finishing 5th.

ooooo

Emmott Robinson's particular contribution would always be fondly remembered long after he left the club in 1913. Curiously, he was to return to play one more match for Rammy on the occasion of 11 September 1915 in a winning league match against Enfield in which he scored 63 runs and took two wickets. It was to be said later that, when he came to play a prominent part in Yorkshire's successful post-war period picking up six county championship wins, Ramsbottom folk took one look at his county averages and derived satisfaction from pressing the point: 'if we larned him owt!'

After he retired from playing cricket, Robinson became a first-class umpire. Although he never gained an international cap as a player, ironically he was to represent his country in the capacity of umpire, officiating in one Test match at Trent Bridge in June 1938 between England and Australia. It is likely he would have stood in more matches had it not been for the outbreak of World War Two in 1939. Emmott Robinson died in Hinckley, Leicestershire in 1969, aged 86.

The obituary that Neville Cardus wrote in honour of him was lavish in its praise of this great man and also laced with anecdotes about Robinson as a singular cricketing character of his time. 'At Bradford in 1920, he took nine wickets in an innings against Lancashire. He obviously thought I'd not done enough justice to the achievement in my report. When Emmott next met me he said, 'Ah suppose if Ah'd tekken all ten Lanky's wickets, tha'd have noticed me'.

Three: The Deadly Duo of Fred Duerr and Bill Hickmott

DURING THE COURSE of a chance conversation with Graham Ratcliffe, ex-Rammy player who is also the club's website co-ordinator, he happened to drop in that he had in his possession a medal that had been awarded to Fred Duerr in the 1920s. Very much aware of the legendary status of this particular player in club history, on account of his remarkable record of success as a bowler, it was pleasing to have chance to view the medal in question.

Putting matters into fuller perspective, Duerr took 50+ wickets for Ramsbottom each season from 1909 to 1916. Then when the league cricket programme resumed, it having been suspended in 1917 and 1918 during the course of World War One, Fred fulfilled the same criterion from 1919 right through to 1927, making it an incredible seventeen seasons in all that he performed the feat.

In addition, it may be recalled from the last chapter that Fred had previously played six seasons for Bacup before switching to play for Ramsbottom after moving job to work at Turnbull and Stockdale's factory in Stubbins. He had already achieved 50+ wickets a season four times during his spell at Bacup.

To say Fred Duerr was a prolific wicket-taker throughout his career is an enormous understatement. Casting an eye over the statistics from one season to the next, it is clear he was a model of consistency over the entire span of his long career. He was destined to take 1,477 wickets, rendering him the leading wicket-taker in club history by a huge margin, those wickets taken at the lowest average achieved by any Rammy bowler at 10.08 runs apiece.

Bowling 'right arm slow', Duerr relied on guile to take wickets, winkling out hapless batsmen through maintaining consistent line and length but also by flighting the ball in such a way that often induced a rash stroke. The sheer number of times he took five wickets or more (142 times) demonstrates how hard he was to play against. Photos reveal a face with a fixed, almost hypnotising stare. Batsmen must have felt intimidated by a demeanour bearing the deadpan expression of a sporting assassin.

ooooo

Despite the outbreak of war in 1914, the League programme initially went on as normal. Ramsbottom came 10th in the table. Following on as pro after the departure of Emmott Robinson, Bert Morgan had Minor Counties experience playing for Staffordshire but his statistics (132 runs at 6.60 and 84 wickets at 12.26) demonstrate that he was much more of a bowler than batsman.

In 1915, pro William Benskin's profile and performance seemed almost a carbon copy of Morgan, in Benskin's case having played Minor Counties cricket with Leicestershire 2nd XI. His batting record was 130 runs at 8.86 and 67 wickets at 13.02. Although finishing 12 points adrift of champions Accrington, 2nd place in the league marked a definite improvement though in team standing from the previous year.

Capably as each of these pros had performed with the ball, it is significant to note that Fred Duerr's seasonal tally was highly comparable, taking 76 wickets at 11.32 in 1914 and 87 at 11.40 in 1915. Fred in fact was set to go from strength to strength. In 1916, during which year the league dispensed with pros, he took 109 wickets at 8.82 with the club finishing 5th in the table.   .

Even though League cricket was suspended during 1917 and 1918, certain localised fixtures did take place between clubs in these years. Ironically, these encounters ended up spawning a cup competition which, since starting in 1919, has continued to grow in status up to the present day. The Worsley Cup competition might not have developed at all but for the particular circumstances of those times.

This prestigious cup award emerged out of three then separate knock-out competitions involving three different groupings of teams. The Hacking family of Clayton-le-Moors had presented a cup to be competed for by local clubs Accrington, Church, Enfield, Rishton and East Lancashire. This was during the time when no conventional league cricket was being played. Meanwhile the Maden Cup, donated by Sir James Maden, had been contested by the Rossendale Valley teams for some years already, Ramsbottom having won it in 1911.

Incidentally, this same Maden Cup was in 1917 to be competed for by eight clubs, including four others in addition to those from Rossendale. Records show that the trophy in that year was won by Rammy with the final against Enfield taking place at Accrington's Thorneyholme Park on 14 July. Enfield had batted first, scoring 75 with Fred Duerr taking 6-37. In reply, Rammy had scored 77-4, opener Jack Redfern making 35*.

In 1919, it had been decided that all clubs should be involved in local cup competitions to be staged in three 'sections'. In addition to the existing Hacking and Maden Cups, the Burnley clubs took part in a new competition which was called the Worsley Cup (donated by Alderman Tom Worsley). The three separate outcomes were that Accrington won the 'Hacking Cup', Rawtenstall the 'Maden' and Colne the 'Worsley'.

It wouldn't be until the year after, in 1920, that the Worsley Cup competition, as it is recognised in modern times, properly became a knock-out competition embracing all 14 member clubs and with an overall victor. Nelson were the winners in 1920.

ooooo

Meanwhile, the whole-scale task of resurrecting the League competition itself in 1919 was inevitably a highly charged and emotional undertaking. The appalling effects of war remained deeply etched in the minds of players and spectators alike. At first, in 1914, the threat hadn't seemed too serious (with thoughts predominating at the time that 'the war will be over by Christmas'), causing the league to trundle on through this year and the next.

However, 1916 was to witness a startling rise in the scale of casualties. Most notably for example, battalions of soldiers, such as the 'Accrington Pals', who had valiantly answered Lord Kitchener's appeal for volunteers to go and serve 'King and Country', had been decimated in a day at the Battle of the Somme. There were many other units made up of young men from East Lancashire killed on other battlefields or returning home badly wounded and scarred from the experience. The moral imperative to suspend the Lancashire league in its traditional format had gone without saying from 1917 onwards.

Now in 1919, with the war finally over, it still remained difficult for authorities to know what to do for the best. As well as honouring the memory of those who had lost their lives, there was also the feeling that life needed to return back to normal as quickly as possible for the benefit of those still alive. In this context, it was perceived that the resumption of the League programme, bringing the fourteen member clubs back together, would have a valuable role to play in helping East Lancashire local communities adapt back to something approaching normal life again.

ooooo

Finishing 11th= in 1919, Ramsbottom had a poor first season back. This was despite Fred Duerr taking 102 wickets. How could he be so effective as a main bowler but the team position end up so low? The problem was that the batsmen hadn't scored nearly enough runs. In addition, the pro all-rounder, A. Smith, had not made much impact achieving only 378 runs at an average of around 18 and taking a modest 66 wickets by comparison with Duerr.

With the next season looming, William Hickmott was signed on as pro in Smith's place. Aged 27, Hickmott had served in the army as a corporal in World War One. Afterwards, he had played in the 2nd XI for his home county Kent. Hungry for a chance to earn a better wage and at the same time make a name for himself in the game, he took the time-honoured step of entering the ranks of Lancashire League cricket.

An out-and-out bowler, Hickmott was no better with the bat than any existing amateur in the team. The Rams taking on such a player seemed a strange choice in many ways. Arguably, if there was a bowler of the quality of Duerr already in the team, surely the crying need was to take on a pro batsman or at the very least a capable all-rounder, someone perhaps in a similar mould to Emmott Robinson, now of course plying his trade very successfully with his own home county.

Not a bit of it - another bowler was taken on! Nevertheless, Hickmott proved a lethally effective operator with the leather in his hands. Bowling medium pace left-arm, he was to prove the perfect foil to the beguiling menace of Duerr's slow right-arm spin. Despite there being 20 years between them (Duerr was born in 1873 and Hickmott 1893), the older man's experience might well have fed through. At the same time, facing a challenge as top bowler from a much younger man might have had a galvanising, almost rejuvenating effect on the seasoned campaigner, now in his 47th year.

Strong hints as to the character and respective mindsets of the two men indeed emerge from those photographs of the time. Whilst Duerr comes across as calm and imperturbable, Hickmott has a restless, hungry look in his eye.

Yet whatever the apparent incongruities between the two of them, the statistics cannot lie in terms of how potent the pairing was in combined wicket-taking capacity. In 1920, Duerr's tally only showed a slight dip from the previous season, eight wickets down to 94 at an average of 7.31 while the new pro took exactly the same number of wickets but at an even lower average of 6.55. Who needed batsmen?!

Those who might have been apprehensive about what might transpire in 1920 were pleasantly surprised by the outcome. In fact, things went so well that Ramsbottom remained strong title-contenders for long stretches of the season. Eventually though, coming down to the wire, the 37 points achieved over the season ended up one fewer than championship-winning Haslingden, leaving Ramsbottom runners-up, as before in 1911. Incidentally, the system of points allocation at this time was very basic: 2 for a win, 1 for a draw and no points for a lost game. That season Haslingden won 16, drew 6 and lost 4 while the Rams also won 16 but drew 5 and lost 5.

In head-to-head matches between the two fierce local rivals, Haslingden had emerged triumphant on 15 May at Acre Bottom.

Although having only scored 79 in their innings (Hickmott and Duerr taking three wickets each), the home team's batting frailties had been cruelly exposed, being bowled out for 35 with no player achieving double figures. A certain degree of revenge was exacted in the return match at Bentgate on 5 June when Ramsbottom posted a total of 127 and then routed Haslingden for 56 with Fred Duerr taking 8-28. However, the overall honours at the end of the season went to Haslingden.

The year after, in 1921, the same two teams were battling it out again to the bitter end. As in 1920, the head-to-head matches between the two of them had been tight, hard-fought affairs with the tally again ending up one win apiece. In the first encounter, on 11 June at Acre Bottom, Rammy pulled off a 3-wicket win after bowling the opposition out for 116 (Hickmott and Duerr taking three wickets each) and scrambling to 119-7 to snatch victory. In the return fixture, on 2 July at Bentgate, Haslingden again batted first, scoring 121 all out. On the day, it proved an adequate enough total to win with Ramsbottom only managing 89 in reply.

Arriving at the last match of the season, on 10 September 1921, and needing to win, Ramsbottom played Enfield away at Dill Hall Lane. Apart from the massive significance of the outcome of this match, it also incidentally marked the final appearance of that great servant of the club, Jack Redfern.

Batting first, the Rams raised a total of 125 all out after 35.1 overs, with Redfern at no. 4 only achieving 7 runs. Even so, the task of bowling Enfield out for a lower score might not have been expected to have presented Hickmott with too much of a challenge. However, uncharacteristically failing to take a wicket in ten overs at a cost of 25 runs, captain Jack Isherwood felt little alternative in the circumstances but to bring on first change bowler Fred Bradshaw in his place. Like Redfern, Bradshaw had pre-determined this was to be his last game playing for Ramsbottom in a career with the club which in his own case had begun in 1900.

In the do-or-die atmosphere of the occasion, Duerr and Bradshaw ended up capturing five wickets each to seal victory by 20 runs with Enfield being bowled out for 105. In a spell of 6.2 overs, Bradshaw had taken 5 wickets for 17. Looking closely at the photograph taken afterwards of that first championship-winning team of 1921, perhaps it should have been no surprise to behold the broad grin on Fred Bradshaw's face that stood out so conspicuously on the team photo!

The miraculous had happened, finally bringing an end to a long, demanding 30-year wait. Having been runners-up to Haslingden in 1920, it must have given an added measure of satisfaction reversing the 1/2 placings of the season before by pipping local rivals Hassy to the post. But putting all that on one side, the joyous reality was that for the very first time, Ramsbottom were now successfully able to lift the league trophy.

The celebrations, in response to this agonisingly long-anticipated first championship win, were said to have been amazing to behold. In a victory parade that ran from Edenfield to Holcombe Brook and back to Rammy at twilight on this last day of the season, virtually the whole of the local community had lined the route to welcome and cheer their heroes home with the procession led by the Stubbins Vale brass band.

Ironically, the Rams' final points score had been two down on the previous year with a record of won 15, drew 5 and lost 6. However, 35 points had been good enough to fend off all other rivals in lifting the coveted championship trophy.

In the final analysis, it could not be denied the Ramsbottom team effort had once more relied heavily on the input of the twin bowling spearhead of Duerr and Hickmott. In terms of their own individual performances, the pendulum had this season swung slightly in favour of the pro with Hickmott capturing 94 wickets at an average of 8.41 while Duerr took 68 at 9.60. The immense value of the two of them in tandem though, complementing one another superbly, was undeniably the decisive factor in the club's monumental achievement of 1921.

With Hickmott now set to enter into a third year's service as pro, hopes ran high for the following season of 1922. He was not about to let anyone down, taking an even higher total this year of 106 wickets at an average of 8.32. With Duerr though only having a relatively modest season by his standards, taking 59 wickets, and the batting line-up still not showing enough consistency in producing the runs, the team finished the season on 33 points with a record that read: 13 wins, 7 draws and six losses. It left the club in 3rd place, trailing two points behind Rawtenstall and Bacup above them on 35.

Unfortunately, as far as Ramsbottom were concerned, Hickmott's bowling feats had been picked up on by Lancashire who seized the chance to sign him up for the start of 1923, requiring Rammy to look for a replacement. Although James McNamara, hailing originally from Victoria, Australia, (again much more of a bowler than batsman) bagged 84 wickets and Duerr raised his game again to take 82, the club only managed 20 points, finishing 11th=. Meanwhile Hickmott appeared to have established himself in the Lancashire county team ably enough to have been retained on their books for the following season.

Ramsbottom fared a little better overall in 1924, climbing to 7th place, even though pro McNamara only managed 63 wickets in his second season compared to Duerr's 67. The season was more notable however for two particular records being broken, one of a positive nature and the other rather less so from a Rammy perspective. In chronological order, Fred Hartley, a slow left arm bowler playing for Bacup, became the first amateur bowler to take all ten wickets in an innings (10 for 16) on 17 May. Unfortunately, the Rams were the fall-guys. Some degree of consolation on the back of this humiliation was derived though from Fred Duerr taking 9 for 15 against Colne on 6 September to create a new club record, which incidentally was not to be beaten until 1997.

Promising news came with the announcement at the start of 1925 that William Hickmott would be returning to the club from Lancashire County. Having found it increasingly difficult to maintain a 1st XI spot, he had bowed to the economics of the matter and signed up again for the club with whom he had enjoyed so much Lancashire League success over seasons 1920-22. Ramsbottom of course were delighted to renew the connection.

Hickmott's return was to coincide with another championship title for the club to add to the one achieved in 1921. The club achieved a record total, to this point, of 39 points made up of 17 wins, 5 draws and 4 losses. Once again with Hickmott and Duerr dictating the pattern of events, wicket-taking capacity was never in doubt. That season, while Duerr was to be back at his best with 96 wickets at 7.58, Hickmott smashed opponents to pieces taking 118 wickets at 7.41. To add icing to the cake for the younger man, he managed to match his senior colleague's 9 for 15 from the previous season, doing so in a home match against Rishton on 29 August. In fact, it was only the one wicket taken at the other end by Duerr that denied him the prize of a ten-wicket haul.

Apart from the 'deadly duo' of Hickmott and Duerr, credit needs to be given to other team-members for the two championship titles won in 1921 and 1925. In leadership terms, Jack Isherwood was captain from 1920 to 1923 while Herbert Walker had followed on from 1924 to 1926. As well as their respective achievements in the captaincy role, both contributed a great deal in different ways as team-players to the club's successes.

Taking Jack Isherwood first, between 1903 and 1933 (allowing for short spells spent in mid-service at Church and Enfield) he played 419 matches in all for Ramsbottom claiming a record combined wicket-keeping haul for the club of 421 victims (282 caught and 139 stumped). Meanwhile, Herbert Walker played 390 matches for the club (with 13 scores of 50 or more) and totalled 4,649 career runs at an average of 13.92 per innings making him ninth highest scorer in club history. An all-rounder, he also took 218 wickets at 16.67, having enjoyed one season in 1906 when he had taken over 50 wickets, the first time an amateur had done this since William Fenwick in 1902.

For a middle-order batsman, Walker's average over the period he played in from 1905 to 1926 was admittedly not a very high one. Nor was that of another stalwart of this period, Albert Wolstenholme, originally from Scotland, who played from 1913 to 1929, scoring 3,929 runs at an average of 16.04. Talking of captaincy, he too had served in this capacity in 1919 and was again to do so in 1927. Neither of these two players though scored more than 500 runs in any one season. Up until 1929, Joe Leach and Jack Redfern (both of them having served stints too as captain) would remain the only two amateurs (3 times each) to achieve this feat.

The fact that ball seemed still to rule over bat was no doubt a factor in the club's decision to invest seriously in new equipment to improve the quality of the wicket. Next season, 1926, saw the advent of mechanical propelled appliances...'a great improvement on the old horse-drawn motor; modern implements are required more than ever to keep a ground such as ours in first-class condition', James Spencer was to recall ten years later. Unfortunately, these technological advances were not to be matched by corresponding success on the field of play in the years coming after 1925.

ooooo

First of all, there was the saga of Hickmott's 'contract'. Despite believing that Hickmott had at least verbally signed up to an agreement to return the next season, the club's interpretation was that he had gone back on his word, allowing himself to be seduced by a better offer to play for Rochdale in the Central Lancashire League.

The ill-feeling that broke out around Hickmott's 'breaking of contract' was not only to prove controversial in its own right but also to present a severe clash of interests for Ramsbottom Cricket Club administrators who had happened to go on to serve in similar capacity at Lancashire League level. Take for example the dilemma faced by William Barlow who was Chairman at Rammy 1894-1904 but then also acted as Lancashire League Secretary throughout a record-breaking stint in that office between 1900 and 1935. During the period that Dr B Crawshaw (President at Ramsbottom 1907-21) had served alongside him in a similar role as President at Lancashire League level, Barlow had experienced few problems in carrying out his role.

Differing interpretations though over the Hickmott contract issue had led to conflict between Barlow and Crawshaw's successor as Lancashire League President, Edward Crabtree, who had adopted an altogether different take on the situation. This was to lead to direct confrontation between Barlow and Crabtree. In administrative terms, although William Barlow survived in office through the crisis of these times and indeed went on serving the League in the role of Secretary for considerably longer, the strong previous link between Rammy club and league administration was destined not to continue beyond Barlow when his longstanding tenure of office eventually came to an end in 1935.

ooooo

After the golden year of 1925, the club slumped to 11th the following season. Ernest Moss, a journeyman on the club pro circuit, who had recently been playing for Todmorden, stepped in to the gap left by Hickmott but only took 66 wickets with Duerr down to 55 compared with his 96 of the previous season. 1927 was even worse with the club 13th and the pro L.V. Vaughan taking only 64 wickets. Sadly, the year also marked the last in a remarkable run of seventeen continuous years that Fred Duerr (53 wickets) would take 50 wickets or more. Certain Rammy folk came to the conclusion that the recent introduction of more modern ground machinery had proved no blessing to the cause of prolific wicket-takers like Fred! Mindful of the fact though that the said gentleman was by now rather getting on in years...

1928 saw a slight improvement up to 10th, mainly due to a good input from pro Hugh Claughton, a player who had once been on Yorkshire's books, although having only appeared in three first-class matches for them. Aged 37 by now, he performed creditably for the Rams, achieving an average of 32.23 with the bat. He also became the first player since Jerry Ellis in 1903, to score a century (115) and at the same time take 5 or more wickets (5-32) in a match. This was in a home match against Rishton. Claughton took 76 wickets across the season at an average of 13.17, with a best bowling performance of 9-25.

However, during a period of continuing instability, Claughton was soon set to be the next to leave through the revolving doors, replaced by Edward Moxham. In a season in which the club finished 10th=, Moxham took a sparse 33 wickets. 1929 was a significant year in other respects though. It marked the first time that Billy Whitworth (who had started playing for the club's 1st XI in 1923) scored over 500 runs in a season.

Also, in this same year, the long distinguished service of Fred Duerr came to an end. By now, he was in his mid-50s albeit with a magnificent career to look back on. His total Lancashire League tally of 1,815 wickets from 1902 onwards (334 first for Bacup and then 1481 for Ramsbottom) would remain a league record for 92 years until finally broken by Rawtenstall spin bowler Keith Roscoe on 8 August 2021.

1930 saw Ambrose 'Billy' Williams as the latest pro in what had become by now an annual merry-go-round. Aged 43, he had played

12 1st class matches for Yorkshire between 1911 and 1919. He was a right arm fast bowler whose other previous claim to fame had been as a member of the Haslingden team that had pipped Rammy to the championship post in 1920. Well past his best by this stage, Williams picked up a mere 43 wickets with the club finishing the season in 12th spot. The only other point of note about 1930, returning briefly to the theme of domestic initiatives, was that 'the appearance of the entrance to the ground was greatly improved by the erection of new pay boxes and gates'.

The club pro, across both 1931 and 1932 was 'Little Jack' Holroyd who had been on Lancashire's books for six years, mostly playing in their 2nd XI. A slow left arm bowler, he took 89 wickets at 9.64 in his first season and topped the century mark (101) in his second at 10.02. However, such bowling prowess had relatively little impact on the club's final placings in these seasons, finishing 11th and 13th respectively.

ooooo

The two 'halves' of the 1920's were like chalk and cheese. The first five years of the decade had proved easily the most successful in the club's history to date, not least with the winning of two league championship titles in 1921 and 1925. However after these two triumphs, including having come second in 1920 and third in 1922, the tail-end years had been as flat as a pancake by comparison. For example, taking the years 1926 to 1932, the best the club had managed was 10th in 1928.

The last few years had witnessed a marked difference as to how certain Lancashire League clubs had come to view the whole remit of signing pros. Up to the start of the 1920s, pretty well every club in the League had invariably relied on obtaining their pro through the familiar process of signing home-grown English players. Such individuals may have had differing degrees of previous experience playing at county level but invariably had in common that they had failed to make the grade and ended up having to resort to League cricket to sustain a living.

Accrington's signing in 1911 of Charlie Llewellyn, a South African Test player, had very much broken the mould. To many, it was seen as a bold move. However, it marked the start of a trend among certain other clubs through the 1920s to import pros from abroad, making every effort to hunt out top-class players.

Nelson's signing in 1922 of the Australian fast bowler Ted McDonald, chiefly responsible for the rout of the English team touring Australia the year before, had especially hit the headlines. Despite McDonald playing his heart out though during the two years he was at Nelson and taking a great number of wickets into the bargain, it had still not catapulted the club to championship success. Even so, Nelson were to persist with the policy of sparing no expense to obtain the services of the best overseas players, preferably with Test experience, as was to be illustrated in the case of the inimitable Learie Constantine. To be fair to Rammy, they had dipped their toes in the water by taking on the Australian McNamara in seasons 1923-4. However, by comparison, he was never to be a household name.

Attracting a big-reputation player, preferably from abroad, inevitably had a significant impact on gate receipts. The epitome of this phenomenon came in the form of the arrival on the scene of the supremely charismatic West Indian all-rounder Learie Constantine. Although at first feeling like a fish out of water, and not just in cricketing terms, Constantine's arrival in Nelson in 1929 sparked a run of highly dramatic batting and bowling feats that would not only go on to secure a remarkable series of championship wins for Nelson from that year onwards but also attract ever-increasing numbers to pay their money at the gate to watch him perform.

While Nelson took over as title-winners in the later years of the 20s and well into the 30s, the Rossendale Valley clubs had clung on to the policy of hiring mediocre English ex-county players. Having managed between them to monopolise the league championship title through from Haslingden's victory in 1920 to Rawtenstall's success in 1926, a certain complacency had built in around method of selection of pros. In Rammy's case, apart from Claughton in 1928, no-one else amongst the string of Hickmott's successors had managed to serve the club with similar distinction.

Having waited so long since 1892 to taste title success, the championship wins of 1921 and 1925 suggested the club had finally built up a head of steam. However, the subsequent years from 1926 to

1932 proved a major disappointment. After suffering for seven years now back in the doldrums, there was a strong feeling within the club that more ambitious steps needed to be taken in advance of 1933.

ooooo

What of Fred Duerr and William Hickmott in later times?

Duerr was unfortunately destined not to enjoy a long retirement after finishing his work at Turnbull and Stockdale's, dying in Ramsbottom in 1941, aged 67. This was only 12 years after he had retired from playing for Ramsbottom in 1929. Incidentally, the commemorative medal, mentioned at the start of this chapter, was one awarded to him in 1925 as a member of the championship-winning team of that year.

Meanwhile, the much younger of the two, William Hickmott, after leaving the club at the end of 1925 to join Rochdale in the Central Lancashire League, achieved a league record 140 wickets for them in 1927. Returning eventually to his home county of Kent, he had relished a second period of celebrity beyond cricket, successfully breeding and exhibiting golden retriever dogs, most notably at Cruft's. He died in 1968, aged 74.

Four: Syd Secures Silverware

CASTING THE NET more widely, in terms of securing their pro for 1933, Rammy finally settled on a certain Australian player. Like McNamara before him though, the individual concerned was hardly a world-renowned figure in the game at the time.

Sydney Francis Hird was born in 1910 in Balmain, a suburb of Sydney in Australia. Before setting off to England to join Rammy for the start of the 1933 season, he had appeared in 32 first-class matches for New South Wales as a right-handed batsman and right arm leg-spin and off-spin bowler. He had to date scored 1,453 runs with a highest score of 130, one of five first-class centuries, and taken 59 wickets with a best analysis of 6 for 5.

Better known just as 'Syd' (sometimes spelt Sid), the nearest he had got to representing his country was when he had been picked as twelfth man for a Test match in the notorious 1932/3 Bodyline Series against England in Australia. The so-called 'legside theory' had been adopted by the tourists in a desperate ploy to unnerve the majestic Donald Bradman who had been in superlative form leading up to the series.

Although widely held to be an unsportsmanlike strategy, particularly by the partisan home crowds, the tactic worked very successfully. Chiefly, it involved English quickie, Harold Larwood, bowling hostile intimidating deliveries aimed at the body. Serious injuries were incurred. Even if a batsman managed to fend the ball off, it often led to catches being spooned up to a ring of fielders positioned close to the wicket on the leg side. England won the five-test series 4-1.

Incidentally, the great Bradman had been wooed in 1932 by Accrington to come and play for them in the Lancashire League. With

Australia in the grip of recession at the time, he had been very tempted but in the end decided to preserve his amateur playing status and stay playing in his country of origin. Accrington had ended up hiring another Australian, Alan Fairfax.

Meanwhile Ramsbottom themselves, as one of many options considered, had sought to attract Donald Bradman to join their ranks for the 1933 season. When the bid was graciously rejected, the Rams turned to Syd Hird. With little to lose, and seemingly not high up in the minds of Test selectors, Hird jumped at the chance.

In his first season, Syd ably demonstrated his skills with the bat, scoring 821 runs at an average of 43.21 with a top score of 152* at Rawtenstall. This amounted to the highest total of runs scored by a Rammy pro in any one season since Jerry Ellis' 837 in 1903. Also performing well as a bowler, Hird took 79 wickets at an average of 14.94. In a similar style to that of Emmott Robinson, he inspired others around him. The team finished 5th= that season.

During the next season though, the club slipped back to 9th even though Hird had scored 752 runs and taken 77 wickets. One league match that would have caused him special satisfaction was that in which he emulated the previous success of Ellis and Claughton in scoring a century and taking five or more wickets in a match. This feat he achieved on 8 September in an away game against Lowerhouse in which he made 108* out of a total of 196-6 before taking 8-30 in the home team's reply of 110 all out.

Another highly memorable match in 1934 was the 1st round tie in the Worsley Cup taking place on 28 May at Bentgate against Haslingden. By the rules of the competition, such matches were played according to a formula classified as 'timeless', meaning that games continued across different dates in the calendar until a final outcome was achieved. In this particular instance, a match that had started out on 28 May did not reach its conclusion until 4 June. Haslingden, batting first, compiled a huge total of 369 with pro George Headley amassing 189 runs, Hird having to settle for figures of 2-135.

However, embarking on an impossible-looking run chase, Syd Hird, batting at no. 4, played the leading role by chalking up 167* out of a match-winning total of 370-6. Those spectators who had watched the match through until 4 June certainly witnessed an epic encounter.

Then, after another nerve-shredding 2nd round tie against Rawtenstall, in which the Rams scraped home by a 3-wicket margin in a comparatively low-scoring match, the scene was set for a second successive season's semi-final contest against Nelson away at Seedhill.

Even though, in both these matches, the opposition's main threat, the celebrated Learie Constantine, was dismissed cheaply for scores of 6 and 1 respectively, Hird would have been annoyed with himself for failing to capitalise on the opportunity presented him, only contributing 17 and 4 in each of Rammy's two unsuccessful run chases. Such comparative failures had the effect though of impelling Syd to do better in future.

1935 was the season that Billy Whitworth was back playing for Ramsbottom. A capable all-rounder, he was returning to the club after a four-year spell as pro at Uppermill in the Saddleworth League. He was just the kind of support act Hird needed, batting high up the order and sharing the new ball.

Despite his professional spell elsewhere, Whitworth was Ramsbottom through and through. Having originally joined the club at the age of 14, he had had to wait two years before gaining formal Junior Membership. He had made his first XI debut, aged 18, against Nelson back in 1923. It had been a baptism of fire scoring a duck batting at no. 9 on a day when the side had been skittled out for 46 with Australian test bowler Ted McDonald going on the rampage with 5-22. It had provided some consolation though to have taken his first wicket at senior level in this same match, finishing with figures of 1-10 in Nelson's innings of 95.

Twelve years later, Nelson were still the team to beat. While Rossendale Valley teams had monopolised the winning of the league from 1920 to 1926, Nelson had taken over the mantle of champions thereafter, claiming the title in 1928, 1929, 1931, 1932 and 1934.

As 1935 opened, there was no reason to believe anything was about to change, not least with Constantine still at the top of his game. In the event though, the current champions were to find a confident Ramsbottom team breathing down their neck throughout that season. In particularly good form as a bowler, Hird took 100 wickets while scoring

725 runs. Meanwhile, able lieutenant Whitworth, re-acclimatising well to the Lancashire League, notched 406 runs and took 50 wickets.

In the vital head-to-head league matches against Nelson, the first occurred at Acre Bottom on 17 June when Whitworth took 4-36 and Hird 2-49 as Nelson (top score of 33 from Constantine) were bowled out for 122. Then the Rammy pair shone brightly in the run chase with Whitworth at no. 3 contributing 19 and Hird 28 batting no. 4. However, reaching a winning total on the day of 123-6 had been largely down to the 43 scored by opening batsman Billy Greenwood.

The return match between the two sides on 6 July at Seedhill was a much tighter affair with Rammy declaring on 231-5 - Alf Tootill scoring a century (103*) - after 58 overs. However, Nelson ended up batting out time during the remaining allocated number of 49 overs, making little effort to chase down the total, managing only 126-3. Sharing a point apiece in a drawn game, the two sides remained locked together in contention for the title.

In the last match of the season at Centre Vale on 7 September, despite achieving a win by 180 runs, having bowled out the hosts for 56 with Hird taking 5-20 and Whitworth 5-33, the title went to Nelson again for the sixth time in eight years. They had gained 37 points (W 13 D11 L2) against second-placed Ramsbottom's 36 (W 14 D8 L4).

An interesting story arose out of that final match of the season at Todmorden. At the end of it, Billy Whitworth had succeeded in taking his 50th wicket of the season and Syd Hird, with the very last ball of the innings, his 100th. The problem arose as to which of the two should receive the mounted, inscribed ball. The matter was only resolved by conducting a raffle competition. Thirty more years were to elapse before the winner of that raffle, Billy Greenwood, was to take it into his head rather belatedly to hand it to Billy Whitworth.

In 1936, the club slumped to 9th=, achieving only 29 points (W4 D17 L5). This was taking into account the revised system of points allocation introduced at the start of the season of 3 pts for a win. Again, with what was becoming monotonous regularity, Nelson triumphed once more as champions, making it now seven times in nine years.

Rammy's leading two players had both had good seasons again. Hird finally broke Ellis' batting record, scoring 918 runs whilst at the same time taking 58 wickets. Whitworth hit 663 runs, the highest number of runs he had scored so far in his time at the club, plus chipping in with 22 wickets. Billy's record as a batsman was to further improve almost season-by-season, but the 50 wickets he had taken in 1935 was to remain his highest tally throughout his time at the club. Although he was to go on turning his arm over until 1955, he was to be increasingly troubled by recurring leg injury.

1937 saw the Rams rising back up the league table to 5th with 39 points (W9 D12 L5). Again, both Hird and Whitworth advanced their run totals from the previous season, the former achieving 920 and the latter 701. Whitworth also contributed to the cause by serving as captain in both 1937 and 1938. While his season's wicket tally for 1937 slipped down to 15, Hird's rose back up again to 76. Meanwhile, Norman Longworth succeeded in taking 50 wickets for the season at an economic rate of 15.08. Almost needless to say, Nelson were yet again league champions, stretching it to eight times in the last ten seasons.

With the prospect of 1938 looming, marking his sixth season as pro, Syd Hird must have realised again that the club's best hope of picking up a trophy lay with the Worsley Cup. Never in serious contention in the league, the club finished in 5th place again with 38 points (W9 D11 L6). Hird himself dipped considerably below his club record-breaking batting statistics of the previous year, only scoring 644 runs, even though raising his wicket tally to 83. Again, as in 1934, he achieved the remarkable feat again of scoring a century and taking five or more wickets in the same match, this time at Thorneyholme Road against Accrington on 7 June. Scoring 101 out of a total of 187-4 declared, he then took 8-28 in the home side's reply of 80.

As for Billy Whitworth, he had enjoyed his most successful year to date with the bat, scoring 739 runs, plus taking 20 wickets. A true measure of his success was that, with an average of 43.47, he had ended up topping the League's batting averages ahead of Haslingden's pro, West Indian George Headley, who had occupied top position in all of the four preceding seasons.

For once, Nelson had failed to win the championship (perhaps no surprise since Constantine had departed to Rochdale, said to have been lured away by a stunning offer in the region of £3,800) with the honour falling Todmorden's way instead.

Meanwhile, in the course of their Worsley Cup campaign, Rammy had progressed through both preliminary Rossendale-based matches to be faced again at the semi-final stage, as in 1933 and 1934, with nemesis opponents Nelson. This time around though, Syd Hird was to blow them out of the water with an astonishing match-winning innings of 205 out of a total of 314. There was no way Nelson could compete and were bowled out for 150 with Norman Longworth taking 5-49 and Hird 3-47.

The final took place on 30 August at Centre Vale against Todmorden. Ramsbottom could not have hoped for a better start to the encounter, bowling their opponents out for 73 with Hird taking 7-35 and John Olive 2-15. In their own innings though, matters could not have fared worse. Opener Jack Pearson went for a duck with the score at 3. Whitworth followed soon after for 2 with the score at 8. Then the hammer-blow was struck with Hird out for 6, making it 10-3. The middle order batting collapsed to 27-8 before a stand of 19 between Jimmy Horrocks and Arthur Waite offered some hope. However with the score at 46, two quick wickets were lost, consigning the Rams to a final total of 47.

Scottish-born Tod pro George Macaulay, whose previous best in the League was 5-26, had ended up on the day with the sensational statistics of: 13.1 overs, 7 maidens, 9 wickets for 10 runs. The Cup had seemed there for the Rams' taking only to have been dramatically snatched away from them by a 26-run margin inside only three and three-quarter hours of play. For Todmorden, it marked the dramatic completion of a memorable year, winning the league and cup double.

Incidentally, George Macaulay served as pro at Tod for the two seasons of 1938 and 1939. This was after playing for Yorkshire - as a contemporary of Emmott Robinson - in eight championship-winning sides on his own account between 1922 and 1935. Although Emmott, ex-Rammy pro, never got to play for his country, George Macaulay did. Not only so but at the same time had ended up joining the ranks of a small elite group of bowlers succeeding in taking a wicket with their first ball in Test cricket. Macaulay however was later sadly fated to die on military service in the outer Scottish island of Sullom Voe during the early years of World War Two.

ooooo

Rammy's league campaign in 1939 was to leave them falling back down the table to 10ᵗʰ=. Again, the club's only hope of glory remained via the Worsley Cup. A first round match against Bacup resulted in a comfortable six-wicket win. The second round match against Haslingden was much closer. Hird took 7-57, keeping the opposition down to a total of 172. Thanks to Hird's 89* and 32 from Whitworth, a three-wicket win was achieved to take the club forward to the semi-final stage, a tricky-looking encounter away against Burnley on 8 August.

Batting first, Ramsbottom scrambled to a total of 101 in 43 overs, Hird top-scoring with 43. Amar Singh, the first Indian cricketer to take part in the league as a pro, took 9-57. In reply, Burnley got off to a shaky start with Hird trapping Singh lbw for 6 before capturing Eatough's wicket, caught and bowled for 8. At the other end, John Hartley dismissed Burnley skipper Olver for a duck, caught by Whitworth. However, it was left arm spinner John Olive, taking 7-9 in a devastating 5.4-over spell, who was chiefly responsible for reducing the hosts to 45 all out and a victory margin of 56 runs.

The final, against Church, took place at Blackburn Road, Oswaldtwistle on 23 August. Unfortunately, the Rams got off to a poor start, losing both openers Pearson and T. Kay for ducks. However, a third wicket partnership of 65 between Hird and Whitworth looked promising before both went soon after one another, Hird for 41 and Whitworth 25. Next highest score was Tommy Kay's brother, Clifford, with 16. Eventually, although the total crept up to 123 all out, there were obvious doubts as to whether it was enough.

Things looked ominous when Church openers Howarth and Sam Pilkington started out confidently with a partnership of 28. At 53-1, it looked plain sailing for Church with their pro Fred Hartley at the crease. However, a breakthrough came when he was caught and bowled by Whitworth for 7. Then with Pilkington going for 44, caught Hird bowled Olive, the floodgates opened with Hird taking 5-43 and Whitworth 3-19. Victory was secured by 23 runs, Church being dismissed for 100.

The achievement marked the end of a 20-year-long wait for the club to win the Worsley Cup competition. The timing of it though could hardly have been more apt happening as it did in the last year of Syd Hird's seven years as pro at Rammy.

In the final outcome, Hird was able to look back over his stint at the club with immense personal satisfaction. The statistics spoke for themselves. During the course of his seven seasons with the club, he had amassed 5,392 league runs in 157 innings at an average of 41.47 with 8 centuries and 35 half-centuries. He had certainly provided the authority with the bat that the club desperately needed. In addition, he had taken 550 wickets at an average of 12.34, not forgetting as an athletic fielder taking 61 catches. Interestingly, if one goes on to assess his record in the Worsley Cup, his record is even more formidable. In 19 innings (including four 'not outs') he scored 1,087 runs at an average of 72.46. With the ball, he took 79 wickets at an average of 13.01, together with 9 catches.

By way of footnote, Syd's next port of call was to South Africa where, after the end of World War II, he played for Eastern Province in the late 1940s and for Border in the early 1950s. After his playing days ended, he coached successfully for East Province and Orange Free State. He remained in South Africa, dying in Bloemfontein, Orange Free State, in December 1980, aged 70, his memory always cherished by everyone associated with Ramsbottom Cricket Club.

ooooo

On 3 September, 1939, the very next day after the last game that Syd Hird played for Ramsbottom away at Enfield, the ominous news was delivered to the nation by Prime Minister Neville Chamberlain to the effect that the country, following Hitler's invasion of Poland, was now at war with Germany.

Despite the sense of horror that Britain, as in 1914, was embroiled in another war against Germany, it was very difficult for anyone to assess at this stage what impact this might have on the home front. The temptation might have been to hope that it wouldn't make too much difference to the usual pattern of life. Purely in practical terms, as far as local cricket was concerned in East Lancashire, League administrators still went about planning ahead to the start of the new 1940 season.

In fact, the only major difference to be made ahead of the new season was a ruling coming in that no pros should be signed on. Otherwise, the fourteen league members committed themselves to an on-going league programme as normal. As it happened, during a period of time called 'the Phoney War', little actual fighting had taken place. This spell of relative inactivity had lasted from the declaration of war through to May 1940. It wasn't until news came of Germany's invasion of Norway that hostilities escalated into full-scale conflict.

ooooo

Meanwhile, most of Ramsbottom's seasoned campaigners from the previous season before were still playing for the club in 1940. One particular match, taking place on 8 June at the Worswick Memorial Ground in Rawtenstall, captured interest with Ramsbottom openers Jack Pearson and Billy Whitworth breaking the record number of runs for a first wicket partnership that had been set back in 1903 by Jerry Ellis and Joe Leach.

In 36.5 overs, the pair scored 240 runs before Pearson was out for 97. With Whitworth on 133*, captain Waite declared the innings. Ironically, despite this longstanding club record being broken, Rawtenstall in the event then coasted to victory, scoring 244-5 in 41.2 overs. Such was always the precarious nature of timing declarations during the long period of time before the latter-day introduction of the limited-over formula.

For his part, Jack Pearson was another outstanding club servant, representing the Rams in 339 matches between 1923 and 1942. His most successful seasons had been in 1933, 1934 and 1937 when he had topped the '500+' mark, with 557, 691 and 518 runs respectively. In all, he scored 5,814 runs, average 18.69, making him the 5th highest run-scorer in the club's history. He had been a member of the 1939 Worsley Cup-winning side.

By the same token, on the bowling side, it had proved a particularly good year for John Olive. He made 299 appearances from 1926 to 1942, taking 511 wickets at an average of 14.78. 1940 saw him capture his highest career wicket-haul of 69 at an average of 9.55, featuring a memorable 9-42 on 6 July away against Haslingden, as the opposition were bowled out for 123. Ironically, such superb statistics had not been enough to win the game with the Rams bowled out for 105. Olive was to achieve two more 50+ wicket seasons in 1941 (57) and 1942 (63).

Despite the war having intensified alarmingly from May 1940 onwards, domestic cricket still somehow managed to proceed smoothly enough towards the culminating month of September. Even on the day marking the fall of France, which effectively led to a position whereby Britain was left fighting alone against the Axis powers, it seems curious to note that Lancashire League fixtures had continued on as normal. For example, during the course of the Dunkirk evacuations taking place between 27 May and 4 June 1940, Ramsbottom entertained Rawtenstall at Acre Bottom in a match on 1 June, ending up in a 7-wicket win for the visitors. This of course was the match preceding the return encounter the week after in which Whitworth and Pearson were to set their new first-wicket stand record.

1940 was indeed to prove Billy Whitworth's most prolific season with the bat for Rammy, amassing a record total for an amateur (surpassing that set by Jack Redfern in 1911) of 829 runs at an average of 55.26. The club finished in 7th position with a record of W7 D15 L4.

In retrospect, it seems amazing that cricket continued to have been played virtually uninterrupted throughout World War II in one way or another. It is difficult to know what this says about the prevailing spirit of the times when Britain remained for long periods seriously under threat of invasion, not least suffering ferocious air attacks. Perhaps the continued playing of cricket served a psychological purpose in amounting to a gesture of defiance in itself as if to say nothing was going to prevent the country from sticking to its normal programme of domestic sports and pastimes?

In the event, the 1941 Lancashire League's cricketing calendar thus unfolded with only one minor adjustment: that being that the number of fixtures went down from 26 to 22. This slightly reduced quota of matches would stay the norm through seasons 1942 to 1945 until reverting again to 26 in 1946, the first full season of play following cessation of hostilities.

In 1941, Ramsbottom had finished 7th= with a record of W7 D7 L8. The club's talismanic player Billy Whitworth fell below his batting record of the year before, scoring 465 runs at an average of 33.21. However, as an all-rounder, he had greater success with the ball taking 25 wickets at an average of 17.44. This season though marked the last season he would play for the club until coming back in 1947.

In 1942, the club ended 9th= with a record of W6 D9 L7. Despite the league programme continuing, wartime engagement meant that teams were increasingly made up of inexperienced players not yet eligible for conscription to the armed forces. Hence it was that John Savage in 1943, at the age of 14, became the youngest player in the club's history to make his 1st XI debut in what is also held to be the youngest ever team to go out on to the field to play for Ramsbottom. Another youngster who, in these wartime conditions, gained opportunity at the tender age of 14 to play first team cricket was Harold Monkhouse.

Although no doubt all Lancashire League clubs were playing under similar constraints, the Rams struggled in these years in terms of league position. In 1943, the club finished in bottom place with a record of W2 D7 L13. It didn't turn out much better in 1944, finishing 11th with W6 D5 L11. In 1945, the club was back in rock bottom 14th place with W5 D5 L12. This season incidentally had seen the re-introduction of pros. Englishman Reg Santall, a right arm bat and right arm medium pace bowler, took up from where Syd Hird had left off in 1939. Now in his early 40s, Santall had played many years pre-war for Warwickshire, having given good enough service to be granted a benefit year in 1935. However his statistics for the Rams in 1945 were to prove poor, scoring 470 runs at 31.33 and taking only 22 wickets at 26.13.

Two particular matches worthy of note though during these years happened coincidentally to involve Rammy's Norman Longworth. Representing the club between 1936 and 1949, Norman took 341 wickets at an average of 14.91. At the same time, he was a more than useful batsman, scoring a season's total of 474 runs in 1944, including a spectacular, match-winning knock of 126* away at Rawtenstall. In another match, against Haslingden in 1945, the Rams found themselves bowled out for 79, only for Norman to bounce into action and take 9-25 in dismissing the opponents for 67. He might well have taken all ten wickets had it not been for one batsman 'retiring hurt'.

Tommy Barnes is another player worthy of note from this period. He played in 397 matches for Rammy from 1919 to 1945. During this time, he notched up 5,509 runs, average 16.59, making him the 6th highest run scorer in the club's history. He had been a member of both the 1921 and 1925 league championship-winning teams as well as the 1939 Worsley Cup-winning side. Furthermore, he had served as captain over seven years from 1928 to 1934 and again in 1944. A highly experienced player therefore, he had a lot to offer as captain to up-and-coming players looking to their future. For example, a young cricketer benefitting from such guidance was John Savage whose own later contribution to the game of cricket was to be immense, both as player and coach, in the years following the end of World War II.

Despite being called up for National Service in 1946, Savage kept his cricketing interests very much alive, representing the RAF in matches against County teams Essex and Hampshire. After demobilisation, he joined Leicestershire, first as an amateur before turning professional in 1953. In the 13 years that followed, John displayed growing mastery of the art of off-spin bowling, playing against and taking the wickets of Ted Dexter, Colin Milburn, Rohan Kanhai and Gary Sobers. He was awarded his County cap in 1958. In 1961, his best season, he took 122 first-class wickets.

In 1967, John Savage was to enter into a one-year contract as player and assistant coach with Lancashire. However, his stay lasted much longer, eventually taking over from Norman Oldfield as the County's Chief Coach in 1973. One of the many players he brought through to later success was the young Michael Atherton, future England captain.

RAMSBOTTOM CC 1885

Backrow: Greenhalgh, Warden, J. Barlow, J. Penny, S. Holden (Bag carrier)
Middle Row: R. Holden, S. Kelly, J.T. Gill, Biddolf, J. Holden. I. Walton
Front Row: W. Moorhouse, H. Holden (Scorer), J. Forshaw

W. FENWICK
PLAYER

W. FENWICK
ADMINISTRATOR

Ramsbottom Cricket Club
Record Opening Partnership
Normal League Cricket Rules

J. Ellis   129 Not Out
J. Leach   73 Not Out
Played 20-06-03
Ramsbottom v Lowerhouse

JACK REDFERN

EMMOTT ROBINSON

FRED DUERR

BILL HICKMOTT

RAMSBOTTOM CRICKET CLUB
LANCASHIRE LEAGUE CHAMPIONS 1921

Back Row L. to R: J. Horrocks, G. Brooks, W. Hickmott, F. Duerr, T. Foster, A. Wolstenholme
Front Row L. to R: H. Walker, J. Preston, J. Isherwood, T. Barnes, F. Bradshaw

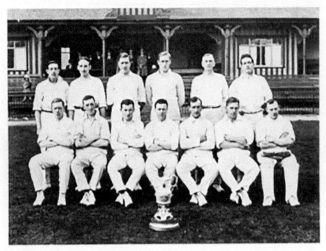

Back Row: W. Whitworth, H. Horrocks, T. Foster, W. Hickmott (Pro), F. Duerr, G. Brooks
Front Row: A. Wolstenholme, B. Fenton, T. Barnes, H. Walker (Capt.), J.F. Horrocks, W. Dewhurst, J. Isherwood.

New Ground Mechanical Appliance 1926

SYD HIRD

BILLY WHITWORTH

RAMSBOTTOM CRICKET CLUB
WORSLEY CUP WINNERS 1939

Back row: H.C. Brierley, T.D. Kay, J. Pearson, W. Greenwood, J. Olive, W. Whitworth
Front row: J. Hartley, S.F. Hird (Pro.), A. Waite (Capt.), T. Barnes, C. Kay, J. Broughton

RAMSBOTTOM CRICKET CLUB
WORSLEY CUP WINNERS 1957

F. Rothwell (Scorer), H. Monkhouse, E. Chamberlain, M. Hetherington, G. Bladen, B. Quinton,
J. Davenport (Wicket-Keeper), A.W. Holt (Bag Carrier)
E.R.H. Fuller (Professional), J. Collinge (Chairman), G. Marsden (Captain), G. Taylor (Secretary), W. Greenhalgh
D. Hodson, W. Savage

Five: Pied Piper, Peter Philpott

FOLLOWING SIX YEARS of war, the prospect of resuming normal community activities again was anticipated with an enormous sense of relief. There was a buzz of expectation amongst those wanting to play the game of cricket again and also those going along to watch.

The Northern Daily Telegraph reported on 10 June 1945 that 'Big crowds, big money and big hitting by batsmen made the Lancashire League "Victory Day Holiday" programme one of the most colourful for many years. At every match something out of the ordinary happened and spectators thoroughly enjoyed their cricket'.

With a welcome sense of liberation from the privations of wartime, these were times when the public flocked back to places of entertainment such as cinemas and cricket grounds. All clubs had felt the financial pinch during the war years and bumper crowds did wonders for the state of club coffers, making it seem possible to go out in search again for the best professionals they could find.

However, as described at the end of the last chapter, the 1945 season had not worked out particularly well for the Rams, finishing in bottom place in the league. At the start of 1946, the club took on Leslie Warburton as pro. 36 years old at the time, he brought a lot of experience but still was young enough to be able to offer his best. Born in Haslingden, he had served as pro there (1931-33) before going on to play for Littleborough in the Central Lancashire League (1934-38) and then one season in 1939 for East Lancashire.

Although a natural all-rounder, right-hand bat and right arm fast-medium pace bowler, it was his prowess with the bat that stood out. In two of the three years he had been at Haslingden (1932 and 1933), he had topped the Lancashire League batting averages, repeating the feat with East Lancashire in 1939.

Warburton was to stay at Ramsbottom for three years (1946-48). Showing he had lost none of his batting skills, he yet again finished at the head of the league's batting averages in 1946, scoring 818 runs at 68.16. He also made a valuable contribution with the ball, taking 43 wickets at 11.18, including a memorable 9-46 against Rawtenstall on 22 June at Acre Bottom. Despite the strength of his own performances, the team had though finished that season in a disappointing 11th place.

Unfortunately, the team was to find it hard to rise up the table in the years that followed, finishing 9th in 1947 and 10th in 1948. However, the latter season had proved a highly successful one for Warburton in personal terms, notching up a club record number of runs in a season - 933 at an average of 58.31 - exceeding the previous highest total of 920 runs scored by Syd Hird in 1937.

ooooo

As referred to earlier, 1947 was the year that the club, with considerable financial assistance from members, had purchased the Acre Bottom site at a cost of £1,000 from Sir Peter Grant Lawson. The land, bought freehold, covered about 8.64 acres and comprised both Cricket Ground and Tennis Courts.

The Cricket Club was granted access - in perpetuity subject to equitable maintenance payments - to Bridge Street via a stretch of roadway lying between the River Irwell and Ramsbottom Paper Mill. It would not be until 1994 that this access route to the ground was superseded by the present road running between the then Trinity Paper Mills (successor to Ramsbottom Paper Mill) and the renovated railway station.

Not long after the purchase of the ground in 1947, the Tennis Courts, first installed in the last quarter of the 19th century, were dug up and abandoned. Part of the vacated site was later used for construction of the new Club House. Incidentally, the original wooden score box, which stood between the tennis courts and the Paper Mill at the north-west corner of the field had been replaced in 1936 with a facility improvised from a caravan at the south-east corner. The makeshift provision lasted until 1949 when a bricked structure was built in its place. This was carried out to coincide with the first Minor Counties match to be staged at Acre Bottom between Lancashire II and Nottinghamshire II.

ooooo

With Warburton due to leave the club to join Leyland in the Ribblesdale League, the hunt was on for a pro replacement. In an era in which it was becoming much more common to sign up a player from abroad, Ramsbottom thought they had struck a good deal by enlisting the services of 'Holland's crack fast bowler', Ary Molenaar, for the 1949 season. In bizarre circumstances though, alternative arrangements had to be put into place after it transpired Molenaar had been committed to prison for ten years for complicity in the murder of a shop-keeper in the Netherlands.

Instead, Harry Lambert arrived on a boat from Australia. Aged 31 and at the time much better known in his native country for playing Australian Rules football for Collingwood, Lambert had made his debut in Sheffield Shield inter-state cricket for Victoria only as recently as the 1947/8 season. If anyone in the Rammy hierarchy thought they were getting another Syd Hird, they were to be disappointed. As a right-handed batsman, he scored 598 runs in 1949 at an average of 29.90 and only 360 the following season at 25.71. As a left arm fast medium bowler, he enjoyed relatively better success taking 66 wickets the first year at 15.37 and 51 the second at 15.96. Meanwhile, the team finished 12th in 1949 and 13th in 1950.

Maureen Smith, a local school girl at the time, was not to forget the occasion she took part in a running event at the refurbished Acre Bottom site and winning the competition. She was kind enough recently to share with the author a photograph she still has of her being presented with a trophy by pro Harry Lambert, smartly-suited with his hair 'Brylcreem-slicked' in the style of the day!

ooooo

A bonus in these years was the return of the indefatigable Billy Whitworth to the club in 1947. Although his performance that first season back had proved modest by his own standards, he was very much back on song in 1948, scoring 692 runs (av. 36.52). Two more '500+' seasons further unfolded (his eighth and ninth to date since his first in 1929), seeing him scoring 757 runs (av. 34.40) in 1949 and 642 (av. 45.84) in 1950. Showing strong commitment to the club, he served as club captain in 1948 and 1949.

Meanwhile, in 1950, Acre Bottom suffered catastrophic flooding with the whole ground coming under several feet of water. The only consolation was that it happened on the last day of the season so that reparation work could be carried out in time for the start of 1951. Much intense labour had to be carried out to restore and strengthen the river banking, involving the planting of small trees leading in time to the disappearance of the view of the field from the off-site, so-called 'Cheeky Stand', where knots of spectators had been accustomed previously to congregate to watch play for free on a mound of land on the far side of the Irwell.

Most notably, the indomitable Les Barrow became engaged in this work, staying on to become official groundsman and maintaining pitches that were always to draw admiration from visiting clubs. At a time when pitches were to increasingly become more favourable to batsmen, Les Barrow presided over his wicket preparation with the ferocity of a guard-dog. Woe betide anyone, whatever their status, who wandered at a wrong moment on to his holy turf!

By way of testament to his longstanding service to the club, a plaque inscription is to be found attached to the front of the pavilion which reads: 'In Memory of Les Barrow, Groundsman, Life Member, 1950-1994'.

ooooo

Gul Mohammad joined as Rammy pro in 1951, aged 30, a left-handed batsman and left-arm medium pace bowler with existing Test match experience playing for India. His main claim to fame though up to that time arose out of sharing in a partnership of 577 runs with Vijay

Hazare in the final of the 1946/7 Ranji Trophy, constituting as it did at the time a world record in first class cricket. Gul had toured England in 1946 and Australia in 1947/8 although it has to be said without much success. His highest score was 34 in the second innings at Adelaide, ironically a match in which Hazare scored two centuries. When Gul signed up to play for Ramsbottom, he no doubt would have asked his friend for advice, aware that Vijay had pro'd at Rawtenstall two years earlier.

Although 1949 had marked another disappointing season for Rammy, it had been a vibrant year for the Lancashire League as a whole. The great Everton Weekes (one of the '3 Ws' – together with two other famous West Indians Frank Worrell and Clyde Walcott) had just joined Bacup. Learie Constantine's massive success at Nelson, not forgetting high levels of remuneration, prompted a host of Caribbean stars to take up residence in Lancashire. Meanwhile, Australians also continued to thrive, none making more impact at this time than Cec Pepper, Burnley's extrovert and decidedly controversial pro.

For Pepper and Hazare, 1949 had been their first year in England as pros. Despite their highly contrasting styles of play and approaches to the game, each of them had managed, for the first time in league history, to achieve the ultimate accolade – the 1,000 runs and 100 wickets double. Pepper was later to enjoy the distinction of hitting the greatest number of runs - 38 - in the new 8-ball-over format that had been introduced in 1939.

Whereas Hazare preferred to let his ability do the talking, Pepper (destined to stay at Burnley for five years) took delight in seeking to psyche opponents out at every end and turn. In this respect, Vijay Hazare would no doubt have alerted his friend Gul as to how he might expect to be greeted in matches against Burnley. Along these lines, Don Ormerod, one of Burnley's leading amateur batsmen in the 50s and 60s, was later to recall the first encounter he witnessed between Cec Pepper and Gul Mohammad on the field of play.

According to Ormerod's recollection, Pepper's usual greeting to players from the Indian sub-continent, when coming to the crease, was something to the effect of 'whether they had brought their prayer mat with them because they were going to need it'. The longstanding

Burnley player remembered on this particular occasion that a series of deliveries then ensued, alternating leg-spin, top spin, googly and flipper. Although unable to lay bat on ball, Gul still had his wicket intact at the end of the over:

'Hands on hips, staring down the wicket, Pepper let out the remark: "As a batsman, you'd make a f****** good snake charmer"'.

Probably Pepper would have regarded it as no more than banter or in cricketing parlance 'sledging', but the anecdote does rather unfortunately reveal the extent to which anyone coming to the league at that time could anticipate being given the 'treatment' for being different in whatever way. The great Learie Constantine himself had suffered racial abuse in his early days at Nelson, not only from other players but also from spectators even if as a result of his huge success with bat and ball, the feedback had soon enough changed to one of awe-struck respect.

Pepper, for his part, would frequently continue to be a thorn in the side of the league authorities over the five years he was at Burnley. Although he was often disciplined, measures taken never seemed to have the desired effect of causing him to modify his behaviour. Unrepentant to the end of his playing days, Pepper stayed on in the game as an umpire (poacher turned gamekeeper) in county cricket from 1964 until 1980, a role which he carried out with an almost exaggerated sense of authority over the players coming under his own jurisdiction. He died in 1993 in Littleborough, aged 76.

ooooo

Across the four-year period Gul Mohammad spent as pro with Rammy, he scored 2,613 runs at an average of 35.05 and took 224 wickets at 17.27. During these seasons, Rammy finished in the league as follows: 1951 - 13th; 1952 - 14th; 1953 - 10th=; 1954 - 8th=.

Throughout these four years though, Gul could not help but have remained acutely aware of the continuing turmoil going on back in his own country. As club pro, he provided good service during a period that must have been very difficult for him on a personal level, ever mindful of the troubles following on from the Independence of India in 1947 and the collateral creation of the new state of Pakistan. Coming originally from the Punjab, an area remaining in the thick of all the tensions that had arisen, he was to return to the Asian sub-continent in 1955, changing his existing Indian citizenship to that of Pakistan.

Gul Mohammad was to play one Test match for Pakistan, against Australia in 1956/7 in which he scored 12 and 27*, in the event hitting the winning runs. Thereafter, he served as a cricket coach for the Punjabi Sports Board and later as a director on the board of the Gaddafi Stadium in Lahore until 1987. He died in 1992, aged 70.

ooooo

Keeping track of Billy Whitworth, he had left to carry out another stint as pro, this time at Bradshaw during seasons 1951 and 1952. But the following season, he was back at Acre Bottom, even if not at his absolute best with the bat, scoring 468 runs at an average of 24.63, to be followed in 1954 with a tally of 417 runs at 23.16.

Another notable Aussie import to the Lancashire League at this time was Bill Alley who, playing for Colne, became the first batsman to score over 1,000 runs across five successive seasons. Apart from his obvious playing prowess, an interesting story arose from a particular match that took place between Colne and Ramsbottom. On this occasion, putting on his boots, Alley discovered a tear in the heel that made standing up in them impossible, let alone going out to play.

In these circumstances, Ramsbottom might justifiably have left Colne to sort out their own problem. However, the Rams happened to have amongst their locker-room staff, a 'clogger' by trade, one by the name of Arthur Holt. In sportsmanlike fashion, 'Owd Arthur's services were proffered. Within minutes of tackling the job, Bill Alley was ready to go out on to the field of play in impeccably repaired footwear.

Incidentally, throughout the years from 1940 to 1961, Holt served the club as 'bag-carrier'. This was at a time when players lacked personal equipment of their own but relied instead on what lay within the club's collective kitbag. Players were always grateful for the role Arthur played in making sure all items of equipment were both well-maintained and also readily available for use on match-days.

ooooo

Peter Philpott, the Australian who joined Ramsbottom in 1955, emerges as the first pro who would put serious pen to paper in recording memories of his time at the club. Although he was to stay at Acre Bottom only for one year initially, he was to return again in 1959 and 1960.

Later on, in 1994, reminiscing in *Forty Years and Ramsbottom*, Peter described how coming to Ramsbottom had originally rested on the toss of a coin. Back in Australia, he and another New South Wales youngster, Pat Crawford, had been approached for two pro jobs being advertised as available in the Lancashire League at both East Lancashire and Ramsbottom. Not knowing anything about either of the clubs, they decided to toss a coin. Crawford won and decided in favour of East Lancs on the basis that they were offering a bit more money.

'It was the best toss I ever lost'. On finally arriving in Ramsbottom, Philpott received 'a warm welcome and it never changed'. Twenty years old at the time, he describes his first impressions on arrival:

'In April, the days seemed short and cold. Practice was difficult on damp, sodden wickets, and my hands certainly felt more comfortable stuffed deep in pockets. I came to know my team-mates better over a pint in a pub than in the nets'.

Recalling his first fixture, 'it was up at Haslingden where Vinoo Mankad was pro. He didn't bother to turn up to the ground, as we were snowed out - the first time I had ever seen snow - and we spent a few hours instead in front of a fire, playing cards'.

Despite a slow start to the season weather-wise, Peter, right hand bat and leg-break/googly bowler, was to enjoy a highly successful season, scoring 861 runs at an average of 43.05 and taking 77 wickets at 12.67, with the team ending the season in 8th position. Again, Billy Whitworth had conjured up another 500+ season, scrambling over the line with 504 runs at an average of 21.91.

Throughout that first season, Peter Philpott remembers fans constantly making him aware of the name of an ex-pro at Rammy, whom he had heard of but never met: Syd Hird. 'Ee, he were a good'un....Did I get Syd rammed down my neck? By the time I had finished in the League,

I hoped my own 4,000 runs and 300 wickets could have caused some other poor beggar to have 'Philpott' rammed down his ear in years to come as I had 'Syd Hird'. God rest his soul!'

ooooo

1956 was to mark the last full season in the illustrious career of Billy Whitworth. During the course of it, he had managed to bang out another '500+' run season to take him to a total of eleven times of accomplishing the feat. Later seasons would see another exceptional batsman, Ian Bell, draw extremely close with ten but the record Billy created in relation to eleven '500+' seasons, at the end of that year 1956, still stands as such in club history.

The service that Billy Whitworth gave to the club was phenomenal, having started playing from 1923 onwards. Within the span of the 483 appearances he put in for Rammy, as opposed to pro spells elsewhere, he scored 10,715 league runs at an average of 27.26 and took 390 wickets at 18.89. With his parting, an era was coming to an end which linked the last championship-winning Rammy side of 1925 to the mid-fifties. Born in Bury in 1904, Billy died in Bury in 1998. Perhaps, the secret to the longevity of his cricketing career, as hinted to latterly by one-time colleague John Cardwell, was that as a teetotaller he always stuck to orangeade in after-match drinking sessions!

Meanwhile, Philpott's successor, Brian Flynn, another Aussie, had struggled to make much of an impression. Having played previously in fifteen matches for Queensland in state cricket between 1952 and 1956, he managed only 362 runs for Rammy at 18.10 whilst his 40 wickets came at a costly average of 21.47. With the club falling back to 13th place, hopes naturally ran higher for the following season.

In 1957, for the first but by no means last time, the club signed up their pro from South Africa. Eddie Fuller's prowess was predominantly as a bowler specialising in right-arm medium-fast cutters whilst also being able to offer valuable lower-order runs. Before he came to Ramsbottom, aged 25, he had already played in seven Test matches for South Africa from 1953 to 1957 and had won the national award of 'Cricketer of the Year' for 1956.

Fuller's performance in the league season of 1957 was in the event to work out very well. Whilst scoring 434 runs at a decent enough average of 25.52 for a player with relatively few pretensions as a batsman, his bowling record more than lived up to expectations, taking 84 wickets at 9.77. From 13th position the year before, the club succeeded in moving up to 5th. However, it was progress made in the Worsley Cup that season which would prove the real pay-off.

In a first round match, played at Thorneyholme Park, Ramsbottom bowled Accrington out for 179 with Fuller taking 5-79 and Harold Monkhouse 4-72. In response, a 71-run 4th wicket partnership between opening bat Hetherington and Fuller saw the Rams home at 181-3 for a seven-wicket victory.

In the second round, Rammy took on Bacup at Acre Bottom. Winning the toss and deciding to bat, the Rams managed only a relatively meagre total of 111, thanks largely to a gusty 30* from captain Geoff Marsden. Subsequently though, Fuller steamed in and ripped the heart out of the Bacup batting line-up, taking 5-46 to finish the opposition of at 89 all out, resulting in a 22-run win.

In the semi-final against Burnley at Acre Bottom, the away team looked in command at 110-1 but dramatically fell away to 146 all out with slow left arm bowler Brian Quinton doing the main damage with 4-50. In response, Ramsbottom had cause to be grateful for half-centuries scored by opener Bill Greenhalgh (50) and Bill Savage (52) - brother of John - to carry them over the line to 147-8, thereby securing a narrow two-wicket victory.

ooooo

Brian Quinton, at the age nowadays of 88, recently recalled in conversation with the author that he had just finished a two-year stint of National Service in time to allow him to appear for Rammy at the particular semi-final stage of the competition described above. Prominent though his role had been in achieving victory in the semi-final, circumstances were ironically such that, although he played in the final, he was destined neither to bat nor bowl in it.

Playing at Rawtenstall on 29 August, Ramsbottom made heavy weather of batting first, getting into trouble at 61-5, despite an innings of 33 from Ernie Chamberlain. Derek Hodgson (38*), having survived a hat-trick ball, then though managed to put on 69 with Geoff Marsden (27*) to steer the Rams to 130-5. Even so, it still seemed a total well within the home team's reach.

However, in a devastating spell of 8 overs, 4 maidens, 7 wickets for 11 runs, Eddie Fuller executed the strike bowler's role to perfection. Rawtenstall couldn't lay bat on ball and were all out for 36. By a 94-run margin, the Rams had succeeded again in lifting the prestigious Worsley Cup. Incidentally, with Fuller bowling one end and Harold Monkhouse the other, the two of them had finished the opposition off inside 16 overs, explaining why Brian Quinton didn't get on to bowl!

The photo of the winning team shows Geoff Marsden sitting proudly behind the Cup Trophy, which is mounted on a plinth. To his immediate right is Chairman Jim Collinge and to his left Secretary George Taylor. Naturally, there are the other ten players on parade but by way of a nice touch, scorer Fred Rothwell - to enjoy a lifelong association with the club in a host of different ways - is standing at one end of the back row and then at the other is the very jovial-looking figure, bag-carrier A.W. Holt, of course known more affectionately as 'Owd Arthur'. The picture succeeds very well in conveying a message that the victory was truly a team effort, including not only the players but also the supporting 'back room staff'.

The partnership between captain Geoff Marsden and pro Eddie Fuller continued on into 1958 but without achieving the same degree of success as the year before. In the league, the club finished 9th. In the Worsley Cup, it was to be 'sublime to ridiculous', following an ignominious first round exit at the hands of Bacup. The Rams were bowled out for 144 with Everton Weekes taking 6-53, before the visitors comfortably knocked off the runs for a nine-wicket victory, Weekes scoring 87* of their total of 145-1.

During this season, Fuller took 67 league wickets at an average of 10.82. His bowling performances over the two seasons had put him third and fourth respectively in the 1957 and 1958 League's bowling averages. Incidentally, the next season, Eddie went to play for Rawtenstall who could have been forgiven for still having in mind his impressive performance against them in the 1957 Worsley Cup Final.

ooooo

The pro vacancy was filled by the return of Peter Philpott for the start of 1959. He was to stay a further two seasons. The second of the two was to prove the more successful all round. In 1959, the club finished in 10th= position, with a record of W5 D13 L8. Philpott's own performance had been outstanding though, becoming the first batsman in the club's history to exceed 1,000 runs, achieving a club record of 1,016 runs at an average of 56.44. Notable amongst his many high totals, as well as two other centuries, was the 155* he scored at Accrington on 24 June. In a drawn match, Philpott opened no. 1 and made his runs out of a total of 235-5 declared. In return, future Aussie skipper Bobby Simpson steered the home team to safety with 122*, reaching 206-3 at close of play. Successful as Philpott was with the bat that year, he was rather less so though with the ball, taking only 23 wickets at an average of 23.43.

In 1960 though, Philpott was back firing on all cylinders. The example he set was also to inspire team-mates to greater things. As the season ran its course, the championship appeared to lie between the Rams and local rivals Bacup who had the fiery West Indian fast bowler Roy Gilchrist as their pro. Two key matches took place between the two sides within the space of a week. On 14 May, at Lanehead, the Rams had won by 75 runs, scoring 152 and bowling their opponents out for 77 with Philpott taking 8-19.

Then on 21 May, another win was achieved at Acre Bottom with the home team scoring 179. Although Gilchrist ended with figures of 5-72, a solid partnership involving Henry Hall (59) and Geoff Marsden (42) had riled Gilchrist into a bout of verbal abuse accompanied by a stream of bumpers and beamers aimed at body and head. This was of course before the time of batsmen wearing helmets! In response though, Bacup were bowled out for 113 with opening bowler John Cardwell doing the main damage - including the prize wicket of Gilchrist lbw for a duck - to capture career-best statistics of 5-56, Philpott mopping up the tail with 4-38.

Although this next game against Bacup had been won comfortably by a margin of 66 runs, the Rams had unfortunately slipped up in an intervening match when losing to Enfield. With Ramsbottom and Bacup vying for supremacy in the final run-in, other factors however kicked into play, namely adverse weather conditions. In two of their last three matches of the season, one against Church (when the match was abandoned without a ball being bowled) and in the rain-affected return match against Enfield, the Rams only managed to pick up one point for a 'draw' on these occasions.

With the system of points allocation having been adjusted from 1956 onwards to make it 4 points for a win instead of 3, Bacup won the 1960 league title reaching a total of 61 points (W13 D9 L4) compared with runners-up Ramsbottom's 60 (W13 D8 L5). In truth, the change in the points system had not made any difference to the outcome. However, although the Rams had won their last match of the season against Rishton, the lack of opportunity to win the two matches prior to this had in the end arguably cost them the title, having to settle in the end for the Holland Cup, the prize for the team coming second in the championship.

Philpott fared even better individually this season with the bat, beating the record he had set in 1959 by scoring 1,069 runs at an average of 53.45. Apart from this, he was very much on song again with his leg breaks and googlies taking 82 wickets at an average of 12.06. Although no doubt he must have felt disappointed that the club had fallen short of winning the title by such a narrow margin, there still remained a great deal for him to look back on with pleasure and satisfaction from his time at the club.

Again, this is evident from all that he was subsequently to write about his experience, not only in terms of matches he played but the club personalities he rubbed shoulders with. Notably, 'the Monk', medium-fast bowler Harold Monkhouse, who apart from his undoubted ability as a player, appears also to have been a great 'mover and shaker' on the social side of club life.

'I still have a great photo of him during a players' trip to Blackpool – an hilarious photo. But' – so Peter continued – 'I won't show it, nor will I tell you about it'. Interestingly though, when coming to speak recently with John Cardwell, the author was informed he too was in possession of evidence of a similar-sounding nature, suggesting perhaps that revealing photos of 'the Monk' were not exactly rarity items!

Peter Philpott was quick to realise that the spirit of togetherness shown away from the pitch contained immense power to pay off in matches on the pitch. 'At the practices, out of the field, in the coaches, then afterwards, in pubs and chippies, over a cleansing ale or even behind some microphone singing – or just talking, laughing, arguing, I'll not forget the Ernie Chamberlains, the Geoff Bladens and Marsdens, Ronnie Bowkers, the Bills (Savage, Whitworth and Greenhalgh), Jacky Ollertons and Jimmy Davenports'.

ooooo

From all Peter's different accounts of matches that he took part in, one highly evocative account stems from a description of playing at Bacup, where he paints a vivid picture of the intimidating atmosphere in which local derbies took place, underlining the intense rivalry operating between the two clubs during these years:

'We arrived at Bacup amidst a thick, grey mountain fog. The ground was totally mist shrouded; we lost the toss, and were sent in on a strange looking wicket. Trevor Morris and I padded up in ominous silence... As I faced up to take strike, I looked up to locate my major opponent (who else but the fiery Roy Gilchrist) who had last been seen beginning to measure out his long, aggressive approach to the wicket. Not only was he invisible, but so were the sight boards, the fence and the crowd. A grey, ghostly wall restricted all visibility to no more than thirty-five yards. But beyond, I could hear the hum of a partisan crowd who could apparently see us, and, as I strained my eyes, the ominous crunch of sprinting feet heralded the approach of our fearsome foe, who, I had little doubt, had me clearly in his sights'.

Whatever followed on this occasion, Philpott does not go on to say. We probably do not need to be told. Suffice it to say that the gladiatorial combat between such renowned pros in 'arenas' such as Lanehead and Acre Bottom provided a spectacle that crowds keenly anticipated and came flocking in their thousands to come and witness. Fog permitting!

Apart though from the time he spent on the field in 1955 and again representing the club across 1959 and 1960, Peter Philpott also played a highly significant part in the life of the community, even if in a quieter and more relaxed way:

'During the week, at Peel Brow School, and through the summer holidays I worked and played at various stages with groups of very promising youngsters - Trevor Morris, Henry Hall, Dally Brooks, Maurice Haslam, Johnny Ashworth, Graham Fallows, John McNutt, Brian Fielding and so many others. We played cricket, ran about in the sun, drank all the coca cola, and ate all the ice lollies that Ramsbottom had in stock. And I think - I hope - we learnt a lot of cricket together and came to love the dear old game that little bit more'.

Despite leaving the club at the end of the 1960, the seeds that Peter had sown in the hearts and minds of these 'youngsters' were to bear incredible fruit in years to follow with so many of the names mentioned above coming to play important roles in the history of the club. Needless to say, they were the first to testify later to the wholly inspiring example served them by their great Australian mentor, Peter Philpott.

By way of postscript, Philpott was, following his experiences at Rammy, later to make his Test debut for Australia in the West Indies in 1964/5, taking 18 wickets in the five Test matches of that series. He was to win eight caps in all. He captained New South Wales from 1963 to 1965. After this, with his vast knowledge and strong ability to read the game, he became a renowned cricketing coach.

In the meantime though, Peter never lost contact with the club, memorably returning on one occasion to Acre Bottom for a notable match 'at fifty years of age'. Very touched at the time to see a sign outside the clubhouse saying: 'Welcome back Peter', he commented further: 'Those who were there will remember a great match and an equally great night to follow'.

ooooo

News of the death of Peter Philpott in early November 2021 came as a huge emotional blow to those, such as Maurice Haslam, who had benefitted so much from his generosity of spirit over the course of the time he had spent at the club as pro. Huge fondness and respect was felt at the club with regard to the inspiring part Peter had played, so ably and with such good humour, in guiding youngsters of those times through their formative cricketing years back in the late 1950s and into the early 1960s.

Six: 'Everyone Down for Practice on Monday - No Excuses!'

IN THE EARLY 60s, the signing up of Caribbean fast bowlers as club pros was all the rage. There were certainly plenty to choose from. Famously, Wes Hall came to Accrington and Charlie Griffith to Burnley. Not all West Indians playing in the Lancashire League were speed merchants though. For example, Barbadian Seymour Nurse, who joined Ramsbottom in 1961, was primarily a batsman although also a useful off-spinner.

After coming close to winning the championship the year before, the club did not do so well in 1961, finishing 12th. This was despite Nurse heading the League's batting averages, notching up 1,129 runs (exceeding Peter Philpott's club record set in 1960) at an average of 62.72. Although scoring two centuries, neither of these feats ended up in victories. In fact, the team only won four matches all season, with twelve matches drawn and ten lost. Nor could any blame be apportioned to the pro in the bowling department with Nurse garnering a respectable tally of 56 wickets at 13.87.

A particularly interesting match that season was one played at home against Enfield on 8 July where Rammy won the toss and chose to field. The visitors scored 156 with Seymour taking 7-62. In reply, although Peter Ashworth and Richard Wheatcroft went for ducks, the pro set off like a train. In fact, he monopolised proceedings to such an extent that, when third man out after an innings of 57, all 57 runs scored to that point had come off Nurse's bat. Unfortunately, the momentum could not be maintained and the Rams were all out for 109, losing the match by 49 runs.

1961 has a place in club history for the fact it marked the first season of the Wolstenholme Cup award for player of the year. The winner in this inaugural year was Bill Savage who took 41 wickets at 13.4, finishing 15th in the league's overall bowling averages.

A process was beginning to unwind in the early 60s whereby the experienced players who had been fixtures in the club's 1st XI throughout the late 50s gradually gave way to a fresh crop of players. This new contingent had in the meantime served their apprenticeship in the junior ranks, starting in the under-18s, then the 2nd XI before establishing a spot for themselves in the 1st XI. Sometimes, admittedly, it seemed to suit such young players to go on playing in the 2nd XI because they could be surer of involvement in matches as compared to batting only nos. 9 or 10 in the 1st XI.

Much credit has though to be given to Peter Philpott for his encouragement of so many of the young players who emerged at this time. The likes of Henry Hall and Trevor Morris, coached by Philpott during his initial spell at the club in 1955, were the first to come through. Many of the other young players, mentioned in the last chapter as having been subsequently mentored by the Aussie pro during 1959 and 1960, featured in the under-18 championship-winning team of 1960. Whilst the 1st XI didn't fare too well during the early 60s, significantly the 2nd XI excelled itself, enjoying two junior championship wins.

The experience of a young player like John Ashworth was fairly representative of these times. He made a 1st XI debut at the age of 15 in 1962 but played mainly thereafter in the 2nd XI, being a member of the teams that won the junior championship in 1964 and 1966. During these times, he had occasional outings in the first team. One particular match he was later to recall was one against Burnley when he faced Charlie Griffith, dubbed the fastest bowler in the world at the time. Arriving at the crease on a hat-trick ball, John stated: 'I never saw it or the next two balls but luckily I came out second top scorer that day with 18, all of 15 of these coming off the bowling of Griffith'. However, this ground-breaking experience aside, it wouldn't be until 1968 that John Ashworth would for the first time play more than ten matches in a season for the club's 1st XI.

1962 had proved another unsuccessful season, finishing 12[th]=. Although Seymour Nurse again achieved high standards as a batsman, scoring a total of 974 runs at an average of 51.26, the number of wickets he took fell to 26 at an average of 20.42. Again though with regard to scoring centuries, only one of his four tons (the highest being 129* against Colne) was converted into a win. The eventual match result breakdown of W4 D11 L11 was virtually identical to the previous season.

For 1963, a 19-year-old Australian by the name of Ian Chappell was taken on as pro. Having broken into State cricket a year earlier, playing for South Australia, he was said at the time to be showing greater promise than any young Aussie since the emergence of Donald Bradman. However, his year-long experience of playing in the League was to prove somewhat disappointing both for himself and the club. He only managed a modest total of 510 runs at an average of 24.28, whilst picking up 60 wickets at 15.06 apiece.

Nor, given the prodigious future he was to have ahead of him in a leadership role, did he appear to have had much of an inspiring effect on others around him at the time, with the side taking the wooden spoon in 14th place with a record of W4 D9 L13. The irony was that when he came to pay a later visit back to Acre Bottom in 1989, he did so with an amazingly enhanced reputation in the meantime that placed him unquestionably in the pantheon of top cricketers in the history of the sport. He had since represented his country 75 times and gone on to be regarded as one of Australia's greatest batsmen and arguably best-ever captain. Notably, in 1976, he had won the Cricketer of the Year Award.

ooooo

Incidentally, on the domestic front, 1963 marked the end of Harold Monkhouse's 1st XI playing career. Born in 1926 in Holcombe village, he had started playing for the club in 1943. Allowing for a break in service from 1945 to 1951, he had gone on to play for the club all the way through to 1963, operating chiefly as an opening bowler, playing in 231 1st XI matches and taking 325 wickets at an average of 19.11.

Going back to mention of him in the last chapter, Harold's influence would be missed both on and off the field.

As another example of emerging talent at this time, a highly promising newcomer bursting on to the scene was a young fast bowler in his early twenties from Summerseat by the name of Terry Stewart. Despite 1963 being a disappointing year for the club in general terms, Terry made his own individual mark with a haul of 51 wickets at an average of 14.70, at the same time winning the club's player of the year award for the first of four times in his career.

Thankfully, 1964, witnessing the return of Seymour Nurse as pro, was to have a happier outcome than the previous season with the club finishing 5th with a record of W8 D11 L7. Ironically though, it was the least auspicious, in personal terms, of Nurse's three seasons at the club. Failing to score a century, his run tally was only 610 at an average of 29.04 whilst taking 48 wickets at 13.37. A low-point of the 1964 season came when the club's scourge from his Bacup days, Roy Gilchrist, now playing for Lowerhouse, captured all ten Rammy wickets (10-41) in a match on 11 July.

The all-round contribution though that Seymour Nurse made over the three seasons he was at Rammy is remembered fondly by those who played with him. In particular, John Steele, who had made his 1st X1 debut in 1963, recalled the way in which the genial West Indian always offered encouragement to young players like himself. Courtesy of the W.I. Test Board, Seymour had several bats in his possession. Generously, he offered the prize of one to any player in the Rammy team scoring a half-century.

In his 80s now, John Steele still keenly remembered a home match in 1964 against Enfield in which the visitors had been bowled out for 143. Opening the Rammy innings, John was on 49* when the home team's total reached 143-3. Facing the bowling, and the chance within his grasp to gain one of Seymour's coveted bats, he played and missed the next ball. The wicket-keeper also missed it and, much to John's personal dismay, the winning runs came off byes! However, understanding the young man's feeling of anguish, Seymour had graciously relaxed the 50-run criterion and granted the John the prize he was desperate to win.

Incidentally, leaving aside for a moment the generosity of Nurse in offering incentives for the scoring of a half-century, it was at the same time the custom in the League for 'the hat' to go round the crowd to reward batsmen scoring a fifty. This could amount to useful money for amateur players. Mention of this reminds the author of talking recently with another veteran from the past, Derek Webster, who happened to recall a particular match he had played in away at Church back in May 1953. Laying no claim to have been a leading batsman himself, Derek prided himself though on his abilities as a fielder. On this occasion he had run out one of Church's all-time greats, Harry Pilkington, (who scored 5,822 runs in his 24 years playing for the club). The unusual aspect about this was that Harry was on 49 runs at the time. Derek still remembered how he was booed throughout the rest of the match for having been seen to deny Pilkington a pay-day!

Going back to memories of Seymour Nurse, John Steele remembered Nurse being another who relished the relaxed atmosphere of club outings to Blackpool, for example playing football on the beach (he was a West Indian international at soccer as well as at cricket level) and having such an affable manner towards everyone around him.

Seymour Nurse represented his country in 29 Test matches between 1960 and 1969. At international level, his greatest success came in the 1966 West Indian tour of England. He scored 501 runs in this series at an average of 62.62, figures only surpassed by his captain, Gary Sobers. He was Wisden Cricketer of the Year in 1967. After his Test career finished, Seymour continued playing cricket in Barbados, going on to serve as head coach of the Barbados National Sports Council, including mentoring famous future West Indian opener, Desmond Haynes.

Nurse died in Bridgetown in May 2019, survived by his twin daughters, and honoured by having a room named after him at the Barbados Cricket Club to commemorate his rich contribution to the game, both at home and abroad.

ooooo

1965 witnessed the arrival at Rammy of the renowned English Test match slow left-arm bowler, Tony Lock who had famously taken the 'other wicket' on the occasion of Jim Laker achieving his world record 19-90 at Old Trafford in 1956 against Australia. In his own right though, Lock was to go on to take 174 wickets for his country at an average of 24.76. In 1954, he had received a Cricketer of the Year Award. As opposed to other pros who had joined Rammy at the start of their playing careers, Tony was by comparison considered very much towards the end of his.

In this light, it had been hoped he would be able to give dedicated time to the club. This was not to prove the case. No sooner had he been signed up than Leicestershire C.C. came hot in pursuit. An uneasy compromise was reached whereby he played for Leicestershire for the greater part of each week while travelling up to honour his Lancashire League commitment as best he could during weekends.

In the event, Rammy finished 7th in 1965 with a record of W8 D10 L8. Tony Lock scored 520 runs at an average of 24.76 whilst predictably doing better with the ball taking 92 wickets at 9.35. Capably as Lock performed over the course of his single season at Rammy, he was destined to last longer with Leicestershire, taking over as captain there in 1966 and leading the side to second place in the county championship of 1967.

As far as the Rams' general pattern of results was concerned during the 1960s, they were never to finish higher than mid-table. 1966 would prove particularly disappointing, finishing rock bottom 14th again, this time with a record of W3 D12 L11. Twenty-six year-old Keith Stackpole was the pro, aged 26, an aggressive right hand bat and useful leg-break bowler from Victoria, Australia. Despite scoring an impressive 824 runs at an average of 45.8 (third-placed in the league's batting averages) and taking 58 wickets at 14.72, his combined efforts with bat and ball could not redeem the Rams from the wooden spoon.

Like Ian Chappell, Stackpole was also ironically to go on to achieve great success representing his country in later years, winning 43 caps and serving as Chappell's vice-captain in the 1972 tour of England, making 485 runs (average 52.88) and topping the Australian batting averages. He was named a Wisden Cricketer of the Year in 1973.

Replaced by fellow Aussie Peter Kelly for the following seasons of 1967 and 1968, the club finished 12th and 10[th]= with records of W4

D15 L7 and W5 D11 L10 respectively. Incidentally, 1968 marked the first year in the League's history that 'bonus points' were introduced. However, the club was only able to achieve a miserly 2 such points in this inaugural season.

Joining at the age of 25, Kelly had played a total of 23 first-class matches for New South Wales in 1962-3 and for Western Australia in 1966-7. A right hand bat and slow left arm bowler, his batting statistics in 1967 fell slightly below those of Stackpole, with 656 runs scored at an average of 38.58 although raising the tempo the next season with 837 at 38.04. In bowling terms, he took 35 wickets at 11.74 in 1967 but the year after only 24 at 18.00.

ooooo

Over the four-year period from 1969 to 1972, the services of Indian all-rounder, R.G.Nadkarni (better known as 'Bapu') were enlisted. Although the batting statistics he achieved were relatively modest - his highest season's total of runs scored being 506 in 1969 at an average of 26.6 - he consistently performed well with the ball over his four seasons at the club taking a cumulative 258 wickets at an overall average of 11.09.

A seasoned Test international by the time he joined the club, 36-year-old Bapu, a left hand bat and slow left hand bowler, had a worthy career behind him going back to the time he had made his debut for India in 1955 at the age of 22. Renowned for bowling an unerring line to batsmen, making it extremely difficult to score off him, he was probably best known for his bowling stint in the Madras Test against England in 1963-4. At the end of the third day of the match, bowling against Brian Bolus and Ken Barrington, his figures remarkably stood at 29 overs, 26 maidens, and no wickets for three runs. Finishing with figures of 32-27-5-0, he had bowled a record 29.5 consecutive overs (equivalent to 131 dot balls) without conceding a run.

At first, 'Bapu' did not find it easy adapting to the Lancashire League. For one thing, bowling conditions were rather different in Bacup compared say to Bombay. Arriving at Lanehead for one of his earliest games in icy April weather, just having come from the heat of India, he had difficulty gripping the ball in his left hand, let alone exercising his customary control over flight and direction.

It was a clear sign though of how well-respected he came to be that he was retained at Rammy four years running. Later, Duncan Brooks was to recall what a pleasure it had been having Bapu, his wife and their children staying with him in Ramsbottom throughout this time, 'delightful to be with at all times'.

In 1969, the club rose to 5th with a record of W6 D16 L4. Trevor Morris did well with the bat scoring 415 runs at an average of 18.9. Despite slipping to 11th in 1970 – W2 D17 L7 – there were further encouraging signs of progress being made by amateur players. For example, Arthur Chapman scored 510 runs at an average of 20.4, the first time the 500+ yardstick had been achieved since Billy Whitworth in 1956. This would have made Billy proud because he happened to be Arthur's great-uncle. Meanwhile, Terry Stewart took 50 wickets at 14.50 and also won the club's player of the year award.

1970 was a disappointing year in which the club finished 11th with a record of W2 D17 L7. The next year, 1971, was notable for the League deciding to move from 'time cricket' to 'limited overs'. Given the fact that the overwhelming number of matches ended up as draws (it wasn't just Rammy who drew most of their games!), the aim was to produce more positive outcomes, mindful also that it might promote healthier levels of crowd attendance and greater sense of entertainment.

Gladly, the 1971 season saw the club climbing back up to 5th place, with Nadkarni coming second in the league bowling averages, taking 64 wickets at 8.5. However, in the light of the change to 'limited overs' cricket, it inevitably brought about a very different results profile: W12 NR5 L9. A 'No Result' outcome was invariably due to adverse weather conditions.

However, the Rams dropped back down to 10th in 1972 with a record of W9 NR 9 L8. Without high run totals from the pro, there was a lot of added pressure on the amateur batsmen. To some extent though, it gave these batsmen more opportunity to shine. For example, it was another good season for Chapman, scoring 440 runs at an average of 22.0.

ooooo

After a brief two-year experiment with 'limited overs' format, the League surprisingly decided in 1973 to return to 'time cricket'. As far as the Rams were concerned, this season was notable for taking on the dynamic South African all-rounder, Clive Rice, as pro. A right hand bat and fast bowler from the state of Transvaal, Rice ('Mr. Motivator') was to prove an inspirational leader who set a relentless standard to players around him, in terms of fitness and attitude.

The club began the new campaign with a vengeance, vying for the lead with East Lancashire. On 26 May, they went four points ahead after defeating Colne in a tight match which could have gone either way. The Rams had been dismissed for 103 but Rice had hit back with a hostile 7-29 to bowl the opposition out for 79.

In mid-June, Rammy opener Arthur Chapman scored a third successive half-century, as the league leaders beat Rawtenstall. However, the Rams were then to suffer their first defeat of the season at home to Bacup. This was after bowling the visitors out for 123 with spinners Maurice Haslam and Bill Savage taking 3-26 and 3-31 respectively. In the event though, the home team was taken apart by Bacup pro Phil Carlson who took 8-18 to bundle the Rams out for just 37, the lowest score of the season to date.

In a vital head-to-head away game against East Lancs, the home team's pro Aussie Neil Hawke took 6-6 to reduce the Rams to 27-9, redeemed somewhat by a last-wicket stand of 21 between wicket-keeper/skipper Duncan ('Dally') Brooks and Mick Galpin which lifted the total to 48. Despite not requiring a massive number of runs to win, East Lancs were rocked by a devastating spell of 6-11 from Terry Stewart before emerging four-wicket victors at 52-6.

The season remained a seesaw contest with the Rams regaining the lead after Terry Stewart, enjoying a purple patch, took 5-47 to dismiss visitors Lowerhouse for 125 with Clive Rice then smashing 74* to take the Rams to victory. A match at Acre Bottom against Haslingden on 26 August was dramatically decided with the last ball of the match. Batting second, it had seemed the visitors had the game in the bag, needing just 30 to win at a run a minute with 7 wickets in hand. However Bill Savage then took 5-31, leaving the visitors two runs to score off the last ball to win. In the event, a run out saw the home team emerge victors on the day by a one-run margin.

With the Rams holding the tightest of leads going into the final day of the season on 16 September, East Lancashire did everything they needed to do at their end by polishing off opponents Bacup by 8 wickets at Alexandra Meadows. All was therefore to be decided by the outcome of Rammy's home game against Todmorden. Batting first, Denis Hardman hit an unbeaten 61, Arthur Chapman 32 and Maurice Haslam 23 as the Rams declared on 133-7. However, despite Brian Fielding's 3-31, Todmorden held out for a draw on 128-7, sadly to consign Ramsbottom to the runners-up spot.

In the end, East Lancashire retained the title with 65 points and an unbeaten record of W13 D13 L0 against Rammy's 63 points, comprising W13 D11 L2. Clearly, had Ramsbottom won their final match against Tod, they would have finished on 66 points. It didn't turn out that way though and the team was left to lick its wounds, having to settle for the Holland Cup.

In personal terms, Clive Rice finished 11th in the League's batting averages with 531 runs at 27.9. Amateur Arthur Chapman wasn't far behind with 498 runs at an average of 24.5. Despite not coming into the side until late in the season, Brian Fielding topped the bowling averages with 14 wickets at 8.6. Bill Savage came 7th with 32 wickets at 10.7 with Terry Stewart 14th taking 51 wickets at 12.8. Clive Rice came 16th with 66 wickets at 13.3. Remarkably, Rammy succeeded in having five of their bowlers in the League's top 20 averages with Maurice Haslam taking 17th place with 19 wickets at 13.5 apiece.

ooooo

Following on into 1974, there was concern that the example Clive Rice had set the year before would be difficult to replicate. However, as captain, Dally Brooks reckoned he had learnt enough from Rice not to let team standards of fitness and commitment slip back.

As far as replacing the unavailable Rice as pro, it had been planned that the highly promising Pakistani all-rounder Wasim Raja would take over, only for him to be called up at the last moment for Test duty.

A frantic scramble to secure a replacement ended in Ray Bright, an Australian all-rounder, right hand bat and slow left arm spin bowler, arriving at Acre Bottom as soon as he could after an ODI set of matches in New Zealand.

Again, as in 1973, the Rams were to enjoy another successful start to a season, competing for top spot with Rishton and Haslingden during early weekends. A home defeat though at the hands of Accrington on 15 June did little to bolster confidence. Nevertheless, instant revenge was wrought with a 7-wicket victory a week later back at Thorneyholme Road. Accrington were bowled out for 143, Ray Bright taking 6-43 and Brian Fielding 3-36. Peter Ashworth hit 12 fours and a six in a swift 72 as Rammy knocked the runs off by the 24th over.

A 60-run win over champions East Lancs at Acre Bottom on 29 June took Rammy to the top of the table. Opener Arthur Chapman made 69 in the home side's 150-7 with Ray Bright taking 7-27 to dismiss the opposition for 90. Leading the table, the Rams then though suffered a reverse on 13 July at Rawtenstall. Things had seemed to be going well after posting a score of 176-5 (Ray Bright celebrating his 21st birthday with an unbeaten century) before the home team dashed the visitors' hopes by coasting to a comfortable 8-wicket victory.

Held to a draw by Rawtenstall in the return fixture at Acre Bottom, Haslingden took advantage to return to the top after shooting Bacup out for a season's lowest total of 31 at Lanehead on 20 July. However, on 27 July, Rammy beat Church at home, dismissing them for 76 with Brian Fielding taking 4-17, Terry Stewart 3-25 and Ray Bright 3-20. John Ashworth (32*) and Ray Bright (29) steered the home team to a comfortable six-wicket victory. This enabled the Rams to capture the lead again after Rishton had done the Rams a favour by defeating Haslingden. Next, Terry Stewart was to have a field day against bottom-placed Colne at the Horsfield, hitting 45* in the Rams' total of 129-9 before taking 5-24 to skittle the home team out for 85.

In subsequent matches, the Rams consolidated their lead until, on Sunday 1 September, they faced Haslingden at Acre Bottom with a clear chance of winning the League title for the first time since 1925. With everything going superbly to plan on the day, Terry Stewart took 5-30 and Ray Bright 5-13 to dismiss the visitors for 63. Bright then made an unbeaten 37 to secure the League Championship title for Ramsbottom with all of three matches still remaining to be played. The eventual margin of victory ended up being a highly impressive 14 points – W12 D11 L3 (59 points) – over runners-up Nelson with a record of W8 D13 L5 (45 points).

To say he had joined the club at such short notice, Ray Bright had achieved everything that could have been asked of him as pro, finishing 6th in the League batting averages with 523 runs at an average of 30.8 whilst heading the pro bowling averages with 73 wickets taken at 9.7. At the same time, it had been a notable team achievement with plenty of outstanding contributions from other players. John Ashworth came 7th in the batting averages with 430 runs at 30.7. Just as 1974 marked John's highest run total in a season in his long career with the Rams, it was also the case for his namesake, opener Peter Ashworth, who scored 423 runs at 21.15. Although Denis Hardman was to have better seasons ahead of him, he also contributed ably with the bat in this championship-winning year, scoring 370 runs at 18.50. Meanwhile, Bright's spin bowling was ably complemented by opening fast bowlers Brian Fielding (35 wickets at an average of 13.4) and Terry Stewart (37 at 13.7 apiece).

ooooo

If the above were the 'headline' contributors statistically, an excellent account provided in more recent times by vice-captain, Maurice Haslam, demonstrates what the winning of the championship meant at the time to the team as a whole:

'There was very little difference in the make-up of the side from the previous season. The team spirit was very high and the confidence was there due entirely to what Clive Rice had taught us in 1973. He was so positive in everything he did and it rubbed off.

'Ray Bright obviously played a massive part in '74, he gave the side a better balance, being a left arm spinner of quality. The opening attack of Terry Stewart and Brian Fielding, followed by Brighty and Bill Savage in the spin department gave us possibly the best bowling line-up in the league.

'What sticks out more than anything was the team spirit and the leadership of the skipper Duncan 'Dally' Brooks who week after week rammed into us what Ricey had preached the previous season.

'We had narrowly lost out to East Lancs the year before, so it was a thrill beating them at the end of June to take us to the top of the table. Even though there were still quite a few more games to play, it gave us lots of confidence for the rest of the season.

'I remember Brighty celebrating his 21st birthday with 100 not out against Rawtenstall but sadly nothing about the match and the night. Despite the disappointment of losing, I expect we would have had a few beers and no doubt Dally would have told us 'Everyone down for practice on Monday, no excuses'.

The following are 'pen portraits' of members of the team, as also provided by Maurice:

John Ashworth – 'John had his best ever season in '74 winning the club's 'Player of the Year'. Very strong on the off-side both driving and cutting. Just loved batting!

Peter Ashworth – 'Tall man who could hit the ball a long way off the front or back foot, also a useful seam bowler who got good bounce. Laid back character.

Duncan Brooks – 'No nonsense skipper who demanded commitment in practice and on match days but knew how to party afterwards! Kept wicket to many top bowlers both spin and pace. Lower order batsman who could stick around and graft a few runs.

Terry Stewart – 'Top quality seam bowler with that extra yard of pace to trouble even the best of batsmen. Handy hitter lower down the order and a brilliant outfielder with the best throwing arm I have seen in league cricket.

Brian Fielding – 'Pace bowler who came into the game late but made the most of it. Good yard of pace and developed a good outswinger. Top-class fielder in the deep. Least said about the batting the better! Life and soul of the dressing room.

Henry Hall – 'Good hooker and puller and good judge of a run. Excellent slip fielder. Good cricket brain.

Arthur Chapman – 'Very effective front-footed batsman who liked a 'word'. Usually found someone to fall out with even if it was a teammate! Always made a contribution at the top of the order. Occasional orthodox left arm spinner. Good catcher close to the wicket.

Bill Savage – 'Off spinner who was not the sharpest turner of the ball, but accurate with good control and variation of pace. Very handy batsman down the order.

Denis Hardman – 'Early order batsman who loved to drive and cut, good temperament. Good fielder catching close to the wicket.

Then characteristically in modest vein about his own contribution – Maurice Haslam – 'I just bowled a few leggers at the end if the opposition were blocking it out. Difficult to get a bowl with our line-up. Batted low to middle order. Took a lot of pride in fielding in the covers and being vice-captain to Dally Brooks in '74.

Seven: Evo Faces 'Whispering Death'

THE 1975 SEASON started in a spirit of high optimism. Apart from unfortunately having lost Arthur Chapman due to work commitments down south, the squad was basically the same. Despite continuing as wicket-keeper, Dally Brooks had felt unable to commit himself to the demands made on his time by captaincy and relinquished the role to his vice-captain from the previous season, Maurice Haslam. Regarding the pro position, 22-year-old Wasim Raja, left hand bat and leg-break/googly bowler, was available to take up the role that had originally been intended for him in 1974.

Meanwhile, the League had decided to switch back again from 'time cricket' to 'limited overs'. The opening day of the season on 27 April happily saw fine weather, good cricket and big crowds. As champions, the Rams started well with a 9-wicket home win against Todmorden. New pro Wasim Raja took 4-22 and Bill Savage 4-9 as the visitors were bundled out for 81. Then Raja hit an unbeaten 63 with four sixes and five fours off just 45 balls to clinch victory.

A second win was gained against Nelson by 17 runs in an exciting match in which Raja scored 84 out of a total of 134, then taking 5-34 as opposing pro Collis King hit a superb 69 before being stumped off Raja, with Nelson bowled out for 117. A third victory came at home against Lowerhouse who had posted a total of 155. In reply, the Rams were struggling at 56-6, despite a contribution of 41 from the pro, before a 7th wicket stand of 100 runs between skipper Maurice Haslam (39*) and Terry Stewart (54*) delivered a memorable four-wicket win.

A fourth victory came away at Rishton. In the next match at home against Haslingden, the Rams were bowled out for 116 only for Terry

Stewart to take 5-28 in the course of dismissing the away team for 91. A four-wicket win in a home match against Rishton, with Stewart taking 5-37, made it six wins out of six. Another four-wicket victory came against Haslingden, with Raja scoring 106 out of a total of 158-6.

On 31 May, the young Pakistani hit 84, including four sixes and seven fours, in a 2nd wicket stand of 117 with Denis Hardman (40) as the Rams passed Church's 191-6 to record another win by four wickets. Remarkably, the team entered June with eight straight wins from eight matches and a commanding lead in the league table.

Just as everything was going so well, and with Wasim Raja in such majestic form, he was whisked away for World Cup duty for Pakistan. Without him, the team floundered to an 84-run defeat against East Lancashire to put a dent in the proud 100% record. Then Burnley inflicted a second defeat in Raja's continued absence before his welcome return coincided with victory against Colne by 52 runs, with the talented all-rounder contributing 75 out of a total of 203-7 before claiming 5-61 in the opposition's response of 151.

Significantly, the first time Raja played but the team lost happened at Enfield. Despite Rammy's pro chipping in with 6-61 and then top-scoring with 44, a 52-run loss was incurred. This led to Burnley taking over top spot in the table. The bubble then very much burst and a series of further losses was suffered, most notably including home and away defeats against Rawtenstall. One consolation in the very last match of the season was Brian Fielding taking a career-best 7-27 in a home match against Nelson. After the euphoria of the season before, 1975 had proved very much an up-and-down year. Runaway leaders going into June, the club had fallen away to 6th, achieving in the end only a virtually breakeven record of W13 NR 1 L12.

Pro Wasim Raja came 4th in the League batting averages, accruing 1,028 runs at a commanding average of 54.1 while coming 10th in the bowling averages, taking 68 wickets at 14.1 apiece. Denis Hardman enjoyed another good season with the bat, scoring 445 runs at 20.2 with Henry Hall totalling 263 at 23.9. Terry Stewart demonstrated his usefulness down the order with 299 runs at 14.2 while a newcomer from Summerseat, Mick Everett, playing in eight matches, scored 107 runs at an average of 13.4. As in 1974, the fast-bowling combination of Stewart and Fielding worked effectively in tandem, the one bagging 47 wickets at an average of 18.3 and the other 40 at 20.0.

ooooo

Wasim Raja started off his second year as pro in great form in the first match of the 1976 season, away at Todmorden, hitting an unbeaten 102 with eight fours and six sixes. After the team had been in trouble at 54-4, he shared a fifth wicket stand of 135 with Henry Hall (34*), enabling the Rams to reach a total of 189-4. With Raja taking 4-35 and Stewart 3-25, the home side was bowled out for 125.

In the next match, at Acre Bottom, Nelson had their tails up after bowling the home side out for 84 with only Denis Hardman (50) proving able to stand up to the fierce pace of West Indian Collis King (7-33). With the result of the game on a knife-edge and Nelson on 48-6 in reply, the match ended up 'no result' after being abandoned at 7.02 pm due to persistent rain.

In their third match, at Thorneyholme Road, the Rams were under the cosh when bowled out by 1975 league champions Accrington for 119. Wasim Raja top scored with 35 off 29 balls with Stewart adding a vital 34. However, losing their first match since September the previous year, Accrington were skittled out for 92 with right arm medium pace bowler Eric Kay coming up trumps on the day with a spell of 5-25 to destroy the champions' middle order, taking the Rams to top of the table.

Although 1976 was to be remembered as a gloriously hot summer in general, 15 May did not work out that way for the Rams when their away match with Rawtenstall was abandoned after just 2 balls. East Lancs took advantage of their plight to seize top spot by beating Accrington. Ramsbottom stayed second after beating Rawtenstall in a low-scoring derby at Acre Bottom in which the home team was bowled out for 97 (Raja 60) but then managed to dismiss their opponents for 74.

Unbeaten to this point, the record was however to be surrendered, losing at Enfield by a comprehensive 8-wicket margin after only mustering a total of 100-7. The side got back to winning ways in their next game, at home against Rishton, making 144 (Raja 88) before the pro took 4-37 and Stewart 6-58 to dismiss the visitors for 119.

The Rams lost for a second time when, despite a valiant top score of 32* by Henry Hall to help them reach 116-7, Bacup's openers struck the runs off without loss to win by ten wickets. Things were not looking much better after a four-wicket away defeat at the hands of Rishton. However, a 40-run victory in the return match against Bacup restored morale when Terry Stewart (39) and Henry Hall (29*) rescued the situation with a 7th wicket stand of 51 lifting the score from 71-6 to an eventual 137-8, before the visitors were bowled out for 97. At this point, the Rams were in 3rd spot, albeit 12 points behind leaders East Lancs.

However, it was proving difficult to achieve any degree of consistency with defeat coming at Lowerhouse. Peter Ashworth top scored with 38 in Ramsbottom's 105 all out but imperious hitting by pro Colin Milburn made light of the total. Then, by contrast, a superb all-round performance by Wasim Raja saw the Rams through to a shock 47-run victory over East Lancs at Acre Bottom. Contributing 87 runs to a total of 164-8, he then took 7-51 to dismiss the league leaders for 117.

The next match, away against Church, witnessed another rearguard action by Henry Hall top scoring with 40 in the Rams' 143-9, only for the home team to knock off the runs to win by seven wickets. A seesaw series of results followed on with a six-wicket win at Acre Bottom against Lowerhouse. Raja took 7-53, leaving the home side a target of 113 to win. Henry Hall (31*) and Peter Ashworth (24*) combined to earn victory with a 5th wicket stand of 48.

On 17 July though, after losing to East Lancs by 48 runs at Alexandra Meadows, the Rams dropped to 5th place, a state of affairs made worse by a home defeat at the hands of Church. Despite Maurice Haslam doing his best to shore up the innings with a top scoring 32, a total of 101-9 was overtaken with eight wickets in hand. Seemingly now in free fall, this was followed by back-to-back defeats against Burnley, firstly at Acre Bottom by 49 runs and then at Turf Moor by 59 runs.

A promising start, as in 1975, had fallen apart at the seams again in the second half of the season with the club ending up disappointingly in 11th position. Pro Wasim Raja hit 867 runs at 37.7 and took 55 wickets at 16.3, on both counts rather below the supremely high standard of his performances from the previous season. Denis Hardman was the leading amateur run scorer with 440 at 18.3, closely followed by Henry Hall, winner of the player of the year award, with 422 at 24.7. Terry Stewart was again outstanding in the bowling stakes with a best-ever season's wicket tally for him of 58 wickets, taken at 16.4 apiece.

The end of 1976 marked Terry Stewart's departure. Although he was to add another year's service as far forward as 1985, his retirement this year effectively put an end to the deadly threat he had in recent years posed for Rammy as a strike bowler. Although in addition having scored very useful runs as a lower order batsman during the course of 385 appearances, Terry is best remembered for the total of 595 wickets he took (at an average of 17.16), placing him 4th highest wicket-taker in club history. He took 50+ wickets in a season four times: in 1963 (51), 1969 (50), 1973 (51) and 1976 (58). As well as this, he won the player of the year award four times: in 1963, 1969, 1973 and 1975.

The club also honoured the retirement of renowned spin bowler Bill Savage who had made his debut for the club as far back as 1949. Making 379 appearances, he had taken 386 wickets (at an average of 19.07) and also scored some useful runs down the order. In common with Stewart, who had captained the club from 1967 to 1971, Bill too had served in the role for two years 1964/1965. He had won 'player of the year' in the first year it had been awarded in 1961.

ooooo

In terms of league position, 1977 was unfortunately to prove an even greater disappointment, the club finishing the season in 12th= place with a record of W9 NR3 L14. Twenty-six year-old Australian Trevor Laughlin was the replacement for Wasim Raja as pro. An all-rounder, left hand bat and right-arm medium pace bowler, he had prior experience playing for Victoria in Australian State cricket.

During his year at Rammy, Laughlin was to score 740 runs at 32.17 and take 62 wickets at 19.75. In 16th place in the league's batting averages and 26th in the bowling, he had performed only moderately well. Yet like one or two other Aussie pros before him, a relatively disappointing performance at this level did not harm his prospects playing for his country. Although reaching nowhere near the heights achieved by Ian Chappell and Keith Stackpole, Trevor Laughlin was also though to go on to gain Test caps, although rather more briefly over the seasons of 1977/8 through to 1979/80.

1977 is perhaps more tellingly to be remembered as the year Mick Everett first became a force within the club. Hailing from Summerseat, he had scored 70 in a game that Henry Hall, Terry Stewart, Maurice Haslam and Peter Ashworth had played in. At this time he also put in bowling stints, reputedly enjoying more success bowling from the end that his Uncle Joe was standing as umpire! Anyway, meeting up for a social drink afterwards, the Rammy players had persuaded Mick, in his mid-20s at the time, to come and play at Acre Bottom. This had been in 1974. Since then, he had mostly been playing for the 2nd XI. It was during the current year that Trevor Laughlin had persuaded skipper Henry Hall that Everett was good enough to hold down a regular spot in the 1st XI.

Opening the batting, usually with Hall, Mick Everett was to emerge by the end of the season with the club's highest amateur batting average, scoring 359 runs at 23.9, earning him the club's player of the year award. A pugnacious striker of the ball, he proved he could also seal up an end when necessary. For example, in a home match against Accrington on 16 July, with the away team desperately trying to defend a total of 110, he came under considerable pressure from the hostile and prolific pro wicket-taker, Accy's Alan Worsick. Scoring a gritty 39 from 106 balls in an innings lasting 124 minutes, his wicket was only taken when the score had reached 107-3 and victory within close grasp.

1978 was to prove an even better year for Mick, again achieving the club's highest batting average, this time round with an impressive total of 551 runs at an average of 24.0. Joining the ranks of Billy Whitworth and Arthur Chapman, this made him only the third amateur batsman since the war to achieve 500+ runs in a season.

ooooo

With Laughlin's departure, the pro in 1978 was Karsan Ghavri, an experienced 27-year-old Indian Test player, an all-rounder who batted left-handed and could bowl either slow left-arm or medium pace. He had won the award of Indian Cricketer of the Year in 1975.

The new season however had started badly with four defeats, the first by nine wickets away to Burnley after having been bowled out for 77 and then at home against East Lancs by 55 runs. A third loss, away to Church, was by the margin of one run. The fourth match was another tight affair with Accrington scraping through to a 2-wicket victory despite Brian Fielding's 5-38.

Fortunately, a win was finally achieved in the away match against Todmorden on 14 May. With the home team deciding to bat, Ghavri dismissed both openers before Maurice Haslam accounted for the middle order, ending with 5-30, his first five-wicket haul in Lancashire League matches. Chasing a modest total of 82, the Rams finally reached their target with the help of a seventh-wicket 19-run partnership between Ghavri (32*) and Haslam (10*) to take them to a 4-wicket win.

Karsan Ghavri grew in confidence as shown by his 99* out of a total of 170-5 in the next match away at Nelson. The same could be said for spinner Maurice Haslam who took a career-best 7-25 in process of skittling the opposition out for 87. In the next match at home against Lowerhouse, Mick Everett had made his mark scoring 63 out of a total of 157-4. Again, the Ghavri/Haslam bowling combination worked well with Ghavri taking 5-26 and Haslam 3-30 to dismiss the visitors for 125. Following the opening stretch of four consecutive defeats, it proved satisfying to follow up with four straight wins on the back of a four-wicket home win against Rishton. Ghavri took 5-52 in containing the visitors to 130-7 with Everett top scoring (56) in the Rams' winning total of 131-6.

The pendulum swung back the other way though after an away defeat at Bacup. Fielding was in fine form picking up 6-64 in the home team's 163-9 but conditions were such that the Rams could only get 21.5 overs in, reaching 94-5, thus losing the match on slower scoring rate. In the next game, away at Todmorden, despite Everett's 73* and Ghavri's 56 contributions to a total of 171-4, a 21-run last wicket partnership enabled the home side to limp through to a one-wicket victory.

The team returned to winning ways at home to Accrington the next day on 11 June even if by a tight 2-run margin. Chasing 128, the visitors fell short at 126-7 with all but four overs bowled by Ghavri (2-46) and Haslam (3-46). A defeat was suffered at home to Rawtenstall despite a stout 69 from Everett helping the Rams to 160-9. In the event, the away team eased to a six-wicket victory. The return match, scheduled for a week later, was a 'no result' washout.

The Rams won the next home game against Enfield, and likewise an away match at Colne. Another home victory against Haslingden continued the winning streak. At Enfield, it was Rammy's turn to win a match on faster scoring rate. A nine-wicket home win against Colne with Ghavri taking 6-28 and Haslam 3-7 to dismiss the visitors for 53 meant the Rams were now motoring up the table. This was followed by an eight-wicket win at Haslingden and another at Lowerhouse by 47 runs with Fielding taking 6-21. At Acre Bottom on 19 August, Nelson's 135-7 (Ghavri 6-52) was overtaken at 139-4 (Ghavri 53*) for a six-wicket win. In another home match, Bacup's total of 86 (Ghavri 6-38) was easily surpassed at 88-3 (Everett 48*). In the home match against Church, Haslam did the damage (5-48), with Ghavri scoring 55* to enable the Rams to win by seven wickets. At Rishton on 2 September, Ghavri (3-41) and Haslam (3-39) kept the home side down to 100-7 to earn a five-wicket victory. Away to East Lancs the next day, yet another victory was conjured up after fielding first with the home side contained to 151-8 and the Rams taking the match by five wickets. This made for an incredible run of 12 straight wins.

Coming to the last game of the season, bearing in mind they had lost their first four, the team had now reached the dizzy heights of second in the table. Ironically, this last match, at home on 10 September, was against the team, Burnley, that was leading the table. Unfortunately, from the Rams' point of view, the Turf Moor club had too commanding a lead at this stage to be overtaken In the event, Burnley won the match on faster scoring rate.

The final standings were as below:

	Pl	W	L	T	NR	Bonus Pts	Pts
1st Burnley	26	19	2	2	3	9	89
2nd Ramsbottom	26	17	8	0	1	9	77

W 4pts T (Tie) 2pts NR 0pts – N.b. in 1979, it was changed to NR 1pt.

The consolation as far as the Rams were concerned was that, finishing in runners-up spot, the club won the Holland Cup. Despite losing those first four matches had been costly, the final outcome to the season had proved most positive.

Although having taken a bit of time to adapt to new conditions, Karsan Ghavri had performed well, scoring 784 runs at an average of 52.3, putting him 4th in the League's batting averages. Taking 77 wickets at 12.7, he finished in 3rd place in the League's bowling averages. It was noted at the start of this section that Mick Everett topped the club's amateur batting averages. Furthermore, he ended up as high as 13th in the League's amateur batting averages. In the bowling department, Maurice Haslam finished in 8th place overall in the League's averages table (taking 49 wickets at 14.3) with Brian Fielding 9th (48 wickets at 15.3). It was difficult in the circumstances to choose between the three of them for the club's player of the year award but in the event, the decision went in favour of Maurice Haslam.

ooooo

With Karsan Ghavri unable to return as pro the following season due to other commitments, in 1979 the club enlisted the services of Greg Hayes, a 23-year-old South African all-rounder with state cricket experience playing for Border since 1974. A right-hand bat and right-arm medium pace bowler, he was to have his work cut out though to match the record of his predecessor in post.

At the end of the previous season, Dally Brooks had retired as a player. In addition to having enjoyed considerable success at junior level in the early 1970s, he had served the club outstandingly well both as wicket-keeper and also in the 1st XI captaincy role in 1973 and 1974. Ending up making 288 first team appearances, he claimed 235 victims behind the stumps and made useful runs down the order. However, he was still to have a continuing link with the club. In the nature of his line of business as a baker, he was to go on supplying the tearoom with such traditional

Ramsbottom delicacies as currant buns, jam slices and gingerbread. It has to be said his meat pies and muffins went down very well too!

Another great loss to the club for the time being was that of Brian Fielding who went on to pro jobs at the likes of Clitheroe and Cherry Tree. It would not be until 1984 when he returned to put in another full season for the club. Without Brian, the bowling attack was to lack the extra pace and cutting edge it always had with him taking the new ball.

Although Burnley were destined to win the League title for the second year running with exactly the same total of 89 points they had the year before, Ramsbottom's own total of points plummeted down to 36 from the previous season's 77, leaving them 13th in the table with a poor record of W7 L15 NR 4 Bonus Points 4.

Pro Hayes had scored 586 runs at an average of 29.3, placing him surprisingly as high as 9th in the League's batting averages. Meanwhile, his take of 76 wickets at 16.2 put him in 15th place in the League's bowling averages. Henry Hall scored 319 runs at 18.76 and Mick Everett 303 at 14.42. All-rounder Maurice Haslam, with 171 runs, headed the club's batting averages at 21.4. By way of a double whammy, Maurice also headed the club's amateur bowling averages, taking 35 wickets at 23.3.

1979 marked the debut year of Ian Bell, a young batsman with immense promise who was later to write himself into the club's history books with a number of outstanding batting feats from 1984 onwards. In this year, aged 20 and cutting his teeth, he scored 221 runs at an average of 13.81.

ooooo

A major development took place at Acre Bottom in 1980 when a large area on site, habitually played upon by the 3rd XI and often jokingly referred to as the 'wasteland', came to be converted for use as a football ground and stadium for local sporting team Ramsbottom United. The club had been formed in 1966 and had been looking for some time to find a more permanent home in place of its existing arrangement hiring a pitch in Chatterton Park in Stubbins.

To be more specific, it was Harry Williams, the major force behind Ramsbottom United, who had been casting a covetous eye on this piece of land for quite a period of time already. A keen cricket player in his youth, one amongst those going back to Peter Philpott's time, Harry had also involved himself since doing voluntary work on the cricketing side and serving on the committee.

The argument he had put to Ramsbottom Cricket Club, in applying to lease the use of this stretch of land, was that it was much more suitable for the purpose he had in mind as a football ground rather than its present use as a cricket pitch. As anyone knew who had played on it, the surface was uneven, plus the fact it was never easy for batsmen to pick up the flight of the ball against the row of trees standing in front of the once busy railway line.

However, an innately stubborn attitude seems to have gone on operating in the minds of some members of the Cricket Club and the argument wasn't a 'given'. Such elements clung to the view that football would prove an unwanted intrusion on the more gentlemanly ambience of cricket. This opposition was only eventually overcome after an agreement was reached that the land would be leased to the football club with the condition built in that the Cricket Club bar would retain sole public licence across the Acre Bottom site and take the revenue from proceeds.

Apart from anything else, the arrangement would turn out to be a very useful money-spinner for the Cricket Club, particularly taking into account the use of it by football supporters during the winter months when otherwise its Cricket Club bar would have stayed relatively idle. For the football club, having access to such a facility, only a short walk away, proved a boon for it too.

It is only fair to add that a strong majority of cricket members would have been in favour of the two sports linking up more closely. After all, many had played both sports. For example, Maurice Haslam and Brian Fielding had been leading players for Ramsbottom United in the late 60s up to the mid-70s.

In this respect, Derek Read's experience is a particularly interesting one to call upon. A notable Rammy United defender from 1966 onwards, he had never though in the meantime been a serious cricket-player.

However, the breaking of a leg at the end of his footballing career had been bad enough to persuade him to encourage his then six-year-old son, Simon, to take up more interest in cricket than football. Incidentally, Dad's 'plan' was to work out well with Simon, who, after working his way through the various ranks, was to become a leading player and eventually club captain. For his own part, throughout the meantime, although Derek continued to put in good work at the football club, he also came to serve as a dedicated R.C.C. committee member in a variety of ways.

ooooo

1980 also saw the start of sponsorship as a means of raising finance for Ramsbottom Cricket Club. John Heys, son of the esteemed Frank Heys (Honorary Treasurer 1957-62 and Chairman 1964-80) was one of the first to become actively involved in the process, recalling later that 'the relationship between club and sponsor was found to flourish best in circumstances where sponsorship was conceived as the act of a good neighbour or friend willing to play a joint role in promoting the welfare of the local community'.

Anyone visiting Acre Bottom nowadays, forty years on, cannot help but witness for themselves the strong level of commitment of so many companies in the local area currently signing up to supporting R.C.C. and also for that matter at the Harry Williams Stadium football ground. The overall situation testifies to the obvious confidence business interests have in wishing to be associated with the life of both cricket and footballing clubs.

ooooo

The return of Karsan Ghavri as pro for 1980 held out hope of a return to the form of 1978. In the event, the team was to finish 7th with a total of 53 points, a kind of halfway house between 1978 and 1979. Ghavri himself didn't perform as well as he had done two years earlier, scoring 659 runs at an average of 27.45. Nevertheless, he maintained good form with the ball, taking 72 wickets at 15.56. Even so, he too must have missed not being able to call on Brian Fielding to open the bowling with him. He did still have though the other element of the three-pronged bowling line-up of 1978 – Maurice Haslam – who took 23 wickets this year at 27.08 apiece.

A batsman who emerged during the course of this year, later to captain the side in 1986 and 1987, was the aptly-named John Ramsbottom. Having joined the club in 1972, 1980 was the year he blossomed as a right-hand batsman, scoring 472 runs at 24.84 whilst hitting a career-best 83 which paved the way to a 67-run victory at Rishton on 16 August. John was to go on to win the player of the year award.

On the bowling side, 1980 was also the year in which 20-year-old Steve Ratcliffe, who had joined the club in 1977, gave notice of his potential for the future as a right-arm medium pace bowler, taking 31 wickets at 16.32, including what would turn out to be a career-best 8-43 at Bentgate on 25 May. On this occasion, he destroyed a demoralised Haslingden batting line-up (in a manner Brian Fielding himself would have very much have approved of!) reducing them to 74 all out. Even so, it had taken a gutsy innings by Mark Price (35*) to steer the Rams to a three-wicket victory on the day.

Only 17 when he had made his debut in 1977, Mark Price (son of Alan Price who had played for the club between 1964 and 1971) firmly established a 1st XI place for himself this year, playing in all 26 matches and scoring 294 runs at 13.36. Although he had been given little chance to turn his arm at this stage, his ability to bowl slow left-arm (modelling his technique on that of the English Test bowler Phil Edmonds) would not only attract attention at club level but at county level for Glamorgan in the mid-1980s. He was also to have a significant role to play down the line as club captain.

In 1980, Henry Hall had another good year with the bat, scoring 402 runs at an average of 22.33. Peter Ashworth had likewise prospered, scoring 393 runs at 15.7. Meanwhile, Mick Everett had had a fairly quiet year by his standards, scoring 228 runs at 15.20. However, 1981 was to bring a transformation in Evo's fortunes, bringing him roaring back into action!

ooooo

On Wednesday 15 April 1981, Mick Everett's name was plastered across the pages of the Daily Mail, with the following story appearing in its sports section:

'Police Sergeant Michael Everett has volunteered this weekend for a duty that carries a high risk of grievous bodily harm.

'He will snatch a few fitful hours of sleep after his Saturday shift before going out to face a missile propelled towards him at up to 93.7 miles per hour.

'Everett is one of the first Sunday afternoon club cricketers to play against West Indian Michael Holding, the world's fastest bowler, hired by Rishton as their professional.

'Last night, in the perfect light and on the true wickets of the Caribbean, Holding was still demoralising the best of England's highly-paid Test batsmen.

'Here, in the gloom of the Lancashire hills on an unpredictable pitch, Michael Everett hopes for no reward save, perhaps, the thrill of hitting the demon bowler for four'.

In such a way was the scene set for a showdown which contained all the movie elements of a gunfight at the O.K. Corral.

ooooo

The debut of Michael Holding, nicknamed 'Whispering Death', drew a crowd of 2,000 to the Blackburn Road ground on 19 April – not bad, considering Rishton's population as a whole stood at only 6,000 – to watch their new star, who had joined them for the princely sum in 1981 of £5,000 for the season.

On an extremely chilly opening match of the year, Rishton won the toss and decided to bat, perhaps to the relief of Mick Everett and his opening partner on the day, Peter Ashworth. Rishton were 56-4 when Holding came to the wicket. He top scored with a brisk 26 runs in seven overs, helping to take the home team to the modest total of 108.

After all the hype, the moment of truth was now at hand for Ramsbottom's batsmen, the confrontation people had paid their money to come and see.

As a precaution against the risk of severe injury, the Rams had invested in helmets and other types of more sophisticated protective gear beyond the traditional 'box' and newspapers stuffed down shirt sleeves and trouser legs.

With Everett and Ashworth spinning a coin for who would face Holding's first ball, Everett won and gracefully decided to let Ashworth have the honour! As the openers walked out to the wicket, Holding was limbering up directly in front of one of the sight screens. Noted as having the longest run-in in cricket, he was bowling off what he was humorously to call 'my shorter run'.

With a roar from the crowd that grew louder the nearer he reached delivery stride, the first ball flew through the air catching Ashworth on the pad and diverting off down the leg side. From the other end, Everett thought there were two runs in it but Ashworth settled for one, consigning his partner to face the next ball.

On an overcast day, the sun suddenly came out almost as an omen of what was to follow. However, despite the odds stacked against him surviving the onslaught, Everett not only held the Rolls-Royce of fast bowling at bay but scored 3 2's to make it 7 without loss by the end of the opening 8-ball over.

With a cracking square cut for four off Holding in the third over, Everett achieved the basic ambition he had set himself of scoring a boundary. Although losing opening partner Ashworth, out for 3 with the score standing at 21 for 1, a 37-run partnership then ensued between Everett and Mark Price, with the no.3 batsman said by some to have been trying his best to escape exposure to Holding.

The official scorecard shows that Price was run out for 23 and that Everett was out 'bowled Holding 29'. To this day though, the latter remains adamant that, as recently made clear to the author, he had scored 30 runs before being bowled by Rishton's pro. In addition, Evo was keen to point out that 22 of his runs had come off Holding.

Meanwhile 'Whispering Death', becoming ever more menacing, had reduced the visitors to 94-7, losing five wickets for 24 runs, before an 18-run stand between Pete Daggert and Maurice Haslam saw the visitors over the line, the latter square-cutting Holding for four to claim a momentous three-wicket victory.

As was recorded in the interviews with the national press afterwards, including one with legendary ex-footballer Jimmy Armfield, Police Sergeant Everett revealed that, apart from one or two bruises, he had lost a thumbnail during the course of his encounter with Holding. Even so, the issue he was keenest to comment on was that, by his reckoning, he had scored 30, not 29.

At the end of a momentous day's events, there can be no questioning the impact Michael Holding's presence had on the occasion. Although, by his own standards, he wouldn't have been thrilled with bowling statistics of 15.2-2-48-3, he had certainly succeeded in paying back a healthy, initial instalment on the money it had taken to bring him to Rishton.

To illustrate the point in economic terms, he had pulled in over 2,000 fans which netted a Lancashire League record gate receipt at that time of £850 (entrance costing 60p). Nor was the profit a slim one made from the sale of 1,200 muffins and 800 pies in the tearoom!

However, back to the business of the cricket being played out there on the pitch, it was Ramsbottom who had enjoyed a winning start to the season. For Mick Everett, it had proved an occasion he would never forget for all kind of reasons, even though he would go on swearing on his sergeant's stripes that he made 30 runs, not 29!

ooooo

By the time of the reverse fixture between Rishton and the Rams on 30 May, Holding was fully into his stride taking 7-51 as the home team was bowled out for 121, with Everett contributing 18 runs to the total. It was a match that Rishton won by five wickets. 'Evo' was to go on that season to score 591 runs at an average of 30.78 while 'Whispering Death' would capture 86 wickets at an average of 10.7 runs apiece.

With all the hype surrounding Mike Holding, it could easily be overlooked that Australian Ian Callen had succeeded Karsan Ghavri as Rammy pro at the start of 1981. Left-hand batsman and right-arm medium fast bowler, he had played State cricket for Victoria from 1976 onwards and also at Test level for his country in 1977/8. His record at

Rammy was not to prove a very distinguished one, only managing to score 97 runs at an average of 7.46 while taking 42 wickets at 19.42.

It is fair to say that the club was left completely perplexed by the fact that, claiming to be suffering serious injury, a medical certificate had allowed Callen to be released from his duties at the club, only for him to take part soon thereafter in a benefit match in the Bolton area.

Irrespective of the vagaries of the pro's performance, or rather lack of it, 1981 saw the Rams finishing again, as per 1980, 7th with a record of W11 L12 NR 3. Mick Everett's 591 runs included a career-best 86 away against Lowerhouse on 1 August, helping him earn the club's player of the year award again.

Pete Daggett, a batsman who had joined the club the year before, was the next most prolific run-scorer with 396 at 22.00. Daggett, whose batting figures were set to improve further over the next two years, was also to serve as captain during the same spell of time. In the bowling department, Mark Price finally was given chance to illustrate his potential as a spin bowler, ending up this season taking 17 wickets at 17.1 to head the club's bowling averages.

Incidentally, returning to Rishton, they would end up 6th in the league, just pipping the Rams by one place. As mentioned earlier, 'Whispering Death' went on to capture 86 wickets at 10.7, with only Rawtenstall's Franklyn Stephenson ahead of him, taking 105 wickets at 9.3 apiece.

Eight: Murray Bennett and Kangaroo Tie Pins

IN 1982, THE club rose to 3rd in the table (W16 L6 NR3 Tie 1, plus 5 bonus points) with 74 points behind top-placed Rawtenstall on 81 and runners-up Lowerhouse on 80 points. Callen had been replaced as pro by Ashantha de Mel from Sri Lanka. An authentic all-rounder, the right-hand bat and right-arm medium fast bowler had already represented his country at Test level. Scoring 672 runs for Rammy this season at an average of 35.36, he also took 63 wickets at 16.92.

Fulfilling his promise from the year before, Pete Daggett joined the club's elite 500+ squad by scoring 501 runs during the season at an average of 23.86. Meanwhile, Mark Price scored 423 runs at 24.88, including a memorable 101* against Colne at the Horsfield on 24 July. In this match, the home team had batted first and made 192 all out with West Indian pro Collis King scoring 104 before being dismissed 'caught Price bowled Monkhouse', the young Rammy fast bowler ending with 5-58.

With King on fire snapping up three quick wickets to reduce the Rams to 7-3, Price defied the rampant paceman by scoring an unbeaten 101 (with seven fours and three sixes) in 101 balls to enable the Rams to win the match by six wickets. Price also had another good season with his spin bowling, not only heading the club bowling averages again but coming 6th in the League's, taking 37 wickets at 15.1, also winning the club's player of the year award that season.

Steve Monkhouse, son of Harold, made an impact this season taking 31 wickets at 21.3. Aged 19, he had come into the 1st XI the year before, taking 29 wickets at 28.55. He too, like Mark Price, was later to be talent-spotted by a county team, in Steve's case, Warwickshire. Just as

'Pricey' was to rub shoulders with the likes of Javed Miandad during his time at Glamorgan, so Steve would later have good cause to recall memories of coming into contact with stand-out Somerset players such as Ian Botham and Viv Richards whilst playing with Warwickshire.

In 1983, the club slipped to 7th but were to have another memorable run in the Worsley Cup. In the league, Zambian pro Neal Radford scored 527 runs at 27.47 and took 77 wickets at 16.25. John Ramsbottom was top-scoring club amateur with 419 runs at 22.1, closely followed by Mick Everett with 372 at 16.91. In the bowling department, Steve Ratcliffe was back on song with 44 wickets at 20.6, earning him the club's player of the year award.

Moving on to the Worsley Cup (incidentally for sponsorship reasons called the Martini Cup at this point in time), the 1983 campaign had proved an interesting experience all-round, particularly for long-serving Henry Hall.

In the first round tie at home against Bacup on 15 May, Neal Radford (4-25) and Steve Ratcliffe (6-39) combined to dismiss the opposition for 72 with the home team scoring 73 for 4 to win by six wickets. The second round match took place at Lowerhouse on 19 June. Winning the toss and deciding to bat, openers Mick Everett and Henry Hall strode out on to the field of play.

As he was later to describe, Graham Ratcliffe, Steve's younger brother, was unexpectedly to find himself called into action in a way that gave him a somewhat more prominent role to play on the day than he might have otherwise anticipated:

'We batted first and Henry Hall opened with Mick Everett. Henry strained his hamstring early on and needed a runner. I had hardly played any first team games but then was sent out to do this job. I got to the middle and Henry said to me: "Guess you've done this kind of thing before?" I hadn't and running with Mick Everett was a nightmare at the best of times. Henry was about 20 not out at the time. He made 100 (his only one) and when he was out, he walked off to applause. I hung back 20-30 yards but felt gratified at receiving a measure of applause for the part played as runner'.

The opening stand of 166 between Henry Hall and Mick Everett paved the way for Rammy's 178-run win on the day. Veteran Henry

Hall (who had made his 1ˢᵗ XI debut for the club back in 1956) had hit his maiden senior century with Mick Everett scoring 77, to help lift the Rams up to 241-3. Neal Radford had then taken 6-22 to roll Lowerhouse over for just 63.

The semi-final match took place against Colne at the Horsfield over 24 and 31 July. The Rams won the toss and batted. There was no epic opening to record this time though. Colne pro Collis King took all five wickets that fell in a total of 226-5, which relied greatly on a stand of 165 runs between John Ramsbottom (71) and pro Neal Radford (93). In reply, Colne fell 22 runs short of the target, Radford taking 4-91 and Steve Ratcliffe 4-32.

In the final, played at Alexandra Meadows against East Lancs, everything began promisingly following another century opening stand of 107. Everett made 58 with three fours and a six in an innings which earned him a hat collection of £108 and 32 pence. The amount was one Evo, with his well-known eye for detail, recalled exactly!

Just as it looked the Rams were set for a really high score, 16-year-old England schoolboy international spinner John Wharton came on and bowled a wondrous spell of 6-42. In combination with Rammy ex-pro Ian Callen (3-53), they managed to confine the away team to 167-9. In reply, despite being in trouble at one stage at 11 for 3, it was Callen, coming in at no. 6 and lashing 56 runs off 59 balls, (ironically scoring more runs in an innings than he had done throughout the season he'd been pro at Acre Bottom), who was chiefly responsible in enabling East Lancs to reach 171-6 to clinch the cup by a four-wicket margin.

ooooo

1984 saw the club having another successful League Championship season – finishing in 3ʳᵈ position – this time with 78 points (W16 L8 NR 2, plus 12 bonus points) behind East Lancs on 96 and runners-up Haslingden on 92 points.

The pro this year was Aussie all-rounder Murray Bennett, a right-arm bat and slow left arm bowler, with experience of playing State cricket for New South Wales. During his season's stay at the club, he was to succeed in scoring 708 runs at an average of 41.64, making him 7ᵗʰ in the league's batting averages, whilst achieving an even better bowling record of 79 wickets at 10.44, putting him top of the league's bowling averages.

After a two-year lay-off, Ian Bell had returned on the scene, aggregating 626 runs at an average of 32.94. 39-year-old Mick Rogers, an opening bat who had played most of his previous cricket in the Bolton League, had lately joined the club, scoring 531 runs at 24.13. From playing in all 26 matches the year before, Mick Everett only played in thirteen matches this season. As a member of the police service, his time was taken up by the outbreak of the Miners' Strike during 1984 which necessitated him being away from Ramsbottom for long stretches, stationed wherever need arose and called upon to put in a lot of overtime. Although making occasional appearances over the course of the next six seasons, he was not to make the same substantial contribution to 1st XI cricket as he had done before.

From the late 1970s onwards, Mick played 229 1st XI matches, manufacturing 3,238 runs at an average of 18.29, twice scoring 500+ runs in a season: 1978 (551) and 1981 (591). He twice won the player of the year award, in 1977 and 1981. No opening batsman could have had a more idiosyncratic playing technique which often left opposing fast bowlers frustrated. Adopting an open stance at the crease, as often as not he looked to step outside the off stump and glance the ball away on the leg side. Never afraid to take bowlers on, as in the famous instance of Michael Holding, he was always up for a challenge. So too it would prove when later taking up the manager's role.

Meanwhile, Brian Fielding had returned to the club this season after various stints as a pro elsewhere. Serving as captain in 1984 and 1985, he had taken 36 wickets at 16.6 apiece to head the club's bowling averages, at the same time coming 6th in the League's. Steve Monkhouse too had made another strong contribution to the club's cause, taking 58 wickets at 16.8 apiece. Incidentally, Steve was to joke with his father Harold that he was the only one of the two of them to manage to pull off the 50+ wickets-in-a-season feat! Although destined to return to play for the club again in later years, Steve would soon however be joining Warwickshire to chance his arm at county level.

As far as player of the year was concerned, it proved difficult to choose between the batting accomplishments of Ian Bell and those of Steve Monkhouse with the ball, so the award was made to the two players jointly.

ooooo

From the host of pros who have come to play for Ramsbottom Cricket Club over the years, Murray Bennett's standing is exceptionally high amongst all those who knew him from the time he spent at the club. Being generous enough in recent times to describe his experience of coming over to play for Rammy in 1984, Murray recalled:

- 'My memories begin at the airport at Manchester following a 24-hour flight from Sydney and a shuttle from Heathrow. At the gate I was met by a large gentleman who addresses me in a deep voice. The only trouble is apart from catching his name - Gerald Dentith - I can't understand a word he is saying. Gerald took me to the baggage area and introduced me to the Club President, Gordon Fish and Secretary, Peter Spencer. Further consternation for me is that I can't understand Gordon's broad Lancastrian accent either, but fortunately, I am able to pick out most of what Peter is saying to me, so not all is lost. The language difficulty continued to be a bit of an issue though. For example in the changing room, with all the boys chatting to each other, I had a hell of a job keeping up with what was being said. Nevertheless, I felt everyone was enjoying my company and laughing along with me. Or so I thought! Three weeks after I had arrived, my wife Jane arrived. The first time she came to the Clubhouse, about six of the players came and introduced themselves. Following a bit of further conversation, they said how pleased they were she was here because they couldn't understand a word I was saying!

- 'I had been forewarned by other Australian cricketers who had played in the Lancashire League that the local team and supporters would be quick to let you know if you weren't doing your job. Fortunately, I never found this to be the case. Everyone was so supportive that I felt instantly at home, and Jane and I were made to feel very welcome. I think the fact that I started the season quite well and immediately involved myself heavily in the club training sessions gave everyone the right message as to what I was about. I was club captain of my Grade team in Sydney, St George, so I was well versed with club practice sessions and particularly fielding drills.

- 'It was requested that I coach the under-11 side. This was a fantastic experience for me. The boys would often chant my name, 'There's only one Murray Bennett', as I walked out to bat on a Saturday afternoon. I was told I was the first pro to coach younger boys since Peter Philpott's days. It was quite emotional for me on the occasion Jane and I returned to visit Rammy in 2010. During a raucous night at the clubhouse, four men, about 35 years old, approached me, saying: 'I bet you don't remember us?' Unbelievably, they were four lads from the 1984 under-11 team, including Jonathan Fielding. I was overwhelmed. One of these ex-youngsters, Simon Read, nearly brought tears to my eyes by turning up on the evening sporting one of the tie-pins, bearing a kangaroo symbol, that I had handed out to the lads at the end of my time at the club.

- 'The camaraderie between the players in the team was special and this was a very enjoyable part of the whole experience. Many of the more senior players including my great mate 'Captain Courageous' Brian Fielding, Maurice Haslam, Henry Hall and Mick Everett had a great bond between them. They enjoyed nothing more than being in each other's company for a few pints and continually taking 'the piss' out of each other and themselves. Wonderful gentlemen who are still involved with the Club and contributing to its future.

- 'The quality of the cricket was very good and the Ramsbottom team of 1984 had some significant talent within its ranks. Fieldo and Steve Monkhouse, opening the bowling, was arguably the strongest combination in the league. Ian Bell was just starting his career with Rammy but it struck me he was good enough to play at much higher levels. John Ramsbottom had the safest pair of hands in the team and took many good catches off my bowling whether at first slip or scouting out at long on when the opposition was opening their shoulders. Paul Marcroft, who liked the nickname I gave him, 'Hub', did a special job behind the stumps where many of the wickets we played on that season spun quite significantly.

- 'The humour is what I remember most fondly. Whether it was in the players' changing room or bar, or simply walking through town there was always humour nearby. A particular example was the day after we had played Haslingden at Bentgate. It was a cliff-hanger of a game and I managed to score 80-odd not out at the end of the day. Opening the bowling for Haslingden had been seriously quick West Indian bowler, Hartley Alleyne. One delivery from Hartley hit me on the instep of my right foot. By the next day, my foot was bruised and sore, nothing broken, but unpleasant. Jane and I were walking through Rammy and passed an elderly gentleman sitting in a bus shelter. I was hobbling along and he calls out to me, 'Teach you to use bat, lad', with a smile on his face. I guess he'd been at the game and seen the incident, but just a great example of the humour.

- 'The 2010 trip Jane and I made back to Rammy was very special. The Club had gone to a lot of trouble to gather various memorabilia and also contact most of the players from that season of 1984 to come for a get-together and welcome us back – all of 26 years later! My memory tells me it was a very special night for both us and many others to reminisce about the great times during that year in which Rammy enjoyed so many successes, including of course coming 3rd in the championship'.

ooooo

Despite Murray Bennett inevitably proving a difficult act to follow, fellow-Aussie David Hookes did his best in 1985. Aged 30 when coming to the club, David had been an Australian Test player from the 1976/7 season onwards. Left hand bat and left arm bowler, both slow and medium pace, he brought with him a wealth of experience at the highest levels.

In the event, David was to score 877 runs for the club at 35.08 (placing him 8th in the league's batting averages), while putting in a relatively more modest performance as bowler, taking 48 wickets at 19.00. Meanwhile, the club finished the season 7th with 56 points and an overall record: W11 L12 Tie 1 NR 2 plus 8 bonus points.

A strong batting input on the club's amateur side came from another Ashworth, Steve (unrelated to either Peter or John), who, joining the club after playing with Bacup and Rawtenstall, totalled 512 runs for the season at an average of 30.1, meriting him the player of the year award. Ian Bell had also predictably surpassed the 500+ mark this season, scoring 539 runs at 23.4. Steve Hall, son of veteran Henry, scored what would prove his career-best total of runs in a season of 345 runs at 23.0. Brian Fielding headed the club's bowling averages, taking 34 wickets at 18.2 whilst Terry Stewart, his longstanding opening-bowler mate, now aged 44, put in a fine swansong year capturing 31 wickets at 20.22.

Henry Hall had only played in two 1st XI matches this season. 1985 marked the end of a successful career going back to 1956 when he had made his debut. Now in his mid-40s, he was happy enough still with his batting - despite never feeling comfortable wearing a helmet - but honest with himself in feeling that his fielding was beginning to let him down. Throughout a long career that had seen him also serve as captain (mainly in the late 1970s), Henry had scored 6,005 runs at an average of 14.47, also achieving player of year award three times in 1964, 1971 and 1976. In addition, he holds the record for the number of 1st XI appearances he made (538), thereby granting him a most special place in club history.

ooooo

During 1985, the freelance writer Tim Heald visited Acre Bottom as part of a tour he was conducting around different grounds across the country in process of putting together his book, *The Character of Cricket*. The match he saw was the one against Rawtenstall on 17 August which in the event the home team, Rammy, won by 31 runs, courtesy of Maurice Haslam's 5-27. However, apart from cricket on the pitch, Tim had come with the intention of soaking up the general atmosphere round the ground.

Tim appears to have picked up fairly quickly that he had better be on his best behaviour, describing how 'the man behind the bar in the clubhouse paused in the middle of pulling my pint, fixed me with a beady if not baleful stare (who else but Harry Williams!) and advised me to take great care about what I wrote'. As Heald goes on to say, the club was still feeling a bit nervous after a recent visit from Clement

Freud (famous writer, politician and chef of the time) who had come and done 'a hatchet job', poking fun at the name of Ramsbottom.

Heald had been warned! Keeping strictly to the evidence in front of him, he really took to the pavilion: 'It's the original Victorian number, newly renovated at a cost of £12,000 and painted in the club colours of green and cream. Because it is heavily timbered it has a striped effect, as if it had been papered in club ties'.

Tim Heald also became very aware on the day of the pride the club took in its history: 'The walls of the pavilion are a veritable scrap-book'. In a section about the range of pros who had played for the club, he mentions 'Ramsbottom's genial young secretary Peter Spencer telling him that at one point during the 1985 Test series against the Australians, the pundits in the Channel Nine commentary box were Ian Chappell, Keith Stackpole and David Hookes, each one of them a former Rammy pro. And when they came to evaluate the performance of Murray Bennett in his curious dark glasses, they were not just passing judgement on another Australian Test cricketer but on yet another Ramsbottom professional'.

The author concluded his piece: 'I was much impressed by what I saw of Ramsbottom Cricket Club. The cricket is reason enough, but there is more to it than that. A notice at Ramsbottom C.C. says, quite properly, "Pleasant Pavilion Bar – Open Seven Days Each Week." Would that they could boast as much in St. John's Wood'.

ooooo

1986 was to prove another mid-table year, finishing 8th (W11 L14 NR1 with 7 bonus points). The pro was South African Craig Norris, a 23-year-old all-rounder from Transvaal, left hand bat and coming with a reputation similar to Ghavri's of being able to bowl either slow left arm or medium-pace. He was to enjoy a good enough season with the bat scoring 769 runs at 45.23 (3rd in the league tables) but only managed to take 18 wickets at a costly 34.50 apiece. Ian Bell was not far behind Norris in run-scoring, notching 741 at 33.7, placing him 7th in the league tables and earning him the club's player of the year award for a third time. Steve Ashworth scored 403 at 23.7 and John Ramsbottom

111

249 at 19.2. Brian Fielding took 46 wickets at 26.3 and Terry Stewart's son Mark, aged 18, had a good season taking 32 wickets at 17.1.

Incidentally, Mark Price had made a brief re-appearance at the club this season, playing in seven league matches and 'part' of a Worsley Cup one! The cup game in question was a first round tie against Bacup at Lanehead which took place over 1ˢᵗ and 7ᵗʰ June. At the end of the first day, Bacup had scored 102-3 with Rammy calling upon four bowlers, Monkhouse, Fielding, Price and Stewart. However, skipper Ramsbottom's choice of bowlers was more restricted on the second day for the reason that Mark Price had left in the meantime to go and play as pro for Kearsley in the Bolton League. It wasn't to be until 1990 that he would chance to return to play for Rammy. When it came to signing up again, longstanding club Treasurer Brian Hutchinson, with his notably dry sense of humour, wasn't in a mood to let him forget what had happened in 1986, inquiring whether he intended now playing whole matches instead of just parts of them!

ooooo

1987 was to prove a reasonable enough season, the club finishing 5ᵗʰ= (W13 NR 6 L7 and 5 bonus points). As in 1983 though, stronger interest developed via another Worsley Cup run. Pre-season, a major new addition to the playing staff had come about with the recruitment of 28-year-old wicket-keeper/batsman Jack Simpson, who arrived at the club in somewhat distinctive circumstances.

Simpson had been on the books of Lancashire Cricket Club before moving to Rochdale and playing for them from 1980 to 1986 in the Central Lancashire League. Whilst there, he had held the League wicket-keeping record for victims in a season, 52. Rochdale was a combined Cricket and Lacrosse club, and though Jack had never played the other sport before, he had also taken to lacrosse, ending up winning 27 caps for England between 1979 and 1993.

The move to play cricket for Rammy happened after he and his wife got married and went to live there. His arrival on the scene came to the notice of Henry Hall, having become club manager at the end of his playing career. Henry had chanced to ask Maurice Haslam to go and pay a call on the town's newcomer to sound out if he might be interested in playing for the club.

In a recent telephone conversation (he now lives in Spain), Jack recalled how 'a man turned up at his door in uniform with 'Norweb' inscribed on it'. This, by the way, was the company Maurice was employed by. He was dropping in on his way back home at the end of a day's work. All Jack could think though was that he had somehow defaulted on paying his electricity bills and was about to be switched off! Two hours later, he had ended up signing to play for Rammy.

The club pro in 1987 was Andris Zesers, who had represented Australia at under-19 level. The son of a Latvian-born construction worker, he was still only 20 but had already built a reputation as an up-and-coming fast bowler. As it happened, he was to play just nine matches for Rammy before being called up for World Cup duty in the full Australian squad playing in India. Zesers was replaced for a fair number of games as pro by Pakistani Test player, Ijaz Faqih.

In the first round of the Worsley Cup, the Rams entertained Church at Acre Bottom on 23 May. The home side reached 236-6, Jack Simpson top scoring with 63, including seven fours and four sixes. In a tightly-contested match, Church came close at 224-7 but, falling below the required rate, suffered two late run-outs before finishing 10 runs short at 226.

In the second round match at Rawtenstall, Rammy batted first and made 152, Ian Bell top scoring with 35. Then Zesers created havoc, taking 8-32 as Rawtenstall were dismissed for 82. This however was fated to be Zesers' last appearance in the cup campaign.

Given the Worsley Cup's standing as a 'timeless' competition, the semi-final against Rishton would more than live up to the description, taking place over five separate occasions: 5th, 19th, 27th, 28th July before finally reaching its conclusion on 2nd August. In the same way as Michael Holding had provided a tremendous boost to Rishton in 1981, this year the club had as their pro the world's top-ranked batsman in the world, West Indian Viv Richards.

Conscious of the damage Richards could do in full flow, Rammy would have felt very uncertain as to whether their score of 165-7 (Jack Simpson top scoring with 40), was good enough. Even more so when

Richards, coming in at 16 for 1, smashed 31 runs off his first 18 balls. Then, at 69 for 1, Viv went to hook Mark Stewart but didn't connect properly and the ball skied upwards behind the stumps on the leg side. However, it suddenly dawned on skipper Simpson that the field he had set had left out having anyone at fine leg!

Instantly, despite encumbered by keeper's pads, he took it upon himself to race 30 metres back towards the boundary in a frenzied effort to pull off an overhead catch. Diving full length, Jack ended up pouching the ball in his gloves only centimetres from the ground. Perhaps no surprise that Simpson was later to recall this as the best catch he took in his entire career. It would no doubt have added extra relish to the occasion that his victim on the day had been the incomparable Viv Richards.

At 69 for 2, Rishton proved unable to recover from the blow. Rammy's stand-in pro on the day, the renowned West Indian fast bowler Franklyn Stephenson, had succeeded in carrying out the main damage with 5-62, bowling the opposition out for 136. Although it was to be a one-off appearance of Franklyn's for the club in this competition (he also played a single match for Rammy in the league), Stephenson had certainly played his heart out on the day, bowling 23 consecutive overs.

The final, taking place at Acre Bottom, pitted the Rams against the same opponents they had faced in the competition in 1983, East Lancs. Again, it was to prove a cagey business all round, taking place over three dates in the calendar: 9th, 10th and 13th August.

At the end of Day One, the Rams had reached 71-2 with Steve Ashworth looking in commanding form on 43* and seemingly set up for a good partnership with pro Ijaz Faqih on 7*. Unfortunately though, Steve Ashworth was pre-booked to go on holiday to Wales the next day and ceded his wicket at the end of play. It was left to remaining batsmen to put together the total of 155-5 mustered by the end of the side's allotted 48 overs.

A strange denouement came about in East Lancs' response where with one ball to go, the visitors had reached 155-4. Technically, it was to transpire they had already won the match at this point. The implications though arising from Ashworth having been declared 'out' as opposed to say 'retired' didn't appear to have quite sunk in at the time. The East Lancs batsmen at the crease certainly weren't aware of the situation and took it upon themselves to try and scramble a run off the last ball. They never looked like completing it though as the ball was returned to the bowler's end without the batsmen having crossed. However, the bails somehow failed to be dislodged, sparing the batting pair huge potential embarrassment. The broader potential irony was that, despite the East Lancs pair only in effect having needed to keep the ball out to win, a run-out would in fact have given the Rams victory on 'countback'.

All ifs and buts aside though, and despite the chaotic end to the game, East Lancs had won by six wickets to prevail over Rammy again in a Worsley Cup Final, just as they had done in 1983.

ooooo

Not that the club was bereft of trophies in 1987. If the 1st XI had not been destined in the end to clinch the championship, the 2nd XI proved capable of filling the gap by lifting the Matthew Brown Cup.

It was a team captained by Maurice Haslam, pictured sitting centre front row in the club's commemorative photo celebrating the winning of the Cup. Mick Everett, on return from his various policing duties, also features in the photo standing four-square solid in the back row. As a proud father, Maurice was bound to have gained extra satisfaction from the fact that, at each end of the back row stood his two young sons, on one flank Jon and the other Michael.

Nine: League Centenary Championship Win

JACK SIMPSON'S FIRST season at the club proved a very successful one. He scored 478 runs at an average of 29.47 and claimed 36 victims behind the stumps. In addition, he had won the player of the year award for the first of five times he would do so over the course of his career with the club.

In 1988, he took over as captain. With a leadership style reminiscent of Dally Brooks, a tougher approach came back into the manner of doing things. Jack was nothing if not competitive, aiming to restore winning ways at the club. In this respect, he set a strong personal example. Apart from his expertise behind the stumps, he again topped 400+ this next season with 453 at 20.6.

Finishing 6th in the league with a record of W11 L12 NR 3 and seven bonus points, many of the amateur players featured strongly. 1988 witnessed Steve Ashworth achieving his highest total of runs in a season with 695 at 31.59 (winning the player of year award) and opener Ian Bell 488 at 22.2. The team's efforts would have benefitted though from a stronger input from pro Ijaz Fakih who, with 426 runs at 28.4, was only 4th highest club scorer.

Similarly on the bowling front, Fakih emerged only 3rd= at club level in terms of the number of wickets he took - 28 at 21.9. Steve Ratcliffe led with 39 at 17.6, the ever-reliable Brian Fielding taking 31 at 18.1 and Mark Stewart 28 at 19.7. Making comparisons with Haslingden, league-winners this year, it had proved a huge bonus for them having Australian Test player Geoff Lawson as pro, who had taken 86 wickets at 11.8.

In 1989, the Rams came 5th – W14 L11 NR 1 with seven bonus points. Brian McMillan, a 25-year-old South African all-rounder, again hailing from the state of Transvaal, performed excellently as a right hand bat this season, achieving a club record of 1,161 runs, scored at an average of 64.50. Topping the league's averages, surprisingly he didn't make a century even if twelve half-centuries rather made up for it. Ranked world no. 1 all-rounder at the time, it had proved an expensive signing. Despite there being no doubt as to him delivering on the batting front, there were many club supporters who were left feeling more sceptical though as to his commitment on the bowling side.

Meanwhile, Ian Bell topped the club's amateur run stakes, totalling 680 at 28.33, making it a fifth season during the 1980s that he passed the 500 mark. Jack Simpson notched up the first of his own 500+ runs in a season, weighing in with 629 at 33.11, including a score of 106 at Colne on 11 June when he and McMillan shared a third wicket stand of 173. Despite this, the Rams were to fall four runs short of the target set them of 217. As well as the runs he scored, Simpson took 38 catches behind the stumps, creating a club record that still stands, although later equalled by Tom Parton in 2013.

Another big plus for the club this season was the return of left-arm medium-fast bowler Steve Monkhouse from his stint in county cricket with Warwickshire and latterly Glamorgan. Incidentally, McMillan too had spent time previously with Warwickshire. Steve's own opportunities to play at 1st XI county level had been limited, having taken 18 first-class wickets at an average of 32.00. However, the experience had obviously sharpened him up for his return to Lancashire League cricket.

More effective than ever, Monkhouse headed the club's wicket-taking tally with 68 at 18.9, winning him the player of the year award, and allowing opportunity to tease his dad about notching up another 50+ season!

The club pro did not capture as many wickets as had been hoped for. As already said, it was felt by some that McMillan did not always put his full back into bowling. For an all-rounder, with such a massive reputation, his quota of 53 wickets at 20.09 felt disappointing. Meanwhile, with Monkhouse and McMillan usually sharing the new ball, Steve Ratcliffe didn't get as much chance to bowl but nevertheless took 19 wickets at 22.2.

With Monkhouse returning and two other pace-options besides, it was an apt time for 'Fieldo' to call it a day on the club's playing side. From 1971 onwards, he had played in 259 matches and taken 362 wickets at 19.60, having headed the League's averages in 1973. In a whole host of different ways, the value he brought to the club was immense. Apart from captaining the side in 1984 and 1985, he always demonstrated the character and ability to raise spirits, on the field, in the changing-room and also by great repute in the bar. A player and personality so highly respected by all he came into contact with, it was inevitable he would go on to serve the club in other capacities in future, including as Chairman and President.

Although the name of 'BR Fielding' was missing off 1st XI scorecards for 1989, there was a very fitting substitution in the form of son 'JM Fielding'. The member of the under-11s side, whom Murray Bennett coached back in 1984, had now matured in his teens, graduating to the 1st XI. Right hand bat and slow left arm bowler, Jon had played a few matches the previous season but had come of age in 1989 taking 33 wickets at an average of 25.5.

ooooo

Rammy fell back to 10th in 1990 – W9 L17 NR 0 with seven bonus points. In an unusual move which had few other precedents in the history of the Lancashire League, Rammy had taken on their own local amateur player, Steve Monkhouse, as club pro for the season. Taking 68 wickets the previous year no doubt strengthened the case. Although examples of such a transition had taken place three times to date at Accrington - Alan Worsick, David Parsons and David Lloyd - it was a very rare phenomenon across the League as a whole.

Monkhouse had few pretensions with the bat so pressure fell on the amateur batsmen to make runs. Fortunately, Steve Ashworth was back to best form, scoring 657 runs at 29.9. Ian Bell fell only eighteen runs short of another 500+, totalling 482 runs at 18.9 with fellow-opener Richard Heaton achieving a career-best total of 485 runs at 25.5.

Talking of Steve Ashworth, despite the excellent form he had been in this season, it was to prove his last full season playing for the Rams. Before joining the club, he had had two six-year spells with Bacup and Rawtenstall respectively but never in those 12 years managed to record a 500+ run season. At Acre Bottom, whilst compiling 3,364 runs at an average of 26.91, he performed the feat four times: in 1985 (512), 1987 (540), 1988 (708) and 1990 (657). Although he was to play eight more matches over the following two seasons, now in his mid-30s, Steve's career with the club effectively came to a close at the end of 1990. He had won player of the year twice in 1985 and 1988.

Meanwhile, Mark Price had returned to the club this season showing what a fine all-rounder he had become, scoring 461 runs at 24.26 and heading the club's bowling averages by taking 60 wickets at 19.26. Winning the player of year award, it was only a fleeting return for Pricey though before he was snapped up as a pro elsewhere. It would not be until 1999 when he returned back at the club again.

For his own part, Jack Simpson had not had such a good season with the bat scoring 319 at 19.9. However, as wicket-keeper, he enjoyed an outstanding season, including a record-breaking feat for the club in a match at home against Colne on 29 July in which he claimed seven victims in the visitors' total of 187 all out, taking three catches off the bowling of Monkhouse (4-65), plus two catches and two stumpings off Price (5-68).

As captain, Simpson was disappointed with the club ending in 10th place and decided to give up the role. Seasoned campaigner Maurice Haslam, although approaching retirement on the playing side and having captained the 1st XI last in 1975, took it on the following season. Incidentally, 1990 was to mark the end of Steve Monkhouse's playing career at the club, subsequently taking on further pro commitments, for example at Greenmount. Steve had played in 149 matches for Rammy, capturing 259 wickets at an average of 21.04, taking 50+ wickets in a season twice, in 1984 (57) and 1989 (68). He had been player of the year in 1989 and also shared the award in 1984.

ooooo

119

In 1991, the club finished marginally higher in 9th place (W11 L14 NR 1 with ten bonus points). The practice had been reverted to of bringing in a pro from overseas. With experience of playing state cricket for Transvaal, it was hoped that South African Rudi Bryson might emulate Brian McMillan. However, despite playing in all 26 matches that season, Bryson only scored 428 runs at 18.60 whilst taking a modest total of 44 wickets at 26.25.

With the pro hardly firing on all cylinders, there was a heavy onus on the amateurs to pull out the stops. Jack Simpson, perhaps relieved at being freed of the responsibilities of captaincy, was back to his run-scoring best, achieving 565 runs at 26.9. The ever-dependable Ian Bell compiled an impressive 642 runs at a slightly lower average of 24.7. A promising 1st XI batting newcomer was Brian Taylor (having climbed up the club's various ranks in a similar way to Jon Fielding), who gave notice of his potential by scoring 400 runs at 17.4.

On the bowling side, the 18-year-old Jon Fielding had proved a revelation, taking 72 wickets at 15.22 (top of the club's bowling averages and fourth in the league's), including what would prove a career-best of 9-53 (including a hat-trick) in a home match against Burnley on 28 July. Having won the toss and decided to take first knock on what looked a good wicket, the home team had only managed to post a modest 151-6 (Simpson top scoring with 40). Looking a difficult total to defend and with the Burnley openers moving smoothly to 41 without loss, the skipper had perhaps not without a sense of desperation tossed the ball to young Fielding. From that moment on, it was a procession of batsmen coming out of and returning back to the pavilion. But for wicket-keeper McLeod being run out, spin-bowler Fielding would likely have taken all ten wickets. No wonder he was voted player of the year at the end of the season for the first of six times he would receive the award.

Another relative newcomer who would also go on to make a considerable impact over future years was Stephen ('Dasher') Dearden. With a deceptive bowling action that disguised his speed and venom, he ended up 7th in the league's bowling averages, taking 33 wickets at 15.5 apiece. He had also scored 323 runs at 17.00, batting in the middle order. Overall, despite the lack of a strong input at pro level, it was evident that a number of younger players were stepping up to the mark.

Opportunity needs to be taken though at this point to pay tribute to Maurice Haslam. This season marked the end of a distinguished playing career since making his 1st XI debut in 1962. He had made 400 appearances, ranking 9th in club history. A batsman who scored many useful runs down the order, he had taken 195 wickets as a spin-bowler at an average of 21.33. A tremendous cover-point fielder, he had captained the side in 1975 and again in 1991. Maurice had enjoyed his best season in 1978, receiving the player of the year award. Although 1991 marked the end of his 1st XI playing days, Maurice was destined to go on making significant contributions to the life of the club in very many different ways up to the present day.

ooooo

Perhaps Jack Simpson's time away from the captaincy role was never intended to be other than a 'gap year'. In any case, he was back at the helm by the start of the next season. The fact that 1992 marked the Lancashire League's centenary year might perhaps have weighed in the back of the mind.

In the opening match of the new season at home to Rishton, Jack demonstrated intent with a defiant innings of 69 out of a total of 127 all out, leading to a narrow victory by 17 runs. However, the next match witnessed a five-wicket away defeat at Todmorden. At home against Accrington, new pro Keith Arthurton made his debut. A 27-year-old left hand bat and slow left arm bowler with Test match experience back to 1988, the West Indian all-rounder set about proving his worth by scoring 57 out of a total of 158-9. In reply, the away team only managed 98 with right arm medium pace bowler Nick Riley taking 6-24. A player who had made his debut for the 1st XI in 1987, it was during this 1992 season that 'Pickles' started to demonstrate his all-round worth to the team.

Yet again, Haslingden set the pace this season. In terms of winning league titles, the neighbouring club had had a strong run of success in recent years, triumphing in 1987, 1988, 1989 and again in 1991. Despite a promising start to the 1992 season for the Rams, league positions seemed very much directed again in Haslingden's favour when the

121

current champions, unbeaten to this point, visited Acre Bottom on Sunday 14 June. At the start of play, Haslingden headed the league table with 37 points. Ramsbottom were in second place with 35 points. It was to be a match that would abide long in the memories of those who were there on the day.

As Jon Fielding was later to recall: 'I remember the band playing before the game and it being a beautiful, hot sunny day at Acre Bottom with a very big crowd, the perfect setting for a Lancashire League local derby'.

The home team batted first. Arthurton held the start of the innings together with 57 and Dearden scored 48. It was 156-5 when Jon Fielding came to the crease at no.7. From this point on though, 59 runs were added with Fielding scoring 51*. To the delight of the home crowd, Fielding had rattled off the fastest half century by an amateur in the season. His unbeaten half-century, including three fours and three sixes, was scored off only twenty-four balls enabling Rammy to reach 215 for 7 by the end of their innings.

Fielding continues: 'Haslingden then went about chasing the runs and the innings ebbed and flowed with the excitement and tension building as the afternoon wore on. I remember a defining moment arriving when Keith Arthurton snaffled their pro Phil Simmons caught and bowled for 72, just when he was beginning to cut loose. We felt in control at that point. However a quick-fire 41 from Mick Tracey brought things back in Hassy's favour. The whole game came to a boil in the last over which was bowled by Nick Riley.

'Hassy needed 3 to win off the last ball with Mick Tracey facing. Before Nick ran up to bowl it, there was some signalling between the bowler and wicket-keeper. In the event, Mick Tracey charged down the wicket with the aim of hitting a boundary, missed it and Jack Simpson removed the bails to secure maximum points and the celebrations began'.

The competition between the two sides went down to the wire. Despite a slight wobble in the last two matches with a 'no result' against Enfield and a loss against Accrington, the Rams held on to win the championship by four points with Haslingden in runners' up spot, as shown below:

	Pl	W	L	Tie	NR	Bonus pts	Pts
1st Ramsbottom	26	19	4	0	3	11	90
2nd Haslingden	26	19	3	0	4	6	86

Following on from 1921, 1925 and 1974, this was the fourth time that the Rams had pulled off victory in the League Championship. Of course, what put the icing on the cake in 1992 was that this latest win coincided with the centenary year of the Lancashire League. As Jack Simpson recalled later, 'I often had cause to remind players of the added significance of lifting the trophy this particular year'.

As for averages, pro Keith Arthurton had achieved a new club batting record scoring 1,185 runs at 69.7. Surprisingly, no amateur batsman had topped 500 runs, even if very decent amounts of runs had been scored by Jack Simpson (425 at 25.00), Brian Taylor (443 at 21.1), Ian Bell and Steve Dearden (both with 400 at 20.0).

On the bowling front, Arthurton headed the club's averages and came 9th in the league's with 57 wickets at 15.0. Nick Riley took 34 at 17.6 and Jon Fielding 38 at 19.7. The fact that Fielding took fewer wickets this season was probably due to the fact that Arthurton was also a slow left arm bowler. Not that, from a wicket-keeping perspective, Jack Simpson would have objected to having two such high-quality spin bowlers to be able to call upon. It was no doubt a factor in him establishing a club record by taking 21 stumpings that year.

ooooo

With Arthurton returning as pro, there was extended optimism for 1993. Unfortunately though, the Rams' bowling firepower was reduced through the loss of the immensely promising Jon Fielding, who had been invited to join Lancashire County Cricket Club on a two-year contract.

Once again, the strongest opposition looked set to be Haslingden who had retained the services of their West Indian pro Phil Simmons. A key match took place at Acre Bottom on 23 May when the away side sought to turn the tables on the outcome from the year before. Winning the toss, the visitors chose to bat and accumulated 221-4 with Simmons scoring 103. In return, the loss of Arthurton for 67 hampered the run chase before Simpson came in and hit 53 in 49 balls. Stumped by his counterpart Marcroft, now playing for Hassy, his efforts were in vain with the Rams finishing 17 runs short on 204-9.

Rawtenstall also were in close contention for the title this year and back-to-back matches against them within the space of a week brought about contrasting results. In the away match on 6 June, Ian Bell carried his bat scoring 64* out of a total of 135 only for the home team to cruise home by nine wickets. On 13 June, at Acre Bottom, the reverse happened with the Rams bowling the opposition out cheaply before going on to win by 10 wickets.

Keith Arthurton was in great form with the bat throughout the season, compiling 1,131 runs at 75.40 to head both club and averages for the second year running. Just as he had scored two centuries and eleven half-centuries over the course of 1992, he was to achieve an identical record this year, with Enfield the victims of his two tons. The first on 27 June was probably the more memorable, 103*, because it coincided with Ian Bell also scoring a century, 101* (his maiden one in the league), in a partnership between the openers of 221 without loss in what turned out to be a 53-run win.

As far as Ian Bell was concerned, a major highlight of his cricket career came in the space of 22 days in June 1993 when, in six matches, including those games against Rawtenstall and Enfield, he scored 319 runs at an average of 106.33.

A crunch head-to-head encounter came on 22 August in the return match at Bentgate. Haslingden clocked up 223-9 but the away team never looked like chasing the total down, finishing on 131-9 and losing by 92 runs. It wasn't to be a repeat of 1992 and in the end the Rams had to settle for a share of the Holland Cup with Rawtenstall, the table as follows:

	Pl	W	L	Tie	NR	Bonus pts	Pts
1st Haslingden	26	19	5	0	2	8	86
2nd= Ramsbottom	26	19	5	0	2	5	83
2nd= Rawtenstall	26	18	6	0	2	9	83

As can be seen, the decisive difference in the end between Haslingden and Ramsbottom, whilst sharing the same record in all other aspects, lay in the number of bonus points acquired.

Apart from Keith Arthurton's excellent batting record, Jack Simpson topped the club's amateur averages with 599 runs at 42.8 while Ian Bell amassed 758 runs at 34.5. Steve Dearden narrowly missed out on 500+ with 491 at 24.6. While Arthurton didn't have as good a year with the ball, having to settle for 40 wickets at 18.6, Nick Riley took 39 at 21.1 and Dearden 38 at 19.2.

ooooo

The start to the 1994 season witnessed a major change to the general landscape of Acre Bottom. Whereas previously, entry to the ground came via the lower end of Bridge Street and a stretch of roadway lying between the River Irwell and Ramsbottom Paper Mill, this access point was superseded now by a newly constructed road running between Trinity Paper Mills (successor to Ramsbottom Paper Mill and now owned by Danisco) and the renovated Ramsbottom Railway Station, with the old road off Bridge Street transferred back to industrial use.

To many people, especially those with more longstanding connections with the cricket club, the old entrance-point held keen associations, For example, Harry Williams recalled operating the 'gate' on the old site for 19 years, during which time he had on occasion been faced with one or two challenging situations. One example was a Bacup Club minibus rolling up and the driver maintaining it only contained himself and the person in the passenger seat. The gate-keeper became suspicious:

'Open up the back, cock!

'Why don't you believe me?

'You're not coming in till you've opened up the back door.'

Reluctantly, the driver agreed. Inside the back of the minibus sat pro Roy Gilchrist and up to fifteen Bacup fans.

'Gilchrist was known to be a fierce character but I didn't give it a second thought. Yes, he got into the ground as a player but the rest had to cough up!'

With regard to the opening of the new roadway, a ceremony took place on 29 May 1994 and a plaque unveiled on the wall of the Gate Lodge by Danisco's representative, Mr Hans Halskov-Hansen. A tongue-twisting name enough at the best of times! Club chairman Brian Fielding, who happened to find it difficult pronouncing aitches, was later to recall having felt uncomfortable having the duty of introducing the Danish dignitary. Thankfully, after a good deal of practising beforehand, he was word perfect on the day.

Meanwhile, during this same year, a rather different type of group photo came to be taken on club premises. Different that is to the normal all-male ones. This particular picture highlighted the important contribution made to the life of the club by the 'Ramsbottom Cricketing Ladies Committee'. With many being players' wives, it reflected another way in which families as a whole tended to provide such valuable service to the club. In this instance, it involved carrying out a range of jobs needing to be done behind the scenes on match days and at other times. The comment had also been sometimes heard said, from those amongst the group, that it was also one way of avoiding becoming a 'cricketing widow!'

ooooo

Returning to the field of play, the prospects for the 1994 season seemed positive enough with Keith Arthurton returning as pro and Jack Simpson continuing as skipper. The feeling was that, maintaining the present formula, the club was bound to end up 'there or thereabouts' again.

1994, however, turned out not quite as well as the previous two seasons with the club only managing 68 points and finishing in 6th place - W15 L10 NR 1 and seven bonus points. This was 24 points off the pace of league champions Nelson on 92 points, with Bacup runners-up on 84 and Haslingden 3rd, 80 points.

Compared to the brilliant form he had shown over the last two seasons, Arthurton found it hard to maintain previous standards. Scoring 849 runs at 40.4, respectable as it was in overall terms, he fell to 11th in the league's batting averages. Although scoring another two centuries, it was noticeable he only achieved four half-centuries in comparison with eleven in each of the last two years.

Even so, the reduction in Arthurton's quota of runs was compensated for by as many as four amateur batsmen achieving 500+ seasons, Ian Bell with 692 at 31.4 (including 105* against Rawtenstall), Steve Dearden with 650 at 32.5, Brian Taylor with 613 at 26.25 and Jack Simpson with 507 at 25.4 (including 106 against Burnley). Taking 48 wickets at 18.0, Arthurton was eclipsed in the bowling stakes by Nick Riley who bagged 61, even if at a higher average of 20.8 runs per wicket. Riley won the player of the year award despite Jack Simpson establishing a new wicket-keeping club record for highest number of victims in a season - 53, consisting of 32 catches and 21 stumpings. Incidentally, this made him only the second player ever in league history, following David Pearson of East Lancs in 1990, to have achieved the wicket-keeper's double of 500+ runs and 50+ victims in a season.

Even if ending in a relatively disappointing final season by his own very high standards for Keith Arthurton, it needs emphasising that the West Indian had given remarkable service overall during the three years he was pro at the club, the highlight undoubtedly being the massive part he had played in the winning of the championship in his first year at the club in 1992.

ooooo

1995 marked the 150th season since Ramsbottom Cricket Club had been founded back in 1845. By way of commemoration, and doing full justice to Roman-style enumeration, a 'Sesquicentenary Committee' was set up to celebrate the anniversary year in a variety of ways. Apart from other forms of activity on the ground, a book was commissioned in order to commemorate many different aspects relating to the history of the club up to the present time.

Casting around for a successor to Keith Arthurton, it was Jack Simpson who suggested enlisting the services of a New Zealander by the name of C.Z. Harris whom he had first seen playing at his previous club, Rochdale. A 25-year-old all-rounder, Harris had been playing Test cricket from 1992 onwards. Batting left-handed and capable of bowling a variety of right-arm spin or medium pace, he was known to have a lively, competitive attitude that accorded well with Simpson's own approach to the game.

However, club chairman Brian Fielding was later to admit: 'We looked at his record, and it wasn't brilliant. One or two on our sub-committee were a bit sceptical, but Jack said Harris was good – on and off the field – at Rochdale. We decided to go for him. We offered him terms and he accepted. It was to turn out the best thing we ever did'.

Chris Harris described later in his autobiography - *Harry: The Chris Harris Story* - how he felt under a fair bit of pressure joining the club at this particular time: 'It was Ramsbottom's 150th anniversary and they were desperate to have a summer to remember'. Even so, the main question he remembered being asked of him was what the 'Z' stood for in 'C.Z.Harris' – the answer being 'Zinzan', a name recurring often in his New Zealand family.

As others before him, such as Peter Philpott and Murray Bennett, Chris testified to how 'the officials at Ramsbottom were very good and made me feel at home and I loved my time there'. This was on and off the pitch. 'Derek Read served behind the bar at the club at the time. And he was forever trying to imitate the New Zealand accent – badly!'

Harris recalled coming across team manager Mick Everett for the first time: 'He's a big man, and on his shoulders rests one of the largest heads I've ever seen. He was a Detective Inspector in the Greater Manchester Police Drug Squad until he retired in 1995. He's a terrific bloke, the sort of person who defines the character of a cricket club'.

As for Everett's reciprocal first impressions, he commented: 'Early on in that season we played Nelson, who were the previous season's champions. He got 42, took 2-43 in 23 overs, bowled tidily, and his enthusiasm shone through. I thought we've got a good'un here'.

With Bacup and Haslingden set to slip off the pace this year, finishing fourth and seventh respectively, it would be left to the Rams to mount a title challenge from amongst the Rossendale clubs. After the match against Nelson, described above, which had resulted in a three-wicket victory, this however was followed by an away defeat at Rishton by a similar margin. Although Harris took 5-48, his batting scores so far hadn't reached the heights they would do later on in the season. His first fifty came away at Enfield but the match was lost by two wickets with another defeat incurred at home against Colne by 21 runs.

It was in the fifth game of the season at home to Haslingden that Harris began to have real impact. The away team had scored 251-7. Manager Everett picks up the story: 'We considered their total massive. We had a relatively good start but we were far behind the run rate. Chris went in. I always hold my breath till he gets to 20. He frightens me to death when he first gets in.

'We wanted about 80 in the last 10 overs. All of a sudden he let loose. He smashed everyone all round the ground. We got the runs in eight overs. The crowd went berserk. It was the turning point of our season'.

Harris finished the match with a score of 117* to secure a seven wicket win. This was followed by 6-46 and a knock of 65 in a win at Lowerhouse. The next match at home against Enfield brought another victory, Harris skittling the opposition out for 66, taking 6-18. The game at Colne was narrowly won on faster run rate, followed by a seven wicket win at home to Lowerhouse, Harris again among the wickets with 5-26. Another winning home game against Accrington, the Kiwi taking 7-39, made it six wins on the trot.

There was to be no letting up. A home win against Tod saw Harris scoring 56*; the next match at Bacup was won by nine wickets. In utterly commanding form now, Harris struck a colossal 156* with 14 fours and 5 sixes in the team's 82-run home win against East Lancs, followed by a win at Turf Moor. Church were dispatched by six wickets, Harris 5-73 and 87*. Then there was a home victory against Burnley, Harris 112* and 5-67. However, the series of 12 wins came to an end away at East Lancs by the narrow margin of 9 runs despite Harris' 5-47. This was followed by further defeat at the hands of Church.

Winning ways were resumed in a home match won on faster run rate at home to Rawtenstall and also the return match a week later by five wickets, Harris taking 6-67. Away at Tod, Harris claimed 4-27 to reduce them to 105 all out. The Rams won by nine wickets, with Simpson scoring 90* in 69 balls out of a total of 108-1. In the next game Harris scored his fourth ton of the season, 114*, in a 49-run win at Nelson, followed by 79 and 5-47 in a 61-run away win at Haslingden.

The Rams headed the table but Rishton were breathing down their necks in second place. The penultimate match of the season on 3 September brought the two teams together in a crunch match at Acre Bottom that looked set to decide which way the title was going. When Rishton took first knock, it seemed they had put the game out of sight after thrashing 290-3.

Imagine the home team's relief then when adverse weather conditions allowed them to bat little more than two overs before stumps were drawn. Ordinarily, this would have ended in a 'no result', with each side awarded one point each, an outcome that would have very much suited the Rams in the circumstances. However, a clause in the league's rule book stipulated that if five or more matches in a day's fixture list were affected in this way, all those matches should be replayed. That indeed was the situation now.

In such circumstances, the two teams were brought together again at Acre Bottom on 9 September. The Rams won the toss and chose to field. A decision which Rishton's pro Phil Simmons obviously relished by way of contributing 96 to a total of 206-9 by the end of 46 overs, with Harris achieving modest figures of 4-84 by his standards.

When it came to Rammy's turn to bat, Simmons proved equally effective with the ball taking the first five wickets, including that of Harris for 18. Finding it impossible to match Rishton's run-rate, the home team's batting effort fell away to 140-8 at the end with Simmons taking 5-62. Following on from this 66-run victory in the replayed game, Rishton emerged with four points to turn the tables at this stage in proceedings.

However, hope remained that the outcomes from final-day matches, taking place 24 hours later on Sunday 10 September, might still tilt Rammy's way. Their own match was at Accrington. In no-nonsense mood, Harris took 7-22 with the home team bundled out for 54, earning the Rams an extra bowling bonus point. Maximum five-point victory was resolved in next to no time with Harris contributing 35* to the winning total of 57-2. Meanwhile, everything hung on Rishton's last match of the season at home against Rawtenstall. Could the visitors do the Rams a favour?

Gallantly as Rawtenstall performed, accumulating a total of 182-5, it did not prove enough to prevent the home team reaching 184-4 and winning the match by six wickets, thereby achieving the four points required to lift the championship trophy. Ultimately, the Rams had to settle for runners-up spot and the Holland Cup in the same way as 1993. Final positions were:

	Pl	W	L	Tie	NR	Bonus pts	Pts
1st Rishton	26	21	3	0	2	10	96
2nd Ramsbottom	26	20	6	0	0	12	92

ooooo

Despite an overall sense of disappointment, there were many strong individual successes to celebrate. For example, on the batting front, Chris Harris had topped the league's averages scoring 1,231 runs at a staggering average of 87.9. Jack Simpson, 716 runs at 29.8 and Ian Bell, 575 at 25.0 had also again contributed magnificent numbers of runs.

On the bowling side, Harris had managed in the end to bag a remarkable 112 wickets. The next leading club wicket-taker had been Garfield Moreton, a slow left arm bowler at the club since 1993, who had shone this year by taking 47 wickets at 17.17. In tandem with Harris, it had proved an effective spin-bowling combination. The thing about Harris though was that he bowled such a rich variety of spin that he could never be pinned down to one predominant type of delivery - hence his diverse range of deliveries sometimes being jokingly likened to 'liquorice all-sorts'. Meanwhile, as a quickie, Steve Dearden had fared well over the season, taking 32 wickets at 22.5.

Coming back to Jack Simpson, always seeking to perfect the art of wicket-keeping, the records he had broken in previous years were further cracked in 1995. His club record of 53 dismissals in 1994 enhanced itself this year to 56, consisting of 30 catches and 26 stumpings. In a similar way, his 26 stumpings also set a new record of its own, superseding that of the year before. As well, he had achieved the wicket-keepers' accolade of the double of 500+ runs/ 50+ victims a second year running. Regular observers of Lancashire League cricket always say Jack Simpson was the finest keeper they ever saw, invariably standing up to the stumps, even for the quickest of seam-bowlers.

In terms of Chris Harris' record that season it needs pointing out that, in scoring a total of 1,231 runs, he had forged a new club record, surpassing Keith Arthurton's previous best of 1,185. By way of taking 112 wickets, apart from Bill Hickmott's tally of 118 in 1925 and of course amateur Will Fenwick's 137 going back to 1900, no club bowler had ever taken more wickets in a season.

The batting and bowling figures Harris achieved make him sound like some kind of obsessive cricketing machine. However that was not at all how he came across to others. As Mick Everett had occasion to comment: 'He's just daft. When you see him walk, if he'd been a horse he'd have been put down. He'd do things like jump from the top step of the pavilion down to the bottom. All the young kids thought he was magnificent. When a ball was thrown in from the boundary he'd catch it between his legs, things like that'.

Everett continued: 'We've got a game we play in Lancashire called threes and fives, which is like dominoes played on a cribbage board. It's a very tactical game and we like to think it's pretty difficult to learn. One night 'Harry' was watching us for a bit. He said he wanted to learn how to play the game. I explained the basic rudiments and within half an hour he was an absolute dab hand'.

Meanwhile, returning to all that he had achieved in statistical terms, Chris Harris' supreme achievement in 1995 was that he managed, in combined batting and bowling prowess, to join the ranks of a remarkably small number of players in the history of the Lancashire League to pull off the 'double' of scoring over a thousand runs and a hundred wickets in a season. Still standing to the present day, the list in chronological order is as follows:

Season	Name	Club	Runs	Wickets
1949	Cec Pepper	Burnley	1,070	113
1949	Vijay Hazare	Rawtenstall	1,075	104
1990	Colin Miller	Rawtenstall	1,078	100
1995	Chris Harris	Ramsbottom	1,231	112

On finer analysis of the above statistics, it can justifiably be argued that Harris stands at the very top of this elite group of achievers in the league's history. Not bad to say that the chairman and others on the sub-committee had felt cause to doubt his credentials prior to him starting at the club!

PETER PHILPOTT
Professional 1955, 1959, 1960

Seymour Nurse 57 for 3

Ramsbottom Cricket Club
Lancashire League Champions 1974

Back l to r: R Brooks, A W Holt, B R Fielding, P N Ashworth, W J Steele, A Chapman, D Handman, H Hall, J Wheatcroft (Scorer)

Front l to r: M Haslam, W Savage, R J Bright (Pro), D L Brooks (Capt), J N Ashworth, T Stewart

1974 Cup Presentation D Brooks, R Greaves, M Haslam, R Bright, J Cropper

Sergeant Everett Wears Helmet

Murray Bennett Wears Shades

136

M.G. Haslam, N. Riley, M. Everett, E. Hoyle, G. Ratcliffe, A. Whittaker, J. Haslam
S. Morris, P. Compston, M. Haslam (Capt.), M. Carter, A. Holt

Ramsbottom CC Ladies Committee 1994

Standing (l. to r.): May Monkhouse, Karen Simpson, Kath Hamer, Marjorie Fielding, Linda Bell, Judith Eardley, Ruth Everett, Chris Spencer
Seated (l. to r.): Elaine Brooks, Betty Jenkins, Kathleen Horrocks, Alice Wright, Annie Walley, Amy Bowker, Marion Haslam

Standing (left to right)
Duncan Brooks   Peter Ashworth
Geoff Bladen   John Ashworth
Henry Hall   Maurice Haslam
Ian Chappell   Ronald Greaves
Kneeling (left to right)
Jim Davenport   Harold Monkhouse   John Steele

**IAN CHAPPELL PAYS A RETURN VISIT TO RIVERSIDE
ACRE BOTTOM AUG. 1989**

138

Ramsbottom. C.C.
Lancashire League Centenary Champions
1892 ~ 1992.

S. Dearden . J. Fielding . N. Riley . I. Bell . M. Mills . M. Gowers.
S. Hall . K. L. T. Arthurton . J. Simpson . B. Taylor . S Ratcliffe .
(Professional.) , (Captain).

JACK SIMPSON
Pincers Action at Church with Nick Riley

KEITH ARTHURTON AND IAN BELL

Chris Harris playing 3s and 5s

RAMSBOTTOM CRICKET CLUB SESQUICENTENARY COMMITTEE

Standing (l. to r.): John Griffiths, Peter Spencer, Des Jones, Chris Wood, Mike Everett, Allan Read, Jack Simpson.
Seated (l. to r.): Fred Rothwell, Harry Williams, Brian Hutchinson, Brian Fielding, Alice Wright, Ronald Greaves, Harold Monkhouse.
(Absent: Barry Miller and Derek Read)

Worsley Cup Winners 2001

MICHAEL CLARKE
New South Wales, Australia
Professional 2002

RAMSBOTTOM CRICKET CLUB
Lancashire League Champions 2010

Back row, left to right: M.J. Dentith, A.W. Bell, A. Hakin, D.M. Bell, R.E. Read, J. Walmsley, A.J. Doolan (Pro), M.G. Haslam.

Front row, left to right: J. Pilling, A. Caunce, J.M. Fielding (Capt), A.I. Holt, K.T. Webb.

Jon Fielding Wins Decision from Umpire

Michael Haslam Cuts in from
the Paper Mill End

Faf du Plessis Catch in 20-20
Semi Final 2010

Rob Read Catch in Worsley Cup Final: 2011

2016 League Champions

Sarah and Daryn Smit at Nelson

The Fielding Dynasty - Brad, Jon, JJ, Brian

Womens T20 Team 2021

Ben Dack
(Treasurer)

Peter Spencer
(President)

Sheila McQueeney
(Secretary)

John Fox
(Chairman)

Jon Fielding
(Vice Chairman)

Current Executive Committee Members

Hall of Fame Five 2021 with Graham Gooch

Ten: Beyond the Boundary

CHRIS HARRIS WAS scheduled to return in 1996 for a second year. The only downside was that, engaged to tour the West Indies with New Zealand, it meant he was unavailable to play for Rammy until the middle of May onwards. Meanwhile, club skipper Jack Simpson was champing at the bit to go one step further in clinching another championship win to add to that of 1992.

However, with Harris missing from the opening away match on 21 April and, despite Nick Riley taking 5-51 to limit opponents Rishton to 145-8, the Rams only made 115 and lost by 30 runs. In the second game of the season at home against Accrington, sub-pro Australian Peter Sleep played a match-winning role in a 70-run win, scoring 102* and taking 5-55. A home match against Colne was won by the tighter margin of two wickets. A third win was gained at Enfield by 74 runs, Sleep scoring 56* and taking 5-20. This was followed by a two-wicket loss at Lowerhouse on 11 May.

A first round Worsley Cup home tie took place the next day resulting in a 76-run win against Rishton, Nick Riley taking 5-38. Significantly, Chris Harris was now back playing again. His first league match came at home against Lowerhouse on 19 May. He opened his account with a score of 50 in a total of 254-6, even though eclipsed on the day by Steve Dearden hitting a whirlwind 106 (in 81 balls with three sixes), his maiden century in Lancashire League matches. In response, Lowerhouse fell short by 54 runs with Harris taking 4-71 and Dearden 3-19.

On 27 May, at home against Enfield, Harris burst back into top form taking 6-39 to help dismiss the opposition for 83 before scoring 53* out of a total of 85-1 to secure a nine-wicket victory. Another win was achieved at Nelson, even if by only nine runs. Harris was again in good form with 77* and 4-61. On 1 June, in a second round cup-tie at Rawtenstall, the Rams scored 187 (Harris 83). The home team looked in contention at 125-4 but fell away to 153 all out (Harris 5-70).

The next week however saw the team suffering league defeat at Colne after being set a total of 226 (Moreton 7-68). Despite 110 from Simpson, the Rams lost by 17 runs. In the following match at home against Bacup on 9 June, a 202-run second wicket stand between Taylor and their West Indian pro Roger Harper enabled the visitors to amass 245-6 to take the match beyond the Rams, who only managed 197-8 in reply. Gladly, the next match at home to Rawtenstall produced a straightforward 8-wicket victory after Harris had taken 7-29 to dismiss them for 105 and Simpson (66*) had batted through the Rams' innings.

Incurring four league defeats to this point hardly looked like championship-winning form though. At least the Rams were still going strong in the Worsley Cup. On 16 June, a semi-final encounter took place away at East Lancs. With Simpson (74) batting almost to the end of the 50 overs, the Rams scrambled their way to a total of 157-8. In reply, things looked promising though with East Lancs wickets going down regularly at the hands of the three-pronged attack of Harris (3 wickets), Dearden (2) and Riley (4). At 123-9, the game seemed as good as over, only for a 10th wicket stand of 27 to produce a dramatic finale in which the Rams were grateful to finish off their gallant opponents, with a run out, after 49.4 overs to clinch the game by a seven-run margin.

Ahead of the Worsley Cup Final, scheduled to take place on 4 August, the team had to return their attention back to the bread and butter of league competition. In an away match which looked to have slipped away after Rawtenstall had scored 255-5, an opening stand of 105 between Jack Simpson and Jon Haslam prepared the ground for Chris Harris (85*) to step in and round off victory at 256-5.

Six more league matches remained up until the Cup Final against Bacup. At home, the Rams beat Haslingden on faster run rate. There then followed a home loss against East Lancs, a close home win against Church in which Ian Bell scored 91*, and another defeat at the hands of East Lancs away from home. Next came a 'no result' from a home tie against Burnley and an eight-wicket win against Church at Oswaldtwistle.

However, all attention was focussed on the match shortly to take place at Lanehead on 4 August. Winning the toss and deciding to bat, the Rams' innings could hardly have got off to a worse start with openers Bell and Simpson both out for ducks. Harris (31) and Dearden (46) retrieved the situation somewhat with a 66-run stand but wily Bacup pro Roger Harper accounted for them both as the off-spinner bowled through the innings taking 5-68. Given Bacup's batting line-up, the eventual score of 160 all out didn't seem nearly enough.

Dearden, having top scored with the bat, picked up the new ball alongside Harris and roared in to bowl. Capturing the wicket of opening batsman Spencer – caught by Moreton – this brought Harper to the crease and the match came to the boil.

In recent conversation with Ben Dack (currently Club treasurer but who had played in this vital match in 1996), he recalled Jack Simpson setting a particular field on the day for Harper. Because it was known he favoured the hook shot, it involved having both orthodox square leg and also a deeper one. To Dearden's bowling, Dack was put in the closer fielding position with Chris Harris behind him on the boundary edge. As 'Dasher' bounded in and unleashed a fast delivery just short of a length on leg stump, Harper took the bait and swung at it. Heart in mouth, ready for the ball coming his way, Dack had felt a certain amount of relief that the ball sailed well over his head in the direction of the deeper field placement. Just as it seemed the ball's trajectory was taking it away from the Kiwi, Harris bolted twenty metres to take a superb diving catch that saw Bacup's main danger-man out of contention with only two runs to his name.

A further couple of runs later, Dearden had Taylor caught behind to claim his third wicket, leaving Bacup clinging on to the ropes at 32-3. Now it was Harris' turn to inflict damage, going on to take 5-44. At one point, at 88-8, the game looked over and done with had it not been for two brave stands, firstly one of 29 between Killelea and Pooler and then another of 31 between Killelea and Chapman raising the score to 148 all out. The Rams had emerged victors in the end by 12 runs.

Although there were many left bemused at the end as to how Steve Dearden hadn't picked up the man of the match award – it went instead to Peter Killelea 'for keeping Bacup in the match as long as he did' – the joy felt at the end by everyone associated with the club was immense, particularly considering this was the first time the Rams had lifted the trophy since 1957.

ooooo

As for league position at the end of the season, the team had done well to claw back into closer contention, in the end finishing 3rd in the table as shown below:

	Pl	W	L	Tie	NR	Bonus pts	Pts
1st Rishton	26	17	7	0	2	15	87
2nd East Lancashire	26	18	7	0	1	12	86
3rd Ramsbottom	26	17	7	0	2	9	81

Although pro Chris Harris hadn't performed quite so well in statistical terms as the year before, he still could proudly look back on the team's achievement in winning the Worsley Cup. From the heady heights of 1995, his run total had fallen to 686 at an average of 57.2. It had though to be taken into account he had missed the best part of a month's cricket at the start of the season.

Meanwhile, Jack Simpson, player of the year, had accumulated a phenomenal total of 810 runs in the season at 36.9. This placed him third highest amateur batsman in club history as per number of runs scored in a season, behind Billy Whitworth's 829 in 1940 and Jack Redfern's 815 in 1911. In the course of recent conversation though, Jack pointed out with a fair degree of justification, that Whitworth hadn't had to face up to professional bowlers during the war-year of 1940 and that Redfern's total had been boosted by the runs he had scored in an 'extra' two-innings match (the play-off title decider in 1911 against Nelson) that made the number of league games he played that season over and above the conventional 26. Not that Jack was grumbling!

151

Steve Dearden had also done well with the bat scoring 587 runs at 32.6 whilst Ian Bell notched 593 at an average of 28.2. On the bowling side, a relative newcomer to the club, Chris Hall, a right hand bat and off-break bowler, who would later to go on to play Minor Counties cricket for Cheshire, took 36 wickets to top the club's averages and finish fifth in the league's.

ooooo

Yet at the end of 1996, despite events on the field of play having made it such a successful one in club history, certain happenings off the field were set to create unpleasant feelings which would lead to two players of major standing at the club, Jack Simpson and Steve Dearden, deciding to leave the club and play elsewhere.

Behind the scenes, tension had been brewing up during the season as to the way in which members of the club's selection committee perceived the captain viewing week-to-week selection of the 1st XI team as his sole prerogative to determine. Committee members came to feel that they were convening merely to rubber-stamp the team-sheet that Jack, in forthright manner, presented them with. Naturally, it was accepted that, as captain, he would have a leading and indeed over-riding say in such matters but committee members came to feel that any tentative views they might put forward were simply being dismissed without opportunity for discussion or involvement in the process.

The view had developed among those members that the time might have arrived for Jack to stand aside and let someone else have captaincy experience. This was felt to reflect the general line adopted at the club, in that rarely had anyone carried out the said role for more than two or three years at a time. The unfortunate aspect of all this though was that, for whatever reasons, Jack himself was not brought into discussions at this stage. Perhaps a sense of apprehension was felt that he might not take too kindly to the proposition. What this led to, however, was a communication breakdown between captain and committee.

It seems from general account that the chairman of the committee, Mike Carter, an ex-player who also at the time carried out groundsman duties, was the one vested with the responsibility of taking the captain aside and transmitting such thoughts to him on a verbal basis. However, a long time passed by without this happening. In the end, at the close of the season, Carter dropped an envelope off through the letter-box of Jack Simpson's home, conveying the message in writing that a decision had been taken to the effect that he would no longer be serving as captain the following season.

Understandably, whatever Simpson thought about the 'decision' itself, he did not take kindly to the method of communication. Almost instantly, it had come into his mind that the way in which he had been treated as captain meant he no longer wished to continue as a player. Pursuing this line of thinking, he was supported by colleague Steve Dearden, who had served as his vice-captain. In these circumstances, the two of them decided they would seek to sign up for another club for 1997, which turned out to be Haslingden.

During the course of conversations in recent times with each of these two players, they both underlined how much they had enjoyed their time playing for Ramsbottom Cricket Club. In fact the main substance of what was talked about related to the actual playing of cricket as opposed to the 'politics' which in the end made them feel they had little alternative but to leave the club at the end of 1996.

Jack Simpson had played in 240 matches for Ramsbottom, scoring 5,499 league runs at 28.79, including three centuries and twenty-nine 50s. He had scored 500+ runs in six different seasons. As a wicket-keeper, he claimed 402 victims, 263 caught and 139 stumped, creating several club records along the way. He had initially served as captain from 1998 to 1990. Then in the League's centenary year of 1992, he had resumed office and led the club to a 4th championship title, continuing as captain up until 1996, the year in which the club had won the Worsley Cup. Since joining the club back in 1987, he had been awarded player of the year five times, in 1987, 1992, 1993, 1995 and 1996.

Steve Dearden, having made his 1st XI debut in 1990, had played in 197 matches, scoring 3,452 runs for the club at 23.32, including one century and sixteen 50s and taken 183 wickets at 23.01 with 5 five or more wicket hauls. In terms of winning honours, he had been a member of both the 1992 championship-winning and 1996 Worsley Cup-winning sides.

ooooo

One aspect of continuity at the club from 1996 to 1997 was the return of Chris Harris for a third consecutive year as pro. With Ian Bell as new captain, the vacant wicket-keeper slot fell to 19-year-old Richard Hevingham who had previously been playing for the club's 2nd XI.

With Hevingham having no serious claims to being a batsman, the main run-scoring onus would now rest on Harris, Bell, Brian Taylor and Chris Hall. In the bowling department, Harris, Nick Riley, Hall and Garfield Moreton were seen as the main lines of attack. Meanwhile, it was hoped that younger players such as batsman Mark Dentith and bowlers Simon Read and Michael Haslam (who had returned back to the club at the start of 1996, after two years away playing for Brooksbottom the first year and then in New Zealand the second), would look to take advantage of chances they may be given.

Fortunately, Chris Harris was available from the word go this season. 1997 in fact started on a bright note with the team picking up silverware straightaway through winning the newly-instituted Colne Cup, which was a one-off encounter, much like football's Charity Shield, between Championship and Worsley Cup winners from the previous year. This success came at Rishton on 19 April. The home team had first knock but been kept down to 132 with Harris taking 5-29. The Rams had struggled for a while to get going in reply but made it through to 135-6 to win the game by four wickets and thereby earn a place in the history of the Lancashire League by being the first winners of the competition.

In the opening league match, taking place the day after at home against Accrington, Ian Bell and Chris Harris shared a second-wicket partnership of 108, contributing 52 and 59 respectively to a total of 175-5. This proved strong enough for the Rams to win the match by 42 runs with Harris taking 5-53, Chris Hall 3-39 plus two run outs.

Harris looked back to his brilliant form of 1995 when scoring 110 in the next game, away at Rishton. Dentith had made an enterprising 32 in 15 balls coming in at no. 8. Then Harris (4-41) and Riley (3-26) did the main damage in bowling out the home team for 91 in a match won by 105 runs.

Alas, the unbeaten start to the season came to an end in the home game against Lowerhouse which the visitors won by 58 runs. Then an away game was lost at Colne on run-rate but a home win against Bacup by 52 runs served as something of a taster for the highly significant match following this one - an encounter between Haslingden and Ramsbottom at Bentgate on 25 May – with of course no need for a reminder that two prominent ex-Rams were lining up against them on the day!

With tensions running sky-high, the worst possible scenario unwound Rammy's way with Dearden packing off Bell (6), Taylor (0), Harris (0) and Dyson (0) in a sad procession back to the pavilion, leaving the score standing at a desperate 17-4. Though slightly recovering to finish on 109-9, Dearden ended with 5-19. Despite Harris (3-31) doing his best to inflict similar damage on Haslingden, there was one batsman he could not dislodge, their opener and captain, namely Jack Simpson, who succeeded in steering his new team home to a five-wicket victory with 42* out of a total of 110-5.

The Rams' next game, at home to Nelson, was won by 37 runs with Harris scoring another ton (104*) and taking 4-38. This was followed by a six-wicket win at Enfield but then came a narrow 11-run loss at Todmorden and a further defeat by 26 runs at Rawtenstall. Despite such an uneven pattern of results, the side still stood in the top half of the table. No one team was forging ahead at this point. Following a tense tied match-result in the return home match against Rawtenstall, Harris took 8-15 at Lanehead and scored 39* of the 57-5 required to beat Bacup by 5 wickets. A 7-run loss at home to Burnley, despite Bell's 55, was made up for by a 99-run victory at Church in which Harris excelled with 84 and 5-41, followed by a dramatic one-run win at Burnley. There followed though an uneasy sequence of six matches made up of three wins, two losses and a no result.

Despite the inconsistency, everything still remained in the melting-pot. On 24 August, the Rams welcomed high-flying Haslingden to Acre Bottom. The Rams were determined not to be taken to the cleaners again. With Harris (6-55) claiming the wickets of Simpson for 6 and Dearden for 8, the visitors were bowled out for 121. In reply, Bell scored

34 and Harris 39* to enable the home team to win by 6 wickets and regain local bragging rights!

The result certainly seemed to fire the Rams up for a strong late run with Harris taking 9-14 away at Accrington and scoring 14* to lead them to a 4-wicket victory. It turned out to be very much Chris Harris's swansong appearance for the club given that he was required soon after to go back and play for his country before the end of the league season was reached. Incidentally, Harris' 9-14 created a new club record beating the 9-15 figures achieved by Duerr and Hickmott back in the 1920s.

With a win and 'no result' in remaining games, the Rams ended the season in 4th= place, tied with Lowerhouse on 75 points. Ahead of them in 3rd place were Enfield with 77. Runners-up were East Lancs with 78. Sitting proudly at the top of the table were Haslingden with 80 points. Although this was a feat that the Bentgate club had achieved many times before, their winning also of the Worsley Cup in 1997 made it a unique year in the history of the club, marking as it did the first time they had achieved the 'double'.

Chris Harris' individual level of success in 1997 had gravitated somewhere mid-point between that of the two previous seasons. Scoring 716 runs at 42.1 placed him 6th in the overall league tables while his 86 wickets at 10.8 put him slightly higher, 4th, in the equivalent bowling averages.

Amongst amateur players, Brian Taylor scored 472 runs at 23.6 and Ian Bell 429 at 17.87. In his new role as captain, he might have hoped this year would have seen him equalling Billy Whitworth's club record of eleven 500+ runs in a season but it was not quite to be. In the bowling stakes, Chris Hall, awarded player of the year, took 37 wickets at 16.5 and Nick Riley 28 at 15.1.

Kiwi Chris Harris had given three years' tremendous service to the club. He was destined to play again in the Lancashire League in years ahead but it was for other clubs, principally Bacup. Chris went on playing Test cricket for his country until 2002 and in ODIs until 2004. With a more successful record of success in ODI cricket, he scored 4,379 runs at 29.00 and took 203 wickets at 37.50. Like so many other pros before and after, he remembered his time playing at Acre Bottom with fondness, recording in his autobiography that 'I owe much to the people of the Ramsbottom club'.

Chris Harris also proudly mentions in the book: 'In 1998 I received a big honour from Ramsbottom. A group called the Horse and Bamboo Theatre Company put on an exhibition called *Beyond the Boundary*. Each club had to nominate the greatest player to have appeared for them in the league, and I was lucky enough to be chosen by Ramsbottom. I was in pretty special company. Among the other players nominated were some great West Indian names, headed by the legendary batsmen George Headley (Haslingden) and Everton Weekes (Bacup), and the famous all-rounder Sir Learie Constantine (Nelson), along with other renowned Caribbean test players Collis King (Colne) and Charlie Griffith (Burnley)'.

ooooo

On the field of play, 1998 proved a relatively quiet season for the Rams, finishing 6th with a record of W6 D11 L3 NR6. During this season, a major change had been introduced in the scoring system, the outcome of a 'draw' coming back into the equation. The system was to prove far from successful though, leading to the more decisive win/lose formula coming back into operation the year after.

At the same time, it was accepted that a more robust points system per game was needed. Rams' manager Mick Everett played a strong role in putting forward a formula that was to prove more workable in subsequent years. All this apart, it has to be conceded that Rammy did not enjoy a very good season in 1998, being well off the pace set by eventual champions Nelson and runners-up East Lancs.

Ian Harvey, replacing Chris Harris as pro, was a right hand bat and right-arm medium-pace bowler who had represented Australia in ODI cricket since 1997. During the course of 1998, he played 19 matches for Rammy, scoring 766 runs at an average of 51.06, including one century (104) in a home match against Colne on 24 May. He finished 3rd in the league's batting averages. Incidentally, Keith Arthurton, pro at Rawtenstall this season, came top with 1,156 runs at an average of 77.1. Harvey also did relatively well with the ball, taking 66 wickets at 12.12, finishing 9th in the league's averages. His best performance of 8-32 came on 8 May against Rawtenstall.

On the amateur side of things, it was a year lacking any outstanding performances. Highest in the batting averages was Neil Richardson, an experienced batsman in his late 30s who played 12 innings for the club scoring 328 runs at 41.0 and picked up the player of the year award. Of the batsmen who had been prolific in recent years, Brian Taylor managed just 241 runs at 15.1 and Ian Bell, disappointingly by his own standards, mustered only 167 runs at 12.84. On the bowling side, Nick Riley took 22 wickets at 23.9 and Garfield Moreton 28 at 26.5.

ooooo

It was in 1998 that a commemorative plaque was installed on the Acre Bottom site: 'In Memory of Gerald Dentith – "A Fine Teller of Tales" – Died 18th June 1998, Remembered By All in Poets Corner'.

The name of Gerald Dentith of course has already been mentioned in the light of Murray Bennett's memorable account of having been met by Gerald on arrival at Manchester Airport in 1984.

As far as Poets Corner is concerned, this famed viewing-point lies at the Paper Mill corner of the ground, situated close to where the original entrance gate stood. Underneath the plaque dedicated to Gerald Dentith, names of other frequenters of this favoured spot are cited as follows: 'Fred A. Rothwell, J. Ryan, F. Rothwell, J.L.Gerrard, Neville Leigh'.

ooooo

Despite the fact that 1999 proved to be not as productive as the season before in terms of league position - down to 11th - there were encouraging signs that the contribution being made by amateur players was picking up again. In particular, Brian Taylor was back to his best form - taking on the captaincy role this year - scoring 573 runs at 24.9 and being awarded player of the year. Simon Lord, a Burnley-born left-hander in his mid-20s who had recently joined the club, made 318 runs at 21.2. The return of Mark Price, after his various travels on the pro circuit, was a welcome one seeing him score 339 runs at 19.9. In addition, 20-year-old Tommy Read had broken into the 1st XI and scored 438 at 17.5. It was fortunate that players like these stepped up to the plate because the pro this year Matt Pascoe, by no means a recognised batsman, could only come 4th= in the club averages with 402 runs at 17.5.

It had been hoped that Ian Harvey would be returning as pro but he had been signed up at the last moment to play county cricket for Gloucestershire. In a scramble to find a replacement, 22-year-old Australian Matt Pascoe was taken on. Young and inexperienced, he had represented his country at under-19 level and been playing State cricket for Queensland for barely a year. Better qualified as a bowler than batsman, he took 60 wickets at 19.93, but even so finished no stronger than 37th in the league's bowling averages. Nick Riley didn't play much this season due to injury. Other wicket-takers this season were left-arm fast bowler Mick Haslam with 23 wickets at 35.73, Garfield Moreton 19 at 18.0 and Mark Price 16 at 26.1.

A remarkable match had occurred at Todmorden on 26 June. The home team won the toss and batted. By the end of their 50 overs, Tod had clocked up a massive 301 for 4. Peter Spencer (Chairman at the time) and Mick Everett (Manager) were later to recall having discussed matters during the tea interval, agreeing that the situation looked somewhat bleak. However, building on a 2nd wicket stand of 151 between Tommy Read and Brian Taylor, the Rams were in due course to make it all the way to 303-7, after 48.5 overs, to clinch the most improbable of victories. Incidentally, the aggregate 604 runs scored set a new League record for the highest total of runs scored in one day.

Another match of note that season was one taking place a few weeks later on 25 July away against East Lancs. Winning the toss and deciding to field, the first wicket fell to Pascoe with the score on 10. Simon Read however, coming on first-change after 13 overs, went on to take all of the remaining nine (including three in four balls), giving him career-best figures of 9-41, as the home side struggled to make it to 118 all out. Despite Simon's magnificent performance and Tommy Read going on to top score with 20, in an innings lasting 96 balls, the visitors were bowled out for 103 and lost by 15 runs.

1999 was significant for the fact it marked the end of the playing career of the remarkably successful opening batsman, Ian Bell (known in the changing room as 'Archie' – apparently derived from America R & B group Archie Bell & the Drells).

Ian amassed 9,014 runs for the club at an average of 23.90 with two centuries and fifty-one half-centuries. In 1993, he had won the League Senior Batting Award after scoring 758 runs that season. Ian felt his greatest challenge had come facing South Africa's 'White Lightning', Allan Donald. Standing second only to Billy Whitworth, 11 to 10 times, in terms of the number of seasons Ian scored 500+ runs in a season, Ian won player of the year award on three occasions, in 1979, 1984 (shared with Steve Monkhouse) and 1986. After retirement as a player, he was destined to go on contributing significantly at the club in many ways up to the present day.

ooooo

The seasoned veteran Mark Price was announced as captain for the millennium season of 2000. A colourful character on all fronts, everyone at Rammy knew he was always committed to giving his best shot to every new challenge he faced.

The pro this year was another Australian, 24-year-old Brad Hodge. A right-hand bat and right arm off-break bowler, his main experience to date had been playing State cricket for Victoria. Believed to be on the fringe of the Australian national team, his decision to play for Rammy in the Lancashire League boded well in terms of the club acquiring a player determined to do whatever it took to further his ambition to represent his country at Test match level.

In the end, a good number of players were to contribute to it being a turn-around season for the club. While Brad Hodge hit 1,183 runs at 59.2, ending up second in the league's batting averages, further significant batting contributions came from Tommy Read scoring 466 runs at 20.3, Simon Lord 311 at 19.4, Mark Dentith 277 at 17.3 and skipper Price 273 at 17.1.

In bowling terms, this season marked a really strong break-through year for seamer Mick Haslam who took 53 wickets at an average of 17.3, winning him the player of the year award. Lee Daggett, son of former captain Pete, alternating his time playing for the Rams and Durham University, took 29 wickets at 15.2. Next was skipper Mark Price with 27 at 16.4 and then Simon Read with 22 at 25.5.

Interestingly, as the new season unfolded, Bacup had lost five of their first seven matches and had at one point been next to the bottom of the table towards the end of May. Nevertheless, they had somehow managed to claw their way back to joint top spot as the season reached its climax. It was to be a season where the weather would play a significant part in affecting outcomes. Meanwhile, three clubs, Bacup, East Lancs and Rammy, all appeared to be in contention for the title. With four matches to go though, the Rams came a cropper away at the hands of defending champions Nelson. Despite Hodge's 81, the Rams were bowled out for 122 and lost the match by nine wickets.

This had let in Bacup who hung on tenaciously to a precarious lead to clinch the title at Turf Moor against Burnley on the final Sunday of the season. Even so, the final table showed the extent to which clubs had been at the mercy of weather conditions influencing match outcomes. As illustrated in the table below, the three 'no result' games incurred by the Rams counted crucially against them in the final analysis:-

	Pl	W	L	Tie	NR	Bonus pts	Pts deducted	Pts
1 Bacup	26	16	9	1	0	51	0	218
2 Ramsbottom	26	17	5	1	3	27	1	212
3 East Lancs	26	16	7	1	2	36	0	209

Well as Rammy had performed, another Holland Cup seemed scant consolation for the season's efforts.

ooooo

Even though Brad Hodge returned as pro in 2001, the Rams were not nearly so successful in the league this year, only finishing 10th with a record of W10, L10 and NR6. Brad Hodge, to his credit though, managed to score a massive 1,246 runs at 77.9 (3rd in the league's

batting averages), creating a new club record by overtaking Chris Harris'
1,231 in 1995. Meanwhile, Mark Dentith was top amateur with 407
at 21.4, earning him the player of the year award. Main wicket-takers
were Hodge with 36 at 21.7, Mark Price 28 at 15.8 (7th in the league's
bowling averages) and Mick Haslam 23 at 31.9.

The Rams' sole surviving hope of silverware was the Worsley Cup.
On 20 May, a 27-run first round win had been achieved at home against
Rawtenstall. The second round match, at Nelson on 2 June, ended up in
a seven-wicket victory.

The semi-final took place at Acre Bottom on 24 June against Colne.
As manager Mick Everett wrote at the time: 'This game provided
considerable excitement, particularly when never-say-die Colne got
much closer to Ramsbottom's total of 204-6 than had seemed possible
for much of their innings. Batting first, the Rams' innings was dominated
by a 140-run partnership between Hodge (73) and Dentith (60). The
key to victory seemed to be the wicket of the Colne pro, Marcus North,
who was in the middle of a spell of prolific run-getting. Lee Daggett
did the trick, bowling him out for just four runs. However, some rapid
scoring from their captain, Gary Laycock (46) with support from the
later order got the total up to 189 before the last wicket fell. Once again,
Brad Hodge's bowling was hugely important as he took 5-49 from his
10 overs'.

The stage, as in 1996, was set for another showdown final against
Bacup. Only this time around, the Lanehead side was much more
fancied on form to deliver the goods. Interestingly, looking back at the
match programme for the day, a section of it concentrated on the 'key
match-ups'. Chief amongst these came 'the hard men' – Mick 'Spider'
Haslam and David 'Dibbly' Ormerod:

'Spider, the uncanny lookalike of Tim Burgess, lead singer of the
Charlatans, is often seen sporting his designer Henri Lloyd & Hackett
gear at Maine Road and various other Nationwide League grounds
supporting his beloved Manchester City...'

Let battle commence! Sunday 5 August duly arrived and skipper
Mark Price, winning the toss, chose to field first. Things didn't look
to be going well with the score at 23 without loss. At this point, the
dangerous Peter Thompson drove Lee Daggett hard to mid-off only

to see young Worsley Cup debutant, David Bell, take a brilliant diving catch.

Another massive turning-point came when Bacup pro Shaun Young, in tremendous form at the time, was dismissed cheaply for 6, cutting a short ball from Tommy Read to gully where Nick Riley clung on to a vital catch. Before the home team knew it, they had slumped to 45-5. A stand worth 44 between Terry Lord and Peter Killelea steadied the ship a bit before Lord was deceived through the air by a delivery from Price and bowled out for 25. An eighth-wicket partnership of 86 between Killelea (eventually out for 46) and wicket-keeper John Chapman (55), enabled Bacup to finish on 190 all out after 49.1 overs.

Despite having to face up to Bacup's much-vaunted opening attack of Shaun Young and David Ormerod, the Rams' reply had mounted safely to 49-0, only for Nick Riley to be struck on the head by a bouncer and have to leave the field of play for treatment. Two quick wickets fell, leaving Brad Hodge and Simon Lord to do their best to keep things going. When Lord was out for 15 with the score on 105, Riley then bravely returned to the crease, going on to record an excellent 40 before being caught behind, making it 132-4. Meanwhile Hodge, riding his luck after surviving two dropped catches, made Bacup pay with some glorious strokes either side of the wicket. Joined by Mark Price, the two successfully knocked off the remaining 60 runs, taking the Rams to 192-4 and a six-wicket victory after 45 overs. Hodge finished on 86* and Price 17* to spark huge celebrations in the Acre Bottom camp.

Again as in 1996, a player on the losing side was awarded 'man of match', this time John Chapman, for his 'fine innings which had made the final into a good contest'. As for Brad Hodge, there was no denying he had had strong cause to have enjoyed the match immensely, even more so for the fact that many of his Aussie buddies were there on the day, including Shane Warne who, incidentally, had played one season for Accrington back in 1991.

By the time Brad came to play his last league match, he had succeeded in re-writing the league's history books by scoring 1,739 runs in all matches he played that season, including seven centuries and nine 50s. As with so many pros over the years, Brad Hodge was fondly to recall his time spent with Rammy, at the same time referring to Mark Price as 'one of the very best of captains he ever played under'.

Brad's ambition to represent his country at both Test and ODI levels was finally fulfilled in the 2004/5 season. For sure he was unlucky to be around at a time when Australia had such an enormous wealth of outstanding batsmen to call upon. However, on those occasions he was selected to play in the Test side he scored 503 runs in 11 innings at a very healthy average of 55.88.

Eleven: Make that Four
Worsley Cups in a Decade

THE PRO RAMMY signed up for 2002 was a little-known 21-year-old by the name of Michael Clarke. Born in Liverpool, New South Wales, Australia, he was a right hand bat and slow left arm bowler who had previously captained his country's under-19 team. Maurice Haslam, having the job of scouting out potential pros, had acted on a recommendation from Murray Bennett.

Clarke's baptism in Lancashire League cricket came on 20 April playing in the Colne Cup against Bacup at Acre Bottom. Rams' opponents on the day would have been thirsting to avenge their Worsley Cup Final defeat at Lanehead. From the start, their bowling attack went all out. Apart from Michael Clarke's 48, no other Ramsbottom player reached double-figures, the home team being sent packing for 88 runs. In reply, Bacup had needed only 15.4 overs to achieve an 8-wicket victory.

As far as the league season was concerned, a loss at home to Burnley on 4 May was disappointing. Even so, the encounter was notable in retrospect for the fact it pitted Clarke against a young, emerging amateur bowler called Jimmy Anderson. On this particular day though, neither of the two future celebrities and later famous Ashes adversaries, enjoyed distinguished games, Clarke scoring 22 and Anderson taking 1-60.

At one point in the season, the Rams reached fourth in the table but were never to come within striking distance of eventual championship winners Bacup. Victorious by a margin of 40 points over runners-up Enfield, the Lanehead club thereby entered into a select group of clubs in League history to have won the title three or more times in succession.

Again, it was the Worsley Cup competition that would by default prove the Rams' focus of attention. On paper, the first round match at Enfield on 19 May looked a tricky encounter with the home team topping the league at the time. However, Mark Price pulled a master-stroke by tossing the new ball to Nick Riley. 'Pickles' didn't let his skipper down with a devastating opening spell which accounted for danger men Liam Jackson and pro Martin van Jaarsveld in his first two overs. Enfield were bowled out for 109, Price himself taking 4-32. Then, Clarke's 64* paved the way to a comfortable eight-wicket win.

Despite Clarke (nicknamed 'Pup') always being keen to enjoy himself off the field as best he could, he invariably proved capable of pulling out the stops when it came to match-time. There were many occasions though when the raw young Aussie turned up at the ground feeling considerably worse for wear after night-clubbing in Manchester.

His captain at the time, Mark Price, recounted one particular episode, prior to a league match on 25 May at Enfield, when not having got back to his digs on Stubbins Lane until the early hours, Clarke had begged his captain to allow him to bat lower down the order to provide more recovery time.

Price was having none of it and sent him out to the crease in his usual slot as opener. Scratching his head but acting on orders, Clarkey went out on to the field, feeling dazed still but doing his best to detect the line of the ball. The upshot was that he ended up scoring 200*, including 25 fours and 7 sixes. The innings surpassed the existing club record of 188* held by Emmott Robinson. Still more significantly, it had set a new league record, superseding the 195* scored by Everton Weekes in 1949, ironically also against Enfield at Dill Hall Lane. Clarke's record was to stand until 2017 when South African Kelly Smuts scored 211 for Todmorden against unlucky-again Enfield!

In the Worsley Cup second round tie against Haslingden at Acre Bottom on 1 June, the Rams posted a score of 221-7 after 50 overs, with Michael Clarke's contribution 116. In reply, the away team only managed 128, Clarke being the main wicket-taker with 4-35. Meanwhile Richard Hevingham had a great day behind the stumps with five victims to earn a well-deserved hat collection.

The semi-final was played against Todmorden at Acre Bottom on 23 June. Winning the toss, skipper Price chose to bat first. At the end of 50 overs, the Rams had clocked up 307-4, Clarke having destroyed the opposition with 178 runs in 148 balls, ably supported by Nick Riley who made a fine 61 in an opening partnership of 150. This overall total, incidentally, set a record for the highest number of runs hit in a 1st XI innings at Acre Bottom. In response, thoroughly dispirited, Tod only mustered 115 runs, Mark Price doing the main damage with a 10-over spell of 4-19 in the middle of the innings.

The Worsley Cup Final took place at home against Church on 11 August. As pointed out in the match programme, forty-two year old Mark Price was captaining a side containing five teenagers, David and Alex Bell, Rob Read, Spencer Woods and Lee Daggett.

Due to adverse weather conditions, the match took three days to complete: 11th, 12th, 13th August. At the end of the first day's play, the Rams had scored 149-7, Clarke top scoring with 40. They were bowled out for 177 on the 12th, although not before John Harrison had completed a well-earned half-century, eventually run out for 53.

In response, Church started menacingly with captain Phil Sykes and Aussie pro Mark Higgs scoring 32 off the first four overs. Then despite Higgs being brilliantly caught by Mark Price at slip off the bowling of Nick Riley, the visitors managed to finish on the 12th still handily placed at 73-2. On the third day though, a devastating spell from 19-year-old Lee Daggett, taking 4-16 in 10 overs, proved decisive in earning the Rams another Worsley Cup victory by a commanding 63-run margin.

John Harrison was named man of the match for his innings of 53 'which had been made in conditions offering assistance to the bowlers'. For the Rams, it constituted a double cup triumph, having won the 2nd XI cup the week before. Also, this particular Worsley Cup victory was significant for the fact it marked the first time the trophy had been retained since East Lancs managed a similar feat across 1987 and 1988.

ooooo

Unfortunately, the Rams' league performance that season had gone downhill from this point onwards with the team eventually limping home 10th - W 9 L 11 NR 6. One exceptional feat, however, occurred in the home match against Accrington on 8 September. This came after Michael Clarke had flown back to Australia, ironically on the same plane as his Aussie mate Mark Higgs. On the occasion, Pakistani Mohammad Haroon was acting as stand-in pro. It was the only match he would ever play for Ramsbottom but proved a memorable one.

With Accrington all out for 156, things were going badly for the Rams at 31-5. At this stage, Haroon was joined at the crease by 17-year-old Alex Bell. The pair added a further 128 runs, leading to an unlikely five-wicket win, Haroon ending on 68* in an innings lasting 127 minutes and Bell 55* in 101 minutes. Incidentally, this still stands as the record total for a sixth wicket partnership in club history.

Over the season as a whole, Michael Clarke scored 877 runs, including three centuries, at an average of 59.1, placing him 9th in the league averages. Nick Riley had proved a reliable back-up opener, scoring 529 runs at 24.0 to earn him the player of the year award. Simon Read (with a top score of 54 against Colne) and Alex Bell had promising years, scoring 257 and 217 runs respectively.

Meanwhile Mark Price (5th in the league table) showed he had lost none of his spinner's guile, picking up 43 wickets at 12.5, including a season's best for an amateur of 8-32 in a home match against Enfield. Of the younger players, Lee Daggett also shone with the ball, taking 7-23 at East Lancs, although injury restricted his ability to bowl in later games.

Even if a lot of the side's successes this season had depended on Clarke and the more experienced players in the team, there were encouraging signs at the same time that younger players were maturing quickly, showing clear potential for the future. Talking to these players more recently, many spoke of the encouragement given them by skipper Mark Price.

Returning to Michael Clarke's involvement with the club, although back now in Australia, 2002 had proved for him a memorable experience he would not forget. Of course, much greater things lay ahead. Between 2004 and 2015, he was to play in 115 matches for his country, scoring 8,643 runs at an average of 49.1. From 2007 onwards, he had taken on the captaincy role. Despite all he would go on to achieve in the international arena, it is evident though that 'Clarkey' always retained a soft spot in his memories for the season he spent playing club cricket with Rammy in England.

When interviewed in 2013 by the Manchester Evening News ahead of a day's play in an Ashes Test match at Old Trafford (with journalist Alex Bell putting the questions), he was more than happy to turn his thoughts back to the year he had played for Ramsbottom. At the same time, he was very keen to point out that he stayed in touch with many of his ex-club colleagues from 2002, particularly captain and mentor Mark Price: 'All the boys are coming to the game. I've put a load of tickets on for my old captain Pricey and we'll have a grand meet-up at the end of the day's play'.

Indeed, from later descriptions provided by 'Pricey', it appears the 'grand meet-up' went very well indeed, lasting into the early hours. It sounded as if 'Pup' might have awoken the next morning feeling much similar to how he had that time in 2002 before that momentous innings at Enfield!

ooooo

As holders of the Worsley Cup, 2003 started with the Rams contesting a Colne Cup match against championship winners Bacup. This took place at Lanehead on 19 April. Winning the toss and deciding to bat, the Rams were reduced to 73-5, having to rely on Mark Price coming in at no. 7 and scoring 61* to lift their innings total to 159-7. In response, without too much difficulty though, Bacup had notched 160-4 to win by six wickets.

New pro Jason Arnberger, another Aussie, came as an experienced player in his early 30s, having spent his career to date playing State cricket for New South Wales and Victoria. Right hand bat and right arm medium-fast bowler, he was to score 1,020 runs at an average of 78.46 in 16 matches played for the club. By late July, Arnberger looked set to break the club's record run score for a season. However, having prior commitments back in Australia, it meant him missing the last ten matches.

Despite the pro's input – he had also taken 30 wickets at 19.4 – the club had only won seven out of sixteen league matches up to this point. Raising their game though, the Rams had then set off on a winning run of eight matches. In the final weekend, both of their matches resulted in low-scoring defeats to leave them 6th at the end.

This particular season, Mark Price had taken on the role of lead bowler, very often reeling off 25-over spells from one end, which resulted in him achieving his best ever return (72 wickets), second only to Bacup's David Ormerod in the league that season. Mick Haslam took 38 wickets.

The return of Brian Taylor and Mark Dentith strengthened the batting that season while Keith Webb was second only to Arnberger in the club's totals, scoring 508 runs, including his maiden century in a match at Rawtenstall. Incidentally, his innings on this occasion also helped create a new club record 2nd wicket partnership, an unbeaten 211 runs made with stand-in pro Pieter Strydom. Spencer Woods showed himself an effective opener while David Bell started to fulfil his potential as a 1st XI player by hitting his first half-century and following it up with another soon after.

At the club Presentation Night on 22 November, skipper Mark Price, who had announced he was retiring at the end of the season, deservedly picked up the player of the year award (making it a third time since 1982 and 1990) on the back of his 72 wickets. Despite all the many other years he had spent as a pro at county and club level, he had still managed to put in 263 matches for Ramsbottom between 1977 and 2003, scoring 2,950 runs at 15.95 and taking 335 wickets at 17.22. He had enjoyed two 50+ wicket seasons in 1990 (60) and 2003 (72). Mark's commitment on and off the field was always exceptional, having also served as captain from 2000 to 2003.

ooooo

The pro for 2004 was 27-year-old Indian Test player Murali Kartik. An all-rounder, left hand batsman and slow left arm bowler, his existing reputation was perhaps higher on the bowling side. This was to be borne out in practice in his time at the club. In 18 innings that year, he scored 460 runs at an average of 27.05 whilst taking 80 wickets at 9.75.

Unfortunately, he had to miss seven matches through an ankle injury and international calls, the club calling upon 'stand-ins' Asif Mujtaba and Mahendra Nagamootoo in the meantime.

On his second appearance for the club, Murali had demonstrated his prowess by taking 9-30 away at Enfield. The season was in fact progressing so well that, at a point in early August, the Rams had taken over as league leaders after beating Rishton at Acre Bottom, thanks to Kartik's 7-65. However, two successive defeats put paid to the club's championship hopes.

An interesting occasion took place on 22 August, prior to a home match against Bacup, celebrating the centenary of the opening of the club's 'Victorian Pavilion' back in 1904. The Lancashire Fusiliers' brass band lent atmosphere to proceedings, while a five-wicket victory over Bacup did justice on the field of play.

The Rams were to finish the season in 3rd place, nine points behind winners Haslingden and four behind runners-up Church. Apart from the loss of Murali for so many games, nor did injuries to key players like Brian Taylor and Simon Read help the situation. However, Keith Webb maintained his form from the previous season by notching 479 runs, followed by John Harrison (360), David Bell (359), Alex Bell (283) and Mark Dentith (264).

Seamer Chris Eardley, who had joined the club in 2001 but only played a total of 28 matches for the 1st XI up to this season, was in good form in 2004, taking 37 wickets and winning the player of the year award. Mick Haslam wasn't far behind with 35. At the same time, Lee Daggett had re-appeared mid-season. In the event, he had proved more effective with the bat, scoring 220 runs compared with taking only 11 wickets. Wicket-keeper/ new skipper Richard Hevingham had an excellent season as the league's leading man behind the stumps with 42 victims.

ooooo

With the return of Murali in 2005, and managing to steer clear of major injuries, the club looked set to challenge strongly for the title. Four clubs, including Ramsbottom, remained in contention at the top of the league table until the final run-in. First, it would be Colne who fell away. Then Haslingden who, despite having defeated Lowerhouse to lift the 20-20 competition trophy in its inaugural year, were the next to drop out of the title race, leaving Lowerhouse and the Rams as remaining front-runners.

Meanwhile though, there was the Worsley Cup campaign. In the first round, a close two-wicket win had been achieved at Accrington. After restricting the home side to 145-8, the Rams had been left on the brink of defeat at 122-8 before Andy Holt and Andy Dalby saw the Rams over the line in the penultimate over of the innings. There had been a further nail-biting outcome to the second round tie at Nelson where the opposition were bowled out after 49.2 overs, falling just four runs short of the Rams' 176-6.

The semi-final stage involved a home match against Haslingden on 3 July. Put in to bat, the visitors only managed a total of 116. In response, the Rams struggled before an unbeaten 46* by David Bell saw them through to 120-6 and a four-wicket victory, leading on to a cup final against Todmorden at Acre Bottom on 7 August.

On this occasion, Rams' skipper Richard Hevingham, winning the toss, put Tod in to bat on a slow surface that seemed to favour bowlers. Despite a determined innings of 65 from their pro, Gyan Pandey, the visitors only managed 145-9 at the end of 50 overs. Not that the home team was destined to have an easy time of it in reply. Starting shakily on 18-2, David Bell and Simon Read steadied the ship with a 45-run partnership that took the score to 63-3 before Read was out for 14. This brought in Kartik who was to remain at the crease (37*) until a five-wicket victory had been secured with the score at 148-5. David Bell was awarded 'man of the match' for his innings of 41, 'scored at a critical stage in proceedings'.

At this point in early August, as mentioned earlier, the battle for the league-title looked to be a two-horse race between Rammy and Lowerhouse. In the final outcome, after having suffered two losses to the eventual winners, Rammy had to settle for the Holland Cup (by a margin of 16 points) as their rivals finally succeeded in pulling off their first championship win of all time since the inception of the competition

172

back in 1892 - an interval of 113 years. Who could have begrudged Lowerhouse their reward after such a long wait?!

For the Rams, Murali had enjoyed another successful year as pro. This was despite missing almost half the season due to international duties. Kartik's 70 wickets had come at a highly economic average of 8.6 apiece while quickies Simon Read (36), player of the year, and Michael Haslam (35) had provided strong back-up.

Murali had hit 429 runs at 39.0. Alex Bell enjoyed his best season to date scoring 508 league runs at an average of 26.73, and also a magnificent 115 on 20 August at Rishton. Keith Webb (390), David Bell (347), Simon Read (345) and Mark Dentith (282) further contributed useful runs that season.

ooooo

The end of the 2005 season marked the retirement as club manager of Mick Everett, who had carried out the job over the last decade. During his time at the helm, the club had won the Worsley Cup four times and been league runners-up twice. He and Maurice Haslam had, between them, also brought a talented array of pros to the club, including Kartik Murali and the Australians Brad Hodge and Michael Clarke.

Interviewed by the Rossendale Free Press at this time, 'Evo' was asked who had been the best pro and captain during his decade in charge. He had replied: 'Chris Harris, who was brought to the club by Jack Simpson, was the best pro and Mark Price the best captain', adding that 'most people at Ramsbottom would have Price as captain of their all-time team. He was not afraid to experiment and do things differently and set some great fields'.

From 2005 onwards, Michael Everett would go on to serve the club in a number of further capacities, including representing the club in vital steps taken at a later date as to the re-forming of the Lancashire League in the late 2010s.

ooooo

At the start of the 2006 season, the Colne Cup was again up for grabs. On 22 April, at Lowerhouse, the home team won the toss and decided to field. Openers Keith Webb and Alex Bell made 46 but then wickets quickly fell to leave the visitors at 86-7. The remainder of the innings was dominated by Mark Dentith's bright and breezy 51* in 44 balls, including four sixes, to lift the total to 158-8 after 50 overs.

In response, the championship title winners of the previous year never got going and were bowled out for 42, leaving the Rams clear victors on the day by 116 runs. In fact, so comfortable was the margin of victory that new pro Sunil Joshi only managed to get on in time to take the last wicket.

Joshi, an established Indian Test player from 1996 until 2001, was in his mid-30s when he joined Rammy. A left hand bat and slow left arm bowler, he had preceded Murali in this role in the Indian team. Bringing very similar qualities to bear during his time with Rammy, Joshi had a better record with the bat than Kartik, scoring 721 runs at an average of 42.41. With the ball, he took 85 wickets at 11.36. Another bonus was that he was able to play in all 26 league matches. With the signing of Joshi and the recruitment to the club of players of the quality of Phil Hayes, Chris Read and paceman Toby McLean, the Rams had started out as one of the favourites to win the title in 2006.

Despite beating Lowerhouse in the Colne Cup, the Rams had been surprisingly beaten the following day in their opening league match at Rishton, even if by just one run. However, a better string of results followed. After victory at Enfield at the end of June, the Rams were riding high at the top of the league table. Going into the last eight matches, they had a 14-point cushion over second-placed Bacup.

However, back-to-back defeats against Burnley would prove costly, ultimately consigning the Rams to 3rd place with the title ultimately swinging the way of the Turf Moor side. With a record of W 13 L 7 NR 6, the Rams ended the season on 187 points below Burnley on 196 and runners-up Bacup on 193.

Phil Hayes, a left-handed opening batsman who had joined the club that year from Radcliffe, was leading amateur run-scorer with 435 runs at 20.71 followed by David Bell (player of the year) with 396 at 20.84. With the ball, Mick Haslam took 30 wickets at 22.36 and Simon Read

24 at 20.12. Skipper Richard Hevingham was again in good form behind the stumps, his 40 victims making him the league's leading gloveman.

Meanwhile the 2nd XI managed this same season to pull off the double by becoming Junior League champions and winning the divisional Cup. Along the way a remarkable game had taken place against Enfield in which Mark Dentith had created a league batting record by scoring 206, including 21 sixes in the course of a partnership of 338 with Andy Holt, 129. Incidentally, the final total reached in the innings of 390-4 is a record score for any Ramsbottom team.

ooooo

With Joshi returning as pro, the club finished in 2007 on 170 points and in 3rd place again behind championship-winning Rishton (192) and second-placed Rawtenstall (184). It was a season badly affected by adverse weather conditions, reflected by the fact that no fewer than eight of the Rams' matches (in common with Haslingden the highest number in the league) ended in 'no result' outcomes.

In the musical world, 2007 would best be remembered for Rihanna's 'Umbrella' which topped the charts during June and July when the whole of the country was dowsed in seemingly never-ending rain. Possibly affected by the monsoon-like weather conditions, pro Sunil Joshi did not have as good a season as before, scoring 328 runs at a much reduced average of 23.4. Meanwhile, Phil Hayes enjoyed a particularly good year scoring 544 runs at 27.2 including an innings of 115 away at Rawtenstall on 19 May. David Bell hit 392 runs at 21.8 with three half-centuries.

Joshi performed better with the ball, taking 69 wickets at 11.1 with a season's best of 8-30 at Nelson. Although having a lean time of it with the bat, new skipper Simon Read had the relative consolation of taking 18 wickets at 17.5. Mick Haslam (awarded player of the year) was the leading amateur wicket-taker with 34 wickets at 22.4. Richard Hevingham was again reliable behind the stumps with 31 victims. Although the season didn't end up entirely washed out, it was one that most clubs in the league, including the Rams, were happy enough to put behind them.

All was not doom and gloom in 2007 though! The club's 2nd XI had again managed to cover themselves in glory by pulling off another league/cup double to leave the club a great deal to cheer about. The nucleus of the group of players instrumental in having achieved the 'double-double' in successive years had grown up together at the club, principally including Rob Read, Mark Dentith, Chris Wood, Sam Price (son of Mark Price), Andy Holt, Chris and Sam Eardley, with the team being ably skippered by Brian Taylor and managed by Pete Daggett. Characteristic of the outstanding pattern of success achieved during these years, a particular high-point from 2007 was a match in which Rammy scored 376-5 before then dismissing opponents Rishton for 18 all out to create a record Lancashire League winning margin of 358 runs.

ooooo

In hiring New Zealander Lou Vincent as pro for 2008, an established right arm batsman and right arm medium pace bowler at Test match level, there was inevitably hope of still brighter prospects ahead. However, it was not to be. Vincent managed only six indifferent league matches although in the one Worsley Cup match he played in, the Kiwi hit a match-winning 122* at Haslingden. At this early stage in the season though, he was signed up for Lancashire as a replacement overseas player for the duration of the 2008 Twenty20 tournament.

Having finished 3rd in each of the last two seasons, 2008 was to see the club drop down to 6th place. Vincent was eventually replaced by Australian Shane Harwood who played the last 15 matches of the season, although not significantly well, only managing 322 runs at 29.3 while taking 42 wickets at 14.1. The club's batting honours fell again to Phil Hayes (player of the year) who hit 629 runs at 28.6 with solid support again from David Bell (340 runs at 17.9) and Keith Webb (305 runs at 17.9). Mick Haslam was the leading wicket-taker with 23 at 25.3, followed by Simon Read with 18 at 12.8.

By way of footnote, the subsequent career of Lou Vincent was to end tragically, being banned from playing cricket for life on 1 July 2014 by the England and Wales Cricket Board on the charge of match fixing, after admitting to 18 breaches of the statutory regulations.

ooooo

Although 2009 started more promisingly for the Rams, with four wins from their first five matches catapulting them into top spot, this proved as good as it got. Fated eventually to finish 9th, the club's attention had soon switched to the Worsley Cup for hope of gaining medal success.

The pro hired for this season was Brenton Parchment, a West Indian in his late twenties with experience from 2007 onwards of representing his country in Test and limited-overs cricket. Playing in all 26 league matches, he scored 697 runs at 33.19, including one century, 131* at home against East Lancs on 3 May. Next highest run-scorer was Rob Read with 323. Although having made his 1st XI debut back in 2002, this season was to mark the first time Rob played in more than 20 matches for the club. Skipper Keith Webb was not far behind on 321 and then David Bell on 300. On the bowling side, Parchment took 55 wickets at 18.36 with off-break bowler Ross Brown (40), Mick Haslam, player of the year, (32) and Jack Walmsley (24) providing the main support.

With hopes necessarily pinned on progress in the Worsley Cup, the first round tie at home against Nelson on 24 May saw Keith Webb winning the toss and deciding to bat. A third wicket partnership of 121 between Brent Parchment and David Bell provided a platform for the home team reaching 197-8 after 50 overs. Then Mick Haslam was in top form taking 3-14 off 8 overs, enabling the Rams to win by 88 runs.

The second round match, away to East Lancs on 6 June, followed a similar pattern to the first round tie with Parchment and D. Bell entering into a major third-wicket partnership, this time of 72 runs, contributing to a final total of 196-7. With the home team fading to 91 all out, the match was won by 105 runs. In the semi-final, at home against Church, another stand of 63 runs between Parchment and D. Bell was pivotal in taking the Rams to 213-9 before the opposition was bowled out for 158.

The final took place at Acre Bottom against Todmorden on 9 August. Watched in a cauldron-like atmosphere by a near-strong 1,000 crowd, with the Red Arrows flying overhead, it was to prove an intensively-fought contest all-round. Winning the toss, skipper Keith Webb decided to bat, a decision he would have had serious cause to worry about when the score reached 44-4, Parchment having been dismissed cheaply for 8 runs. Magnificently though, David Bell had again come to the rescue. In partnership with no. 6 batsman, Andy Holt, a stand of 110 runs developed to take the total to 154. Bell's innings of 71 (later to result in him being named as man of the match, following on from his 2005 award) and Holt's of 43 were to prove the highest scores in the Rams' total of 187-7. Even so, it could hardly have seemed a match-winning score at the time.

In Tod's response, with the score on 63-2, a controversial moment arose when their pro Chinthaka Jayasinghe, appearing to be sailing along on 34, skied Rammy bowler Jack Walmsley high and wide. Although looking for all the world like a six, Alex Bell managed to pull off a stupendous catch on the boundary. A strong contingent of Tod fans though, stationed nearby, went all out to claim that Bell had stepped over the ropes. Nevertheless the umpire gave the Sri Lankan out. Rammy fans in the vicinity thought it was a clean catch. All the same, the incident was to give vent to ill-feeling between the two clubs for a good while after.

However, back to the day in question, despite losing their pro, Tod managed to keep track of the target they were chasing. Despite the fall of the ninth wicket at 165-9, their last-pair partnership succeeded in staying together until the start of the final over. At this point, 12 runs were required. With tension mounting, and as David Bell recalled later the presence of a dog on the field not helping, the match still hung very much in the balance. Eventually though, after a stubborn innings of 34, Tod's no. 8 batsman Harrison was run out with four balls left, thus delivering a seventh Worsley Cup victory to the Rams, albeit by a slender 5-run margin.

The day's outcome had unquestionably represented heartbreak for Todmorden, losing in a final for the third time in five seasons and a second season running. By contrast, massive celebrations broke out in the home camp, success on the day rounding off the decade in style, making it the Rams' fourth triumph in this competition, building on the victories gained to date in 2001, 2002 and 2005.

One further interesting aspect to the season was a visit to Ramsbottom Cricket Club in 2009 by sports author Duncan Hamilton, looking to collect material for the compilation of his book *A Last English Summer (2010)*. In this study of the current state of cricket, the line he pursued was that the game as a whole was facing an unprecedented crisis in terms of economic viability.

Hamilton's visit to Acre Bottom on 23 May coincided with a home match against Accrington, which ended disappointingly with the Rams losing by six wickets. However, as well as what was happening on the field of play, the author was seeking to explore issues relating to financial hardships being faced at grass-roots level by local league clubs like Rammy.

Hamilton was already aware of the heightened difficulties in recent years of clubs in meeting the demands placed on them of hiring professionals. Not receiving the same kind of gate-money as in the past, it was clear that clubs were having to rely more than ever on profits made through social facilities to help meet financial commitments.

Returning to the question as to how clubs could go on affording the fees being sought by the hired pros, the situation had been aggravated by the fact that richer pickings were now more readily available for the best players arising from recently established competitions such as the Indian Premier League. This left it much more difficult for Lancashire League clubs to compete to 'buy in' pros of any renown. The strong bargaining position this put all potential recruits in had led to clubs having to think more carefully than ever about extracting value for money from their 'paid man'.

Indeed, this was the exact dilemma facing Rammy at the end of 2009, with Brenton Parchment negotiating for a higher wage to stay. This was despite him not having performed convincingly well in a season that, despite the Worsley Cup win, had also seen the club slip further down the league table to 9th place.

Twelve: A Shot in the Arm from Fielding

THE BREAKING NEWS of 2010 was that Jon Fielding was set to return to the club. Having had so many successful pro commitments in the meantime, including playing for Lancashire and Cumberland, it was a distinct boost to Rammy that a player of his proven quality was signing up again to the cause. The last full season he had played for the Rams was during the championship-winning season of 1992, eighteen years earlier. Given the amount of time in between, there may have been a certain amount of speculation as to the impact it might be possible for him to make. In the event, his return would prove a complete turn-around for the club.

At this point in time, Andy Dalby was team manager. He had been in post since the year before. To date though, he had found it frustrating to influence matters in the way he would have wished. It had hardly helped when at the end of the 2008 season, twice 500+ run-scorer Phil Hayes had gone off to play for local rivals Haslingden, taking others like Chris Read with him.

A former Rammy cricketer himself, though having played mostly for the 2nd XI, Andy had kept in touch with close friend Jon Fielding as to the possibility of him re-joining the club. Negotiating terms for his return, the latter had expressed a preference to take on the captaincy role.

For Andy, implementing such a wish may no doubt have involved ruffling a few feathers in the home camp. Not least those of existing skipper Keith Webb who had skippered the club's Worsley Cup-winning side of the season before. However the executive club decision was taken that Jon Fielding should captain the side from the start of 2010 onwards.

Further seeking to bolster player-strength for the season ahead, Dalby had brought in additional reinforcements including batsman Jamie Pilling, bowler Andy Hakin and wicket-keeper Andy Caunce.

Much as he was aware of the importance of delivering at 1st XI level, Andy Dalby at the same time actively promoted the philosophy that all three teams, 1st, 2nd and 3rd should enjoy equal rights in other more basic ways. One example of how this policy manifested itself in practice was that all three teams started each home match with a 'new ball'.

oooo

The curtain-raiser at the start of 2010 was the Colne Cup match against Accrington at Acre Bottom on 24 April. Winning the toss, the home team batted first and scored 233-5 with Aussie pro Clinton Perren top scoring with 109 after sharing a 3rd wicket partnership of 151 with David Bell (64).

In response, Accrington had largely kept up with the target, going into the final over needing ten runs for victory. This became six from five balls after Fielding's first ball went for four byes. However big-hitting Graham Lloyd, on 71, was run out two balls later. Two were needed off the last ball but only one was scored with Graeme Sneddon run out chasing the second. The visitors finished with an identical total of 233 runs, but with seven wickets down, the Rams lifted the Cup by virtue of having lost fewer wickets.

Incidentally, the club had been fortunate to be able to call upon the services of Perren for this game. It was the only time Clinton ever played for the Rams, a stopgap move on a one-match basis. The original decision had been to hire Aussie Usman Khawaja as the contracted pro for the season, but his arrival had been delayed. As it happened, he was never to make it to Acre Bottom, after having been selected for the Australia squad for the series against Pakistan which was staged in England that year. Ultimately, in varying circumstances, five different players were to carry out the pro role over the course of the season.

Meanwhile, the Rams' opening league match was at Nelson, the day after winning the Colne Cup. This match would provide a first illustration of the devastating effect of Fielding's bowling. With the away team scoring 164-5, Nelson were always struggling in reply. In a spell of six overs, Jon Fielding took a decisive 5-12 to finish them off at 95 all out.

On 1 May, the side briefly moved clear at the top of the table with a second maximum points win of the season in a rain-reduced match at East Lancs. The Rams had only managed 117-7 in 39 overs. The adjusted target for the home team ended up being 109 in 35 overs. Mick Haslam (4-62) and Jon Fielding (5-45) bowled all of these unchanged. At the start of the last over of the 35, the home team needed six runs with three wickets in hand but a superb last over from Haslam saw him taking two wickets and there being a run out on the last ball to earn the visitors an improbable two-run victory.

On 8 May, the Rams took on Todmorden at Acre Bottom without the benefit of a pro in their midst. However they managed 255-6 with Alex Bell hitting an unbeaten 106. Jon Fielding recalled that 'there were a few words spoken between some of the Todmorden lads and Alex over a controversial piece of fielding in the Cup Final. The thing with Alex is that you are probably best advised not to wind him up because he really digs in.' The match was won in the end by 64 runs.

Rammy suffered their first defeat of the season by 52 runs at Rawtenstall on 9 May. It was a turning wicket. In those circumstances, it was regrettable that Jon Fielding had been forced to miss the match due to work commitments in Germany.

The inability to field a pro for the Tod game was indicative of an issue the Rams would face throughout the season, often having to scramble around for stand-ins and never being able to count on a settled situation. Despite needing to call upon a range of different pros though, the individual whose performances stood out was the South African, Faf du Plessis. Making his debut at Haslingden on 22 May, he shone immediately, scoring 83 out of a total of 268-4 to help gain the Rams a crucial victory over the current league-leaders. However during the course of this match, he sustained a hip injury which caused him to miss several matches.

At this stage, alongside Rammy, the other two main contenders for the championship title were Haslingden and East Lancs. While Hassy, having won their first six matches, still led the table at the end of May, two points ahead of Ramsbottom in second place, East Lancs had managed to claw their way back into contention after losing all three of their opening fixtures. Following an impressive run of eight successive wins, they had climbed up to top spot in early June. Meanwhile, back-to-back league defeats against Burnley and Haslingden saw Rammy slip to third.

Talking of du Plessis, once he had recovered fitness, his various exploits in cup competitions would prove memorable. Although only playing a total of seven league matches, scoring 392 runs at an average of 65.3, it was in the Worsley Cup and 20/20 matches that his contributions would prove most telling.

In helping the Rams win the 20/20 trophy (the competition that had been introduced in the Lancashire League in 2006), du Plessis had hit a brilliant match-winning 112* at Haslingden in an earlier round. Touted at the time as perhaps the world's greatest fielder, the vital catch he took in the semi-final match against Nelson on 2 July to remove Thomas Lord (68), diving to cling on to the ball on the boundary, was described by skipper Fielding as 'the best catch that anyone had ever seen'. But for this catch, it is doubtful whether the Rams would have finished victors by 9 runs.

In the final, at Church on 9 July, du Plessis took 4-16 in his 4-over spell to help contain the home team to 97-8. Despite losing two early wickets, the Rams reached 100-4 in their innings to snatch victory by six wickets, Jon Fielding taking the side home with an unbeaten 64.

Having now won the Colne Cup and 20/20 trophies, and at the same time still in serious contention in both the league and the Worsley Cup, the prospect remained alive of the Rams achieving the unprecedented feat of the 'quadruple', namely sweeping up all four major Lancashire League trophies in the same season.

Tracking progress in the league, East Lancs had now slipped from pole position after suffering a 'no result' against Nelson. Despite regaining some temporary momentum with two victories, they had then crashed to a disastrous run of five consecutive defeats. A surprise defeat for Haslingden at Rishton enabled the Rams to turn an eight-point deficit into a two-point lead after beating East Lancs on 7 August.

Meanwhile, in the Worsley Cup, a superb innings of 125 from Keith Webb had been a key factor in Rammy achieving a total of 265 in their second round tie at Enfield on 5 June. Even so, the home team had fallen only six runs short in reply with a total of 259 all out in a match yielding 524 runs.

The semi-final against Burnley at Acre Bottom on 4 July proved even more of a cliff-hanger. Taking first knock, skipper Fielding must have had cause to regret his decision when the Rams found themselves 8-4 with Webb, Pilling and the Bell brothers all back in the pavilion. Gritting their teeth though, du Plessis and Fielding set out to repair the damage. Despite three stoppages for rain threatening their concentration, the pair succeeded in putting on a record 5th wicket partnership of 191 until Fielding was out for 95. Du Plessis went on to make 111 with the home team finishing on 249-9 at the end of 50 overs.

The drama had only just begun! Even though the match seemed to be going the Rams' way when the visitors sank to 148-8, the trouble was that their South African pro, Farhaan Behardien, was not only still at the wicket but looking all-conquering. There followed a 9th wicket partnership of 93, with Behardien managing to farm the bowling all the while. Looking unstoppable on 175 out of the 241 runs scored, it meant at a certain point that only nine runs were needed off nine remaining balls. The added advantage was that the Burnley pro was on strike. Sensationally though, he was then caught and bowled by du Plessis.

In the final outcome, victory had miraculously fallen Rammy's way by the narrowest of 2-run margins. Given the various rain interruptions, the match didn't finish until 9.42 p.m. when, according to eye-witness account, 'it was virtually pitch black'.

ooooo

The Worsley Cup final took place at Acre Bottom on 8 August, coming the day after the win over East Lancs had taken them to the top of the table. Du Plessis, however, was unavailable to play and it was Tasmanian Aussie Alex Doolan who stood in as pro on the day.

Despite the enforced change, everything though still seemed lined up for a Rammy win. Certainly if the form-book was anything to go by. Very much underdogs on the day, Colne had endured a miserable season to date, on course to finish the season in 13th place, winning only five of their 26 league matches. Nevertheless, in terms of a one-off match, the occasion presented the much less fancied team with a perfect opportunity to redeem themselves.

Winning the toss and deciding to bat, the away team's openers put on 30 runs before the first wicket fell, bringing in 37-year-old Justin Nutter. A stand-in on the day, appearing only because of an injury to regular batsman Gary Hunt, Nutter was to go on to play a hugely important anchor-man role. Defiantly sticking at the crease while wickets tumbled all around him, he was still there at the end of the innings, having contributed an invaluable 46* to Colne's final score of 145 all out after 49 overs.

Even so, it seemed a modest enough total for the home team to chase down. Colne's pro, Anwar Ali had different ideas though. Dismissing openers Keith Webb and Alex Bell for ducks, he later held on to a catch off the bowling of Ellis to end the innings of Rammy pro Alex Doolan (15), reducing the match favourites to 65-5. The game fell away from the Rams, ending 113 all out and 32 runs short of their target. Anwar Ali had inflicted the main damage, finishing with 10-4-22-5, thus denying the Rams their dream of the 'quadruple'. For his gritty innings of 46*, Jason Nutter won the 'man of the match' award.

Despite the inevitable sense of disappointment that the team felt after losing the Worsley Cup Final, Fielding's men successfully put it behind them and never looked back in the league after establishing a two-point advantage at the start of August. From that point on, they chalked up a further seven straight wins including taking revenge for their cup defeat by thrashing Colne by nine wickets, after bowling them out for 80 with Jon Fielding taking 8-29. How much though the team wished they had managed to perform like that on 8 August too!

The championship title was finally sewn up after the home match win against Accrington on 5 September with wild celebrations taking place in the evening. In fact, since losing to Haslingden on 17 June, Rammy had gone on a record-breaking unbeaten run of sixteen league matches finishing with the win at Church on the last day of the season.

This particular match at Oswaldtwistle, on 12 September, was one that Alex Bell, looking back on later, singled out as the 'favourite game' of his cricketing career. Acknowledging that the trophy had already been won the week before, he commented that 'while it could clearly have been a game to go out and just enjoy, I recall everyone, especially our captain Jon Fielding, approaching the game no differently to the previous 25 matches we'd played'.

As Alex further explained, there still remained quite a few personal landmarks needing to be achieved on the back of this game. For example, could Michael Haslam succeed in getting to 50+ wickets for the season, plus the challenge remaining for batsmen Keith Webb and Alex himself to reach 500+ as well as brother David achieve 600+? The answer to such questions still hung very much in the balance on the day...

ooooo

Over the season as a whole, the Rams were to take the title with 264 points after a win at Church. This still stands as the highest number of points achieved by a club since the present points system had been introduced in 1999. The 264 points number of points came as a result of winning 23 of their 26 matches plus gaining 34 bonus points. Incidentally, throughout the period of time from the 1890s onwards, in which 26 matches have been played each season, 23 remains the highest number of matches ever won in a season. The triumphant Rams had ended the campaign taking the title by a convincing 27-point margin over runners-up Haslingden.

Although the team had cause to feel a shade disappointed at having fallen just short of the 'dream' outcome of winning all four major trophies in one season, the winning of three of the four major Lancashire League competitions was still a fantastic achievement.

Putting the team's 2010 success into closer perspective in terms of significant individual contributions, enormous credit has to be given to Jon Fielding in his dual capacities as captain and player. Inspirational in leading the side to such an unprecedented record of achievement in winning three trophies, he also set an unbelievably high standard in terms of his own level of performance. There can be little doubt that

Fielding's feat of capturing 113 league wickets, at an average of 10.32, was a major factor behind capturing the title.

This was indeed the first time an amateur bowler had passed the century mark since Church's Tommy Lowe in 1939. A model of consistency, Fielding took five or more wickets in no fewer than thirteen matches. Ever maintaining an enthusiastic approach to his bowling, particularly when it came to pursuing lbw calls, Jonny always succeeded in maintaining an impeccable consistency of line and length, with an added degree of guile that often reduced even the best of batsmen to tears. Needless to say, on the club's Presentation Evening on 19 November, apart from receiving a special accolade for his outstanding achievement of taking 113 league wickets in a season, Jon Fielding also won the club's player of the year award.

ooooo

The next highest wicket-taker was Mick Haslam who, on the back of his three wickets at Church, ended up taking 51 wickets at 17.47. Tellingly, skipper Fielding was later to say of 'Spider': 'A key factor in us winning the league. His bowling enabled us to build pressure every week on batters. Very rarely bowls a bad ball. Enables me to set attacking off-side fields. Mr. Consistent'.

As referred to earlier, three amateur batsmen had gone into the last game at Church looking to surpass particular personal targets. In the event, Alex Bell and Keith Webb both exceeded the 500-run mark while David Bell enjoyed his best-ever season scoring 644 runs at 35.8 with four half-centuries, including a career best 90 against Accrington. Brother Alex's season had got off to such a great start with those scores of 106* and 90* in consecutive games against Todmorden and Enfield. He finished the season with 510 runs at 25.5. Keith Webb had succeeded in scoring 526 runs at 22.9 with two half centuries. Of Webby's input, Fielding was to note that 'he often laid the foundations for us to go on and get a good total' adding that 'Keith has been fully supportive of me as the captain and has been a great lad in the dressing room'.

There were also useful contributions with the bat from new signing Jamie Pilling (323 runs at 17.9 with two fifties), Jon Fielding (287 runs at 22.1), Mark Dentith (165 runs at 20.6) and Andy Caunce (129 runs and 32 victims) and Andy Holt (75 runs and 20 victims) who shared wicket-keeping duties. The outfielders also supported the bowlers in fine style, not least in taking valuable catches, with four players in double figures. Fielding pouched 20, Dentith 17, D. Bell 16 and A. Bell 15.

Andy Dalby's strategic plan of action for the season had been based on an approach set out to utilise Jon Fielding's return to the full, but also to have counted on others making significant contributions. The strong degree of success achieved by so many of the club's amateur players this season was all the more welcome given that the pro situation had proved so uncertain from one month to another.

Testimony has already been made to the tremendous exploits of Faf du Plessis, a player still very much at a formative stage of a cricketing career which would later see him become an established South African Test player and eventual captain. Reference also deserves to be made to the contribution of fellow South African Ross McMillan who played in just seven league matches but achieved a similarly impressive record to du Plessis, scoring 279 runs at an average of 69.75. Meanwhile, Tasmanian Aussie Alex Doolan, playing in nine league matches towards the end of the season, scored 400 runs at an average of 57.14. He had entered upon the scene at a highly tense stage of affairs when, as Alex Bell was later to comment, 'the team was grateful for him bringing a sense of calm'. There might have been a lot of chopping and changing but it cannot be denied that the various pros, in their own distinctive ways, each performed extremely well for the club over the course of 2010.

Apart from all the great individual performances that season, it was clear that a wonderful team spirit had shone through, without which it would not have been possible for the side to achieve everything it had. Despite celebrations continuing long and hard after what had been the most successful year to date in the club's history, the tactical minds of Fielding and Dalby remained alive to the need though to do whatever it took to keep the momentum going into 2011.

ooooo

Another key figure with a massive say in the direction the club took during these years was Chairman Rod Hamer who had taken up the post in 2005. It was largely down to him that Andy Dalby had been made manager in 2009. Going back to Duncan Hamilton's visit to Acre Bottom, the author had also picked up strongly on Hamer's appetite for work and the passionate way in which he carried out his role:

'Rod Hamer, the club's chairman, is tanned and silver-haired with a sharp peak of a nose. In short-sleeved check shirt and pale khaki shorts, he buzzes from one corner of Acre Bottom to another like a wasp in an upturned jar. One moment he's announcing the scorecard changes from the secretary's office, the next he's dealing with a complaint in the bar about cold pie and chips and lumps in the gravy'.

Behind the scenes, on another tack, Hamer could not help but be aware at the same time of the harsh financial circumstances facing clubs like Ramsbottom in current economic times. For example, as pointed out by Hamilton, 'recession has forced the packaging company, whose factory walls border one end of Acre Bottom, to withdraw sponsorship for next season'.

As Chairman, he of course understood all too well the challenges facing Ramsbottom Cricket Club to sustain itself on a viable basis. The amount taken on the gate was never enough in itself, leaving the club dependent on what extra monies it could accrue from hiring out facilities, for such as wedding events, to keep solvent. In order to go on conducting core business, Hamer, like so many chairmen before him, had to rely on enlisting an army of local volunteers to help carry out the work that needed to be done on match days and at other times.

Hamer did everything he could to keep the club afloat financially. One particular money-spinning activity he was proud of having pioneered was the use of the ground for the Ramsbottom Music Festival, 'Head for the Hills', which had taken place in the month of September over many years already.

Chairman Rod Hamer gave great service to the club from 2005 onwards and would continue to do so until 2021 when his period of office as Club Chairman was however fated to come to an end in most unfortunate circumstances.

ooooo

Looking to the following season, 2011, Andy Dalby had Faf on his radar to re-join as pro. The South African had appeared more than keen to come. In the end though, he was snapped up by Chennai Super Kings for the Indian Premier League, keeping him in India until June, rather too late into the Lancashire League season. With Plan B needing to be put into operation, the club signed up New Zealander Shanan Stewart, a right hand bat and right arm medium pace bowler who had experience playing ODI cricket for his country from 2009 onwards.

Stewart was available from the start of the season and the first match he took part in was the Colne Cup Trophy decider at Colne on 23 April, a rematch of the two sides who had contested the Worsley Cup Final in August 2010. Opening the batting, Webb and Pilling put on 95 for the first wicket before Stewart came in at no. 3 to score 57, taking the Rams' total to 214-4 after 50 overs. Colne struggled in reply, bowled out for 134 with Jon Fielding carrying on from where he had left off in September, ending with figures of 10-5-20-4 to enable the club to acquire yet more silverware. Could it mark the start of another quest for 'the quadruple'?

Signs in the league looked good with four wins out of four to extend the side's run of unbeaten matches to twenty going into May. In three of these matches, Fielding had taken seven wickets. With the Rams topping the table, a crucially important match took place at Acre Bottom on 8 May with high-flying Lowerhouse as visitors.

The game seemed to be following a predictable enough pattern after Lowerhouse, opting to bat, had been reduced to 70-5 with Haslam taking three wickets. The demolition job that might have been expected to follow on from here failed to materialise though. Instead, captain Cottam and partner Bailey made light of scoring 132 runs to hoist the Lowerhouse total up to 202-5 after 50 overs.

Losing Pilling early, Alex Bell and Shanan Stewart then put on 74 before three quick wickets fell to leave the score at 92-4. However, Stewart was still there and was joined now by Rob Read. Together, they took the score to 155-4 with Stewart on 78* and Read 15*. There were still nearly eight overs left to make the 48 runs required to win. With wickets in hand and the batsmen at the crease having put on 63 already, the Rams looked in good position to accelerate the scoring pace and achieve victory.

Unfortunately, adverse weather conditions kicked in to prevent this happening. Persistent rain caused the game to be halted on 155-4 after 42.2 overs. No further play was possible. The match outcome had to be determined on 'adjusted target' calculations, based on respective run-rates. It boiled down to the fact the home team would need to have scored 182 runs by the point the game had finished. Thus, by such reckonings, Lowerhouse emerged as winners by 26 runs. The defeat led to Accrington taking over at the top.

By coincidence, Accrington were scheduled to visit Acre Bottom on 21 May. In a tightly-fought contest, the Rams posted a score of 189-7. In response, the away team, relying heavily on their pro Ashar Zaidi, who scored 100 before being given out lbw to Fielding, fell 10 runs short of their target, Haslam ending up with 4-31 and Fielding 5-77. Though the tables were turned, it was not for long, with a six-wicket defeat following for the Rams at Haslingden.

At this relatively early stage of the season, the title lead was swinging back and forth between the Rams, Accrington and Lowerhouse without any one side able to establish a clear advantage. Behind those three, Todmorden also still seemed more than capable of mounting a challenge down the line.

Meanwhile, the 20/20 programme started on 27 May with a series of four group matches against fellow Rossendale sides. Winning all four matches against Edenfield, Bacup (during the course of which match Fielding took a hat-trick), Haslingden (coincidentally Rams' Andy Hakin snatching another hat-trick) and Rawtenstall, a semi-final home match against Enfield took place on 1 July. Taking advantage of being put in to bat, Stewart and David Bell put on 117 for the first wicket to help establish a total of 160-5. Tight bowling and keen fielding kept the visitors down to 144-7, producing a 16-run victory.

The final was staged at Acre Bottom on 8 July against Nelson who were restricted to 133-6 from their allotted 20 overs. Stewart and David Bell again started like a train with a partnership of 77 by the end of the 11th over. At this point, the weather was set to have the last word, preventing any further play. Taking into account their 'adjusted target', the Rams ended up clear winners by ten wickets. A second trophy had been achieved.

The Worsley Cup campaign had started on 22 May with a first round tie away against East Lancs which was won by 21 runs thanks largely to a half-century scored by Stewart, followed by Fielding taking 5-27. In the second round tie at home to Enfield on 4 June, Stewart (76) and D. Bell (60*) were the main contributors to a Rams' total of 227-5. The visitors had looked handily placed on 177-3 before Simon Read, having taken one wicket in his first spell, came back fired up to capture six more quick wickets to finish with 7-31, reducing the opposition to 210 all out.

Next came a memorable semi-final match at Todmorden in which the home team pro Quaiser Abbas scored 132* out of a total of 217-7. In reply, Rammy had looked to be going comfortably enough at 113-2 with Stewart and D. Bell at the crease. But then wickets fell quickly and with the score standing at 152-7, the chances of winning the match now looked highly remote.

The fall of the seventh wicket had brought to the crease no. 9 batsman, young 16-year-old Tom Parton, to join Rob Read. Until now, Parton's main claim to fame was having broken John Savage's club record for being the youngest player to make a 1st XI debut at Bacup on 20 June 2009 at the age of 14 years and 113 days. In 2010, he had been a regular member of the 2nd XI, ending up winning the player of the year award at that level. From the start of 2011, he had earned a regular place in the 1st XI but principally on the back of his wicket-keeping talents, without any real record so far of scoring runs.

Neither of the two batsmen at the crease were to be daunted by the scale of the challenge facing them though. In the final outcome, Read (41*) and Parton (36*) put bat to ball to such devastating effect that 66 runs were scored in rapid time to take it to 218-7 after 49.4 overs, the Rams triumphing at the end of the match with an incredible three-wicket victory.

The Worsley Cup Final took place at Church on 7 August. The match had remained very much in doubt at around midday after a torrential downpour. More in hope than expectation, the umpires had indicated a 2.15 start. Luckily, worse weather held off. Skipper Fielding put the opposition in to bat. Church's innings heavily depended on the input of their young opener Levi Wolfenden. Well-placed on 74 and intent on stepping up a gear or two in the last five overs, he appeared to have connected perfectly with a ball bowled him by Hakin. For all the world it looked to be sailing over the boundary ropes for a six before, seemingly out of nowhere, Rob Read burst on to the scene to pull off a remarkable catch.

The sheer spontaneity of the moment was to be caught in a marvellous photo which succeeds very well in capturing the look of sheer amazement on the faces of those spectators standing just behind the boundary rope, beholding Rob Read's leap into the air to take the catch.

Church's final score was 168-9. In response, driven on by the vociferous support of their 'banana army' fan-base, the Rams made light of the challenge set them, reaching 172-4 after 39.2 overs following a 94-run 5th wicket partnership between Stewart (69* at the end) and A. Bell (27*) to lift their third trophy of the season. Meanwhile, Wolfenden had been awarded 'man of the match'.

Given this latest success, and bearing in mind how narrowly the team had fallen short of achieving the quadruple the previous season, the question arose again as to whether the Rams could possibly pull off the feat in 2011?

Thus, everything hinged on the fourth remaining element of the equation, the league championship. The three-way tussle throughout May between Rammy, Accrington and Lowerhouse had continued on into June. The Rams' defeat at Haslingden on 29 May had allowed Lowerhouse to take the lead but only for a week.

Accrington returned to top spot after Lowerhouse lost at Rawtenstall but they too were defeated to let in Todmorden. However after Tod lost away to the Rams on 2 July, Lowerhouse and Accrington jointly headed the table until Lowerhouse pulled away in mid-July. Eventually, they were to clinch the title in the penultimate match of the season's campaign.

Final league championship positions emerged as set out below:

	P	W	T	L	NR	Bonus Pts	Pts
1st Lowerhouse	26	20	1	4	1	38	248
2nd Accrington	26	18	0	6	2	32	218
3rd Todmorden	26	16	0	8	2	44	210
4th Ramsbottom	26	16	0	9	1	42	205

Finishing in the end all of 43 points behind title-winners Lowerhouse, the Rams had only themselves to blame after losing nine league matches as compared with only three the season before. However, they could take some consolation from having remained in contention for the greater part of the campaign. It had only been during the final month or so that the ultimate prize slipped away from them. Thus, for the second year running, despite having again performed superbly well to capture three titles, the elusive fourth element of the equation had ended up evading them again.

In individual terms, pro Shanan Stewart had notched up an impressive 937 runs at an average of 46.85. Keith Webb had totalled 512 at 23.27 while both Bell brothers exceeded the 400 run mark. Once again, skipper Jon Fielding had exceeded the century criterion in the bowling stakes taking 106 wickets, earning him the club's player of the year award for the second year running. Next was Michael Haslam (32), then Stewart (22) and Simon Read (15).

ooooo

2012 staked a claim for being the coldest and wettest summer in living memory. As a sign of conditions to follow, rain prevented any play in the season-opening Colne Cup match with the trophy being shared between Ramsbottom and Lowerhouse.

Although amongst the favourites to win the championship, the league season got off to a poor start for the Rams at Rishton when, winning the toss and deciding to bat, they were skittled out for 77 and beaten by six wickets. Fortunately, the second match, at home against Haslingden, had a better outcome. Containing the visitors to 167-8 with Jon Fielding taking 5-60, openers Keith Webb and Tom Parton put on 152 before Webb was out for 84. A nine-wicket victory was achieved with Parton (64*) and new pro Pieter Malan (14*) guiding the team home with 173-1.

Aged 22, a right hand bat and right arm medium-fast bowler, Malan had experience playing club cricket and for South Africa under-19s behind him. It wasn't to be as late as 2019 that he would represent his country at full Test level. Recommended to Andy Dalby and Jon Fielding by Faf du Plessis, Malan adapted well to the Lancashire League and would finish the season top of the batting averages, hitting 947 runs at an average of 63.13 with three centuries and six fifties to his name. On no account though an all-rounder, his wicket tally was just three.

Despite Malan impressing with the bat, 2012 was not to prove such a good experience for those amateur batsmen who had performed so successfully in recent seasons. For example, Keith Webb, David and Alex Bell each mustered little more than 200+ runs. Skipper Fielding had ended up promoting himself to open and hit 284 runs at 17.8.

The next highest individual total of runs, after Malan's, was accrued by young wicket-keeper/batsman Tom Parton who scored 307 at 19.2. Apart from the 64* against Haslingden, he made 118* at Colne, becoming at the age of 17 years and 5 months one of the youngest players in the history of the Lancashire League to notch up a century. All those at Acre Bottom, who had followed his meteoric rise to success to date, were thrilled by the achievement, none more so than John Steele who had spent a lot of time coaching Parton. For his part, Tom would always remain grateful to John for the time and effort he had put in during his formative years towards helping him blossom so well with the bat.

ooooo

To take some time out at this point, by way of paying tribute to John Steele, it needs adding that it was not only in Tom Parton's case that John proved such an able coach. As a player in his own right, after making his debut in 1963, Steele had played 158 1st XI matches for Rammy. It would no doubt have been a lot more had his career as a secondary school English teacher not taken him away from the area from 1976 onwards before eventually returning to the Bolton area to take up post as a Deputy Head Teacher. In a cricketing capacity, it was as a coach that John was ultimately destined to make most lasting impact.

John's latter time at Rammy had involved the setting up of Ramsbottom Junior Foundation, the start of which process also witnessed the likes of Phil Croft and Iain Round coming on board as team-managers. Both initially became involved when their sons had started playing cricket at the club at an early age.

John Steele's undoubted coaching skills were such that his services were also in demand at county level at Lancashire C.C. In a way somewhat similar to John Savage's earlier input at Old Trafford, John was to coach many players later to make names for themselves on a broader stage such as Haseeb Hameed, who would make his international debut for England in November 2016.

All the while, John Steele's residual enthusiasm for the game saw him going on to commit his energies at Rammy in other ways, for example taking responsibility for conducting fitness sessions for the 1st XI. In this context, it was no wonder that he was dubbed at the time: 'the fittest septuagenarian ever!'

ooooo

Returning back to 2012 though, apart from his success with the bat, Tom Parton had also fared very well as wicket-keeper, claiming 39 victims (24 catches and 15 stumpings) to share top league spot with Burnley's Chris Burton.

Unfortunately though, the season would see the club finishing only 7th in the league with a mediocre record of 12 wins, 10 losses and 4 NR. Managing 171 points, this total left them 46 behind Lowerhouse, title-winners for the second year running.

In the bowling stakes, Jon Fielding's performance however was again outstanding, capturing 89 wickets at 13.56, yet again emerging as the league's leading amateur wicket-taker whilst ten times achieving five or more wickets in a match. For the third season running, he was the club's player of the year. Mick Haslam had again supported his skipper well with 37 wickets at 20.6 with both players passing 500 league wickets during the course of this season.

Meanwhile in the Worsley Cup, the Rams went out ignominiously to East Lancs in a first round tie played at Acre Bottom on 20 May. Dumped out for 90, the visitors went on to secure victory by a margin of four wickets, despite Haslam's 4-17. Fortunately, the 2012 season was to be somewhat salvaged in the 20/20 competition. The highlight of the Rossendale group matches was Pieter Malan's record-breaking 165* against Rawtenstall. The semi-final draw saw the Rams pitted against Todmorden at Acre Bottom on 29 June. The visitors only managed to reach 85-8 at the end of their 20 overs with Fielding taking 5-16 from his 4-over allocation. The Rams made 87-6 to win by four wickets.

Against Church in the final, described on the occasion as 'a cool, damp, murky night' at Acre Bottom, the Rams had won the toss and chosen to field. Despite a productive second wicket stand of 51 between pro Anwar and no. 3 Aspin, Church were contained to 118-7 at the end of their 20 overs. In response, despite looking insecure at 41-4 at one stage, the Rams recovered to 121-5 by the end of 19 overs to win the match by five wickets. Fielding (33*) and Dentith (21*) were there at the end pushing the home team over the line and achieving for the club a hat-trick of consecutive wins in the competition spanning 2010, 2011 and now 2012.

ooooo

As mentioned earlier, it had not been a particularly productive season with the bat for either of the Bell brothers or Keith Webb. All three of them left Acre Bottom at this point. Alex went to play for Stand while David and Keith joined Woodbank. Each left with magnificent records of run-making behind them, having played pivotal parts in the club's striking recent successes, particularly in relation to seasons 2010 and 2011.

Elder of the brothers by two years, David could remember in earlier days making his debut for the 1st XI, batting together with dad Ian in a home match against Enfield in 1999. Overall in his career, David went on to play in 285 league matches scoring 4,018 runs at an average of 18.95. He had won the player of the year award in 2006. His most prolific season's run total had been in 2010, scoring 644 runs at an average of 35.77. Perhaps though, it was in relation to the Worsley Cup that he had made his most indelible mark, representing the club in four different finals, all ending in victory, whilst picking up the 'man of the match' award on two occasions.

Alex had made his 1st XI debut in 2000, starting to have real impact from 2002 onwards. He played in 205 league matches scoring 2,815 runs at an average of 18.40 with two centuries to his name. In two different seasons, he managed to score 500+ runs, 508 in 2005 at an average of 26.73 and 510 in 2010 at 25.50. Like David, Alex too had many memorable moments in the Worsley Cup, one being when he held on to a catch on the boundary in the 2009 final against Tod to take the wicket of their pro Jayasinghe. In recent conversation with Alex, he felt that by the end of 2012 'everything had been achieved that could be by this point and that now was the right time to go'.

Keith Webb had started playing for the club in 2002 and since that time played in 247 league matches scoring 3,879 runs at an average of 18.38. Making a century (105*) in 2003, a season in which he also registered 500+ runs (508), Keith was also to notch up 500+ run tallies in two further seasons: 2010 (526) and 2011 (512). On so many occasions, as an opener, he had laid solid foundations for the team. As in the case of the Bell brothers, Keith also featured strongly in the Worsley Cup success-story of these years, his most notable contribution being the 125 he scored against Enfield in a second round match on 5 June 2010. He also served the club as captain in 2009.

ooooo

Things looked up again in 2013 in the league with a 4th place finish. The fact they only managed to complete 21 matches (15 wins and 6 defeats) with five 'no results' - the largest number among the top sides - cost dearly. In the end, title-winners Accrington accrued 259 points, well ahead of Rammy's 194.

Pieter Malan resumed as pro and made 1,053 runs at 56.3, with nine fifties and an unbeaten 111 at Rawtenstall on 26 May. At the same time, he moderately raised the number of wickets he took this season to 23 at 18.7. Victory over Lowerhouse in mid-May had taken Rammy as high as second place and the club stayed there until successive defeats were inflicted on them by fellow challengers Haslingden and Lowerhouse in mid-June. The team remained in contention until losing at Accrington in the penultimate match of the season.

High points for the club had been ending Accrington's 20-match unbeaten sequence in the home match at Acre Bottom with a 20-run win. Also, the Rams reached the 20/20 final for the fourth year running even if it wasn't to lead to a fourth successive win. In response to Lowerhouse's 171-9 on 12 July, the Rams collapsed from 19 without loss to 59 all out, inside 13 overs, defeated by an emphatic 112 runs.

There were many outstanding individual achievements though this year. Chief among these was the form of wicket-keeper/batsman Tom Parton who became only the third player in league history after David Pearson, in 1990, and Jack Simpson, twice in 1994 and 1995, to perform the double of 500+ runs and 50+ victims. Up until July, Tom had languished down the batting order but, promoted to opener, he had hit 587 runs from this point onwards to finish the season with 670 at 35.3, including five half-centuries. His best performance behind the stumps came at Bacup on 25 August when taking six victims, three caught and three stumped, five of them coming off the bowling of Fielding who took 6-15 on the day in an eight-wicket victory. Tom deservedly won the player of the year award that year.

Skipper Jon Fielding proved himself in good form again taking 64 wickets at 15.7. For the fourth year running, he won the award for being the leading amateur wicket-taker in the league. The evergreen Mick Haslam took 29 at 25.1, newcomer Sam Halstead 23 at 23.4, Andy Hakin 13 at 21.4 and Dale Gabriel 11 at 17.4. Matt Sutton also made his mark with a maiden five-wicket haul at Accrington.

On the batting front, a father and son pairing made very useful runs: the Deardens, Steve and Harry. New recruit to the club Harry made 393 runs at 24.6, with a season's best of 78* at Rishton. Dad Steve, returning to play at Rammy following his time spent at Haslingden, scored 333 at 24.6, including a decisive 75 in the match that broke Accrington's 20-match unbeaten run. Incidentally, it was the only season that Harry

Dearden played for the club before going on to play 1ˢᵗ class county cricket for Leicestershire. Meanwhile, Rob Faulkner hit 284 runs at 18.9, Rob Read 224 at 17.2 and Mark Dentith 155 at 22.1.

This was Mark's final year before going on to follow in the footsteps of quite a few Rammy players in recent times by joining Woodbank. Since making his debut for the 1ˢᵗ XI in 1990, he had scored 2,701 runs at an average of 15.35. His best seasons, statistically speaking, had been from 2000 to 2005 and also in 2010. A magnificent striker of the ball, he came more latterly to be selected to bat lower down the order with the aim of coming in and slogging quick runs. Of course, Mark's career would also be remembered for his innings of 206 when playing for the club's 2ⁿᵈ XI in a match against Enfield on 22 July 2006, creating a record individual score at this level.

Although Jack Simpson was destined not to retrace a path back to Acre Bottom in the way that Steve Dearden had, he was to share the same distinction with 'Dasher' of having a son very notably following in his footsteps. In Jack's case, it was John who, after a spell of keeping wicket at Bentgate, would later go on to play county cricket for Middlesex, eventually to be honoured in 2021 by selection to play for England in ODI matches against Pakistan.

Meanwhile, if 2013 marked the first year since Jon Fielding's return that the 1ˢᵗ XI had failed to pick up silverware, this omission was made up for by the 2ⁿᵈ XI, who not only succeeded in becoming Junior League champions but did so with a record number of points, 259, and also record margin of 49 points since the introduction of the system of 12 points for a win.

ooooo

However, in advance of 2014, it was perceived that changes needed to be made if the club was to mount a serious challenge for the 1ˢᵗ XI league title in the year ahead. With rumours rife about Jon Fielding leaving, a statement was issued on 6 September announcing that the club had signed South African Daryn Smit as their professional for 2014.

The initial decision not to renew Pieter Malan's contract had already been taken in late August. Now, in early September, Director of Cricket Andy Dalby went public on the situation: 'It was a really tough decision not to retain the services of Pieter Malan who was a popular professional with all the players and supporters. However, as a Cricket Committee, we felt that to move this club forward we needed a professional who had the potential to not only score a large amount of runs but also take a good number of wickets during the season. This is aimed in the direction of complementing current leading wicket-taker Jon Fielding who will be at the club in 2014, contrary to all the rumours'.

Even though the statement was reassuring in many ways, not least in confirming that Jon Fielding was staying on at the club, Rammy fans were still left holding their breath as to how Daryn Smit, the new pro South African, would manage to perform when put to the test.

Thirteen: Near-run thing at Nelson

DARYN SMIT WAS 30 years old when he started as pro at the club in 2014. He was known for being a particularly versatile player. In 2009, he'd been pro at Littleborough, scoring over 1,300 runs and taking 78 wickets. In South Africa, he had captained his club side, Nashua Dolphins, also keeping wicket.

Apart from his batting credentials, it was the extra dimension Daryn could provide as a genuine leg-spinner that was the clinching factor in the Rams going after him. As far as the wicket-keeping element was concerned, the club felt confident that 19-year-old Tom Parton would maintain the excellent form he had shown the previous year.

The 2014 season did not get off to the best of starts though with a defeat at Accrington where the side was bowled out for 94 and lost by six wickets. A win at Nelson in the next match gave greater grounds for optimism with Simon Read, returning from his spell at Woodbank, looking sharp again in taking 4-30. Andy Dalby and Simon's cousin Rob Read, new captain this season, had set out to persuade Simon to re-join. Later, he recalled jokingly that: 'I made them sweat though. It took four cans of Guinness and about an hour before I agreed!'

In the next match at home against Todmorden on 27 April, Daryn Smit gave first notice of his bowling ability with 7-29 in a 54-run victory. Following the opening day defeat, the Rams won their next five games to head the table. Team spirit was high. To his credit, Rob Read had taken on the captaincy role at a time when the mood in the changing-room had undoubtedly needed some picking up. With an infectious brand of enthusiasm, he had successfully gone about the business of lifting spirits and encouraging everyone around him to go out on to the field of play to do their best for the team.

A defeat against Haslingden at home on 31 May however stalled the promising opening run, despite Smit taking 5-42. Only Parton (26) and Smit (36) reached double figures as Rammy were bowled out for 92 in response to the away team's 161-9.

It was to prove another outstanding season for Tom Parton, going on to score 743 runs at 35.4. His most notable innings came at Todmorden on 8 June when he batted through the 50 overs to finish with 129*. Parton had such a prolific start to the season that he looked set to challenge the club's batting record only for the chance to slip away in the closing stages of the season.

Meanwhile, Daryn Smit was handsomely repaying the faith put in him, particularly with the ball. He was to pick up 88 wickets at an average of 7.2 with eleven five-wicket hauls. Apart from 7-29 against Todmorden, he also took seven wickets (7-10) in a home match against Bacup on 1 June. In all competitions, he would top the hundred mark (103) with an average of 6.99, easily making him the top pro bowler in the league.

Not that he was any slouch with the bat! Scoring 790 runs in the league at 60.8 with six half-centuries, he was also the leading scorer in the 20/20 with 282 runs, including his 128 at Edenfield. His figures of 5-15 against Haslingden were a season's best in the competition on the bowling side. In all matches across the season as a whole, he scored 1,073 runs at 67.1 with seven half-centuries and one century.

Despite all this, scant progress was made in the cup competitions. The best hope of silverware remained with the league. It was a blistering pace though that Lowerhouse had set. In second place from mid-June onwards, the Rams eventually were left having to settle for the Holland Cup with 20 wins and a total of 243 points as runners-up to Lowerhouse - 22 wins and 261 points. Affording a measure of consolation, the Rams had come out on top against the title victors in the final league match of the season at Acre Bottom, with Simon Read taking 6-27 to bring the away team's club record of 19 straight wins to an end.

Smit had been well supported with the ball by Jon Fielding who took 45 wickets at 14.1, Simon Read 36 at 12.4 and Mick Haslam 36 at 17.5.

It had been a well-balanced and penetrating 4-pronged bowling attack that the Rams put out that season.

Tom Parton, as well as claiming 28 victims behind the stumps, headed the club's amateur batting averages and also again won the player of the year award. Of the other main batsmen, Callum Kay, who had joined the club from the Cheshire Premier League, hit 343 at 26.4. A particular high spot for Kay had come at Enfield on 7 September when, together with sub-pro Saliya Saman, the pair scored 190 runs for the third wicket, amounting to the highest partnership in the league that season. Meanwhile, after being promoted up the order, Jon Fielding notched 305 runs at 19.1 with a top score of 92 at Colne on 17 May.   Other useful runs were contributed by Dale Gabriel (289), Jamie Pilling (203) and skipper Rob Read (166) who also took 12 catches.

ooooo

2015 was the year in which Daryn Smit found himself involved in an epic bid to break Brad Hodge's record of league runs scored in a season. Starting out as he meant to go on, by scoring 137* in the first match at home against Rishton, Smit was to smash two more centuries, 102* against Church and 114* against Colne, as well as eleven half-centuries.

The question of whether he could surpass Hodge's record of 1,246 runs hung tantalisingly in the balance until the home match against Haslingden on 23 August. Scheduled to fly back to South Africa soon afterwards, it was his last match for the club that season. At this point, he was still 52 runs shy of the target.

Having taken over the captaincy role by this point in the season, Smit won the toss and chose to bat. After a first wicket partnership of 59, he came in at no.3. However, weather conditions suddenly took a dramatic turn for the worse. With heavy clouds scudding across the skyline, and the familiar view of the Peel Tower becoming increasingly enshrouded in mist, the South African was left with little choice but to chance his arm.

Farming the bowling as much as he could, he drew ever nearer to the total required. Only a matter of minutes after joyously reaching 53*, thus breaking the record, the heavens opened and a torrential downpour brought play to a close for the day.

ooooo

2015 was completely dominated by Burnley in all other respects, succeeding in pulling off the quadruple goal that the Rams themselves had fallen so narrowly short of in 2010 and 2011. Compared with the Turf Moor team's 21 wins and 257 points that season, the Rams only managed 16 and 211 respectively. Although in second spot from mid-June onwards, a poor finish, with three defeats in the final six matches, ended up leaving them 3rd.

Whatever else, matches played against Burnley that season never lacked drama. In the second round Worsley Cup tie at Turf Moor on 27 June, the home team had flayed Rammy's bowlers all over the park. Their 371-7, a Worsley Cup overall team record, included 199 from Jon Clare, thereby establishing an individual record amateur score. The Rams had been bowled out in reply for 244 in 38.2 overs.

Only a few days later, on 4 July, a chance to redress matters came in a home league match against the same opponents. Ahead of this game, Rob Read, struggling for form under the pressure of also skippering the side, had stood down from the captaincy role, the baton being passed to Daryn Smit. Batting first, Smit contributed 51 to a Rammy total of 187-9. In the circumstances, it still did not seem too ambitious a target for the run-happy Burnley batsmen to chase down. Pace bowler Simon Read though had other ideas. Tearing in with a vengeance, his 6-27 saw the vaunted Turf Moor team skittled out for 74 in one of their rare humiliations that season.

Despite suffering two unfortunate league defeats late in the season, the Rams had managed to hang on to second spot until the last match of the season on 13 September, which was at home against Nelson. Needing a win to be able to claim the Holland Cup for a second year running, things though went very wrong with the home side bowled out for 72 and losing the match by six wickets.

Daryn Smit would no doubt have more than willingly sacrificed some of his own outstanding individual achievements that season if it meant the side as a whole gaining greater success. However, nothing should be taken away from the colossal effort he had made in the team cause. Not only breaking Brad Hodge's run-scoring record, with 1,248 runs, achieved at a staggering average of 113.45, Daryn had ended way out in front as the league's top wicket-taker. Prior to his having to return home with four matches to play, he had already taken 74 at 8.2. As for other key players, wicketkeeper/batsman Tom Parton, even though suffering different forms of injury and illness during the course of this season, had still finished with 436 runs at 24.2, at the same time adding 20 more victims to his career's wicket-keeping tally.

The only ever-present this season was Mick Haslam who took 30 wickets at 23.0. The end of the year marked his official retirement. A great servant to the club, Haslam had made his debut for the 1st XI back in 1991. Operating from the Paper Mill end, his bohemian appearance, with flowing locks, almost belied the reality that he was a model of conformity in terms of line and length bowling. His eventual haul of 611 wickets, including two 50+ seasons in 2000 (50) and 2010 (51), placed him third behind Fred Duerr and Jon Fielding in club history. His 498 appearances put him second only to Henry Hall in this respect. 'Spider' was awarded player of the year three times, in 2000, 2007 and 2009.

Meanwhile, Simon Read was the club's top amateur wicket-taker during the course of this season with 55 at just 10.90, earning him a second player of the year award to add to that from 2005. Jon Fielding, who had temporarily taken over the captaincy after Daryn's return to South Africa, took 40 wickets at 16.2 and also hit 207 runs at 13.8. Callum Kay scored 363 runs at 18.2, including an unbeaten 98 against Todmorden while Dale Gabriel made 347 at 19.3. Relative newcomer Martin Cropper scored 260 at 14.4. Another young player to have emerged in the 1st XI this season was Brad Fielding, grandson of Brian and son of Jon, illustrating his promise for the future by scoring 198 runs at 12.4.

ooooo

In 2015, longstanding club official Brian Hutchinson sadly passed away. His famously dry wit has already been mentioned in relation to the episode of Mark Price signing back on at the club in 1990. Revered for the length and quality of his service to the club, a special seating structure was erected in Brian's honour, looking out on to the field of play and bearing the inscription: 'In Memory of Brian Hutchinson, Honorary Treasurer, 1964-2015'. Incidentally, the pavilion had in due course become named 'the Brian Hutchinson Pavilion'.

In the same way that he had previously put together the area known as Poets Corner, Andrew Rothwell (local stonemason and longstanding committee member) also created a seating construction tribute to Brian Hutchinson, sited in front of the clubhouse.

ooooo

With Daryn Smit set to return as pro for a third year running in 2016, hopes naturally ran high as to chances of success. It was also a bonus that, free this year of other commitments, Smit was scheduled to take part in all 26 league matches.

Other practical matters though had needed dealing with prior to the start of the 2016 season. Following the River Irwell breaking its banks on Boxing Day and causing huge flooding on the Acre Bottom site, a great deal of work had to be put in to make sure ground facilities were back in acceptable condition for the beginning of the new season. Such necessary repair work was admirably undertaken by the club's ground staff, principally Roger Davies (who had been groundsman since 1973), assisted by a host of volunteer helpers.

A significant aspect to the start of 2016 involved the opening of more formal discussions amongst club representatives as to how the Lancashire League structure might look to re-constitute itself for a year ahead. The significance of such a move must have seemed enormous at the time. After all, since the time Todmorden had joined in 1897, Lancashire League membership had been limited to the same fourteen clubs. However, the question was now being put forward as to the feasibility/desirability of broadening the membership base. For the consideration of such matters, representatives were sought from each

207

club to enter into discussions. Michael Everett was chosen to act as Rammy's spokesperson.

ooooo

At the start of the 2016 season, Rawtenstall were early pacesetters after taking maximum points from their opening two games. Rained off at Rishton on the opening day, the Rams were quickly back in contention though and topping the table by the end of Match Day Three after wins against Enfield and Lowerhouse. Then at home against last season's champions, Burnley, the visitors had made 109-9 in their innings. Replying, Rammy were in massive trouble at 30-6. However, a brave 57-run partnership between Jon Fielding (50) and Rob Read (18) helped the Rams make something of a recovery. By the time of the fall of their 9th wicket, having reached the same score of 109-9, it was left to Simon Read to come in at no.11 and score the winning run to clinch a tight one-wicket victory. Incidentally, the batsman at the other end at this point was Tom Booth on 6*. It was by no means the last high-pressure situation the pair were going to have to face during the course of the season.

Following on from the winter floods, it was also to be a dismal summer weather-wise with a record 50 games across the league set to finish as 'no result'. One such saw the Rams' fifth match, away at East Lancs, rained off without a ball bowled. The vagaries of weather conditions this season were to remain a constant factor throughout, leading in the end to as many as nine of the club's matches being declared 'no result'.

Once again though, despite everything else, pro Daryn Smit was in brilliant form, still managing to score 774 runs at an average of 86.0 with two centuries and seven half-centuries. With the ball, he picked up 69 wickets at 8.1 including 5 five-wicket hauls and a season's best of 7-15 at Colne.

Though at the mercy of the weather, Rammy managed to remain in top spot until 20 August when Burnley took over after the Rams' match against Tod was rained off. However, a defeat at the hands of Accrington the day after didn't help. Fortuitously, the match in hand that the Turf Moor team had over their rivals fell victim to the weather to slip the advantage back the Rams' way. A subsequent run of victories against Bacup, Haslingden and Rishton saw them entering into their final match at Nelson with a five-point lead over second-placed Burnley with the stage promisingly set for a triumphant end to the season.

If ever things were so easy! Only the season before, the club's hopes of lifting the Holland Cup had been scuppered at the hands of the same side they were now set to face on 11 September.

In the decisive match that was to follow, away at Nelson, the home team won the toss and decided to bat. However, never settling to the task, they were bowled out for a paltry 78, Smit ending up with 6-10. Despite news filtering through that their title-rivals had already banked 12 points at Todmorden, the challenge facing the Rams still looked something of a formality.

A somewhat less straightforward story however was to unfold, not least on the Smit household front! Texting his wife Sarah, who wasn't able to arrive at the ground until later on in the afternoon, Daryn had gladly informed her of the situation at the end of the Nelson innings. Arriving at the ground not long after, she had come all smiles, expecting to find Rammy players and fans in happy and delighted mood. However, it was a very different scene she encountered. Looks on faces were not only tense but almost glum.

Devastatingly, the first three Rammy wickets had already fallen with the run-total still only on 10. Openers Parton and Turner were back in the pavilion and, even more devastatingly, Daryn Smit had gone soon after. Despite having given the team a strong talking-to at the interval as to taking no unnecessary risks, he had impulsively looked to cut a ball before getting his eye in, missed it and been bowled for a duck.

Wickets went on going down like ninepins. With the score standing at 54-8, and the situation frankly desperate, the two batsmen left at the crease at this stage were veteran Simon Read and relative newcomer Tom Booth. Both of them owed their places in the team to being bowlers as opposed to batsmen. Of the two, Read had proved himself useful on occasion with the bat during the course of his long career to date. By comparison though, in the 23 matches Booth had played that season, he had managed only a meagre 31 runs in total. With title prospects now riding very much on the outcome of this stand, fellow-players and supporters alike could barely bring themselves to watch.

Re-living the tense atmosphere of that moment, Simon recalled later that the situation felt even more alarming for the fact that, chasing only 78, he had never expected to find himself in such a situation to start with. Even so, the main thought hammering through his head was that, after missing out on the 2010 league title win through injury, this was a heaven-sent opportunity to be part of a title-winning team that he just had to make sure he capitalised on.

Thus feeling a great weight on his shoulders, he took it upon himself to drop anchor as firmly as he could just to keep the ball out. Equally though, he saw it as imperative to provide support and advice to young 19-year-old, Tom Booth, at the other end. However an added pressure built up for the two of them from the fact that, while doing everything to stay out there, the run-rate became so slow that it was now drawing close to the end of the allotted 50 overs.

With every odd run or so being cheered on almost hysterically by the large gathering of attendant Rammy fans, Simon Read and Tom Booth miraculously somehow conjured up 24 runs between them to level up with Nelson's score of 78 during the course of the 50th over. At this point, Booth was out stumped by Bradley off the bowling of Hussein.

Technically, the worst outcome at this stage was a tie (worth seven points - with the Rams only needing five from the match). In effect, the Rams had already succeeded in picking up the championship title. For his part though, Read wasn't for relaxing. Urging in-coming no.11 batsman Josh Dentith to make sure he laid bat on ball, Dentith edged a boundary off the penultimate ball of the innings (49.5 overs) to secure the Rams an outright one-wicket win, so bringing the game to a triumphant conclusion.

Whilst the famous victory was naturally celebrated like mad, an enormous sense of relief echoed through the camp. A sixth championship had been won, in the end by a five-point margin over runners-up Burnley. Apart from this, the victory contained added significance from the fact that Rammy had in the process secured the last traditional Lancashire League title, marking as it did the closing of a chapter in the League's long and illustrious history. Despite all this, the abiding memory of those who were there witnessing events on 11 September was just how sorely the nerves had been frayed on the day!

ooooo

In all matches for Rammy that season, Daryn Smit hit 1,143 runs at 87.9, also capturing 81 wickets at 8.8. Tom Parton was the leading amateur batsman scoring 483 runs at 34.5 with five half centuries, together with picking up 24 victims behind the wicket. Five other amateurs also made half-centuries – Dale Gabriel, Callum Kay, Will Turner, Michael Howarth and Jon Fielding. In the bowling stakes, Jon Fielding took 46 wickets at 8.7 and in so doing surpassed the 700 mark in the Lancashire League. Meanwhile, Simon Read reached the 300 mark in taking 31 wickets at 16.2.

At the end of Daryn Smit's third year as pro at Rammy, he was signed up to play county cricket for Derbyshire the next season. The final outcome to 2016 proved for him, as well as for everyone else associated with the club, immensely satisfying to reflect back on.

ooooo

Dependent on one's point of view, the advent of 2017 came either as a shock to the system or else a fresh lease of life. To traditionalists, it marked the end of a cricketing way of life that had remained virtually unaltered since the 1890s. To those with an eye to the continued viability of the Lancashire League though, change was not only seen as necessary but arguably long overdue.

In essence, the 2017 season saw Lancashire League membership expand to seventeen with Clitheroe, Darwin and Great Harwood joining the fourteen existing clubs. A new format was put in place which involved all clubs playing each other in Phase 1 and then splitting into two divisions to play against other clubs in the same division in Phase 2.

As 2016 champions, under new skipper Tom Parton, the Rams opened their season on 9 April in a Colne Cup match against Burnley at Turf Moor. Winning the toss and deciding to bat, their innings got off to a sticky start. The score had been 58-5 before stand-in pro Usman

211

Tariq played a commanding innings of 102 to take the team's total to 210-8. Despite an opening stand of 41, Burnley lost wickets at regular intervals before ending up all out for 149, Jon Fielding chief wicket-taker with 4-19.

Pleasing as it was to start the season with a trophy win, the Rams' league campaign was to fall somewhat flat by comparison. The team finished Phase 1 in sixth place with eight wins. At the end of Phase 2, admittedly with half of their games ending up 'no results', they had dropped to seventh.

The performance of new pro Grant Thomson, 29-year-old right hand bat and right arm medium-fast bowler, proved to be in rather stark contrast to that of his predecessor. Another South African joining the club with strong recommendations from back home, Thomson only scored 422 runs at an average of 42.20 in the sixteen matches he played, whilst taking 14 wickets at a costly 28.28 apiece. In his defence it could be said that, with the new system, there were more matches played against tougher teams in the upper echelons of the revised structure.

Tom Parton was the club's leading amateur batsman with 389 runs at 22.9, also taking 20 victims behind the stumps. Meanwhile, 14-year-old JJ Fielding (younger son of Jon) had a promising start to his career scoring 248 runs at 24.8, including two half-centuries. His brother Brad hit a career-best 81 in the win against Accrington in process of making 171 runs at 21.4. Martin Cropper scored 244 runs at 20.3, including his maiden Lancashire League half-century. The Kay brothers also chipped in with Callum scoring 134 runs at 16.8 and Fraser 193 at 17.5. Jon Fielding made 210 runs at 19.0 to add to his 33 wickets at 15.7. Simon Read took 21 wickets at 16.3 apiece and newcomer Matt Burdaky 17 at 14.8.

For Simon Read, this marked his last season playing 1st XI cricket for the club. Since making his debut in 1993, he had played 334 matches, scoring 1,934 runs at an average of 13.24 and taking 337 wickets at 19.30, highlighted by his 55-take in 2015. He had served as club captain 2007/8. A player often contending with injuries (for example having played few games in 2009 and none at all in 2010) he had transferred to Woodbank (2012-13) before coming back to enjoy a final flurry at Rammy from 2014 onwards. Simon was twice awarded player of the year, in 2005 and 2015. The icing on the cake had come in 2016 when he helped steer the club home, in that nail-biting encounter at Nelson, to a 6th title-win.

∞∞∞

The transformation process in terms of the Lancashire League structure was far from over! Seven more new clubs were accepted into the fold at the AGM for the start of 2018 – Crompton, Littleborough, Middleton, Milnrow, Norden, Rochdale and Walsden – all former members of the Central Lancashire League that had folded in 2015. The number of clubs, who were now members of the Lancashire League, had suddenly risen to twenty-four. During the forthcoming season, they were scheduled to play against each other once in a single division with the league set to split into two divisions from the start of 2019 onwards.

Accrington emerged as the early leaders after winning their first three games. However, following an away match against fellow contenders Lowerhouse on 19 May, the Rams took top spot. In this particular match, Jon Fielding demonstrated his continuing value to the club by coming in at no.7 at 102-5 and scoring 73 to take the Rams to 220-7, with Rob Read also contributing a useful 46 on the day. Then, opening the bowling, Fielding took 3-28 in a highly economic 14-over spell. The match was also notable for Tom Parton, captain and wicketkeeper, bagging five victims (two caught and three stumped) as the home team, at 205 all out, fell 15 runs short of their target.

The Rams managed to hold on to the championship lead until an away fixture at Walsden on 3 June. Winning the toss, the Rams chose to bat. Despite half-centuries from Tom Parton (51) and new pro that season, South African Sen Muthusamy (60), the last eight wickets fell for 82 runs. All out for 189 after 48.3 overs, Walsden made light of reaching the target, emerging comfortable winners by seven wickets, and seizing the title lead. Incidentally, J.A. Gale had enjoyed a particularly good match for the home team, achieving personal Lancashire League bests with both ball and bat, 4-23 and 106* respectively.

The pro contracted for 2018, Sen Muthusamy, was destined to play just seven games for the club after arriving later than anticipated, then having to leave for a training camp and finally returning home for good in mid-June. Muthusamy scored 250 runs at 35.7 and took 24 wickets at 11.0 in the league and also hit an unbeaten 146 in an early round of the Worsley Cup against Rawtenstall.

The Rams though were to be edged out at the quarter-final stage of the Worsley Cup away at Todmorden on 23 June. After Tod posted 224-5, the visitors tried their best but in the end had fallen agonisingly short of the target by a mere three runs, despite a magnificent 120 by Rehan Udwadia, an amateur player at the club for whom it would prove a season's highlight. Meanwhile in the 20/20s, the Rams reached the semi-finals before being beaten by five wickets by Burnley in a match reduced to 10 overs each side.

Back to the league and Walsden never looked back from the moment they had snatched the lead off the Rams on 3 June. They were to go on to take the league title with 240 points. Apart from winning the senior competition at the first time of asking, Walsden further achieved the feat of being the first club in the whole history of the Lancashire League to win, in addition, both the 2nd and 3rd XI competitions in the same season. A perhaps even more interesting detail was that the 3rd XI side was skippered by a spry 67-year-old by the name of Albert Ross.

The Holland Cup was picked up by Lowerhouse who, in winning 19 of their matches, finished with 234 points. Meanwhile the Rams had to settle for 3rd place. Despite winning an equal number of nineteen matches to Lowerhouse, they lost one more match and finished on 228 points. Overall though, to say there were 24 clubs vying for contention this particular year, 3rd place marked a solid enough success in the circumstances.

In terms of individual achievement, team captain Tom Parton had performed outstandingly as an opening batsman, amassing 754 runs at 47.1, including two centuries and six half-centuries. This was despite being handicapped by a knee injury which prevented him from keeping wicket for most of the season. Simon Hanson had a successful first season, hitting 498 runs at 33.2, including a maiden senior century at Colne. J.J. Fielding scored 402 runs at 28.7 with four fifties, Martin Cropper 346 at 19.2 and Rehan Udwadia 266 at 38.0. On the bowling side, Jon Fielding led the averages with 65 wickets at 10.8. Matt Burdaky picked up 32 wickets at 19.31.

The pro situation had failed to provide the club with much extra boost this season. Given that Muthusamy had only been able to play a handful of games, his replacement Werner Coetsee came in and scored 260 runs at a relatively low average of 23.6, whilst proving more effective in taking 29 wickets at 9.8. In comparison though with Daryn Smit's input in recent seasons, pro contribution had fallen short.

ooooo

Talking of Daryn Smit, he was back playing in the Lancashire League the following season in 2019 in the guise of a sub-pro, playing twelve matches in all, six for title-winners Burnley, five for Rammy and one for Worsley Cup winners Darwen. All twelve matches had victorious outcomes for the clubs he represented. In league matches only, Smit topped both the batting and bowling averages in Division One, hitting 558 runs at 93.0, whilst taking 46 wickets at 7.0 with six 5-wicket hauls.

After taking maximum points from their first three fixtures with Daryn Smit playing as sub-pro, the Rams lost three out of the next four league games played without him, falling to fifth place. The club's contracted pro for the season, George Linde, a 27-year-old left hand bat and slow left arm bowler who had played most of his cricket at State level back in South Africa, came late and returned early, being away for a training camp in the meantime. In fairness, 2019 was the season he was called up to represent his country at Test level. In the ten league matches Linde played for the Rams, he scored 301 runs at 30.1 with two half-centuries and picked up 13 wickets at 28.4. With regard to Smit's five-match input, playing in the first three and last two matches, he scored 228 runs at 76.0 and picked up 14 wickets at 8.0. In the end, the Rams finished the season in 4th place.

Another pro player who featured for the Rams this season was Ashar Zaidi, who played four league matches, scoring 172 runs at 43.0 and taking 9 wickets at 9.4. Most notably, Ashar was the club pro on the occasion of the 20/20 Finals day held at Bacup on the Bank Holiday Monday of 26 August. Having fallen out of contention in the league and knocked out of the Worsley Cup, the 20/20 still gave hope for the Rams to pick up silverware. The first match in the campaign had taken place against Haslingden on 31 May, a comfortable 7-wicket victory, leading on through the group stages to a quarter-final home win on 5 July against Todmorden by 46 runs.

In the semi-final against Church, on 26 August at Bacup's Lanehead ground, the Rams clocked up 193-5 with pro Zaidi smashing 97 runs off 59 balls - five fours and no fewer than nine sixes. A fifth wicket partnership of 113 between Zaidi (97*) and JJ Fielding (45 in 30 balls) had in the end seen off Church, pitting Rammy against Bacup in the final.

ooooo

Winning the toss and opting to bat first, Rammy scored steadily from the start with the rate accclerating in the latter stages of their innings. A combination of Udwadia (25* from 21 balls), J.J. Fielding (a 'tour de force' of 27 from 7) and Hanson (20 from 13) lifted the total in the end to 159. In reply, Bacup were restricted by tight bowling to a final total of 113-7, resulting in a victory by 46 runs for the Rams and another trophy win. Not that this was the only silverware the club collected that season, for the 2nd XI won their own knockout cup while the 3rd XI emerged top of their league competition, making it a rewarding season at all levels.

Apart from the various pro inputs, skipper Tom Parton scored 429 runs this season at 25.2 and claimed 27 victims behind the stumps. Four other batsmen scored more than 200 runs in the league season: Alex Olpin (286 at 17.9), Simon Hanson (259 at 17.3), Rehan Udwadia (250 at 20.8) and Brad Fielding (238 at 13.2). Meanwhile Jon Fielding (player of the year), took 49 wickets at 13.3, making him not only the club's leading wicket-taker but also again across the league as a whole.

Rob Read retired at the end of the season. Variously a medal-winner on the back of 2 League titles, 2 Worsley Cups, 3 T20 Cups, 2 2ndXI league titles and 3 3rd XI titles, he was a genuinely one-club man from playing in junior sides to serving as club captain. In 237 1st XI matches, he scored 1,704 runs at 13.74. Undoubtedly, he had major impact in motivating others around him, as recalled by Daryn Smit: 'Rammy through and through, with him as captain, it was the start of a journey with a new regime heading in a new direction'. Mick Everett referred to 'Rob's leadership qualities bringing back a spirit of unity which was much needed at the time and succeeded in making the club a force to be reckoned with'.

Another considerable loss, in relation to playing strength and much besides, was that of Tom Parton who left to go to Australia for work purposes at the end of the season. Although hope is still held out of him returning to play again for Rammy in the not too distant future, losing a player of Tom's quality came as an undoubted blow at the end of 2019. Still only 24, he had up to this point in his career played 208 matches for the club, scoring 4,358 runs at an outstanding average of 29.64, and served as captain. In addition, as wicket-keeper, he had taken 259 victims. With numerous medals and records to show for his efforts, he had won the club's player of the year award three times to date.

ooooo

Having due regard also for services provided by long-term volunteers working at the club, this was also the year when 'Life Member' Jack Wolfenden officially retired. He had carried out a tremendous amount of work across the Acre Bottom site, on behalf of both the Cricket and Football clubs. Dubbed by the Lancashire Evening Telegraph in 2014 as 'the oldest ball-boy in non-league football, Jack was now in his mid-80s. He was honoured with an event at the Cricket Club, at which respective Chairmen Rod Hamer and Harry Williams, expressing their appreciation, made a special presentation to Jack as a token of appreciation for all he had done in the way of service at both the clubs.

Meanwhile, the cricket club had found itself embroiled in a two-year struggle to avoid an unsightly mobile phone mast being erected on the ground. Due largely to the efforts of veteran administrator Peter Spencer (now approaching his 50th year of service on the club's committee in a range of capacities), the said project was eventually staved off.

ooooo

As the latest of an impressive list of cricket writers to have visited Acre Bottom, author Michael Henderson in his book entitled *That Will Be England Gone – The Last Summer of Cricket* (2020) describes coming to watch the match at home against Clitheroe in 2019. As a social commentator to boot, he had also carried out a 'recce' in the surrounding township beforehand, conversing with locals as to how they saw Ramsbottom itself having changed in character in recent years - not always it transpired for the better.

Curious to find out how the cricket club managed to sustain its own distinctive identity in a climate of accelerating 'modernisation', Michael talked to Maurice Haslam, 'a club stalwart'. Although stating that Maurice says 'it seems the same people do the work from one year to the next', Michael added that 'he doesn't sound angry'.

Drawing broader conclusions, Michael Henderson states: 'If there is such a thing as a hub of the community in a town like Ramsbottom, that has changed so much in character in recent years, then it can be found in this clubhouse…Here you will find decent folk, who were born in the town, and will die here. The club is part of their lives, a part they are pleased to hand on to those who follow'.

ooooo

The following season, 2020, was massively affected by all matters Covid-related. With Ramsbottom United Football Club's season having come to a premature end in mid-March, major doubts ran into the summer months as to whether it would be possible to put any sort of cricketing programme in place.

Inevitably, lockdown led to the postponement of the start of the Lancashire League. Later on in the season, a so-called 'President's Cup' competition was devised, which took place over a seven-week period in August and September. Conditions allowed clubs to play without pros. Games were restricted to forty overs a side, organised on the basis of four different groups of teams competing against one another, leading through to knock-out stages.

The Rams, having welcomed back Daryn Smit, had been placed in Group One, consisting of five teams, Burnley, Middleton, Littleborough and Norden, in addition to Rammy, all of whom had committed to taking on professionals for the season. The competition as such adopted the Worsley Cup 2019 rules, including powerplays and fielding restrictions. In statistical terms, runs scored and wickets taken were counted in players' career records as Worsley Cup games.

Although the season was foreshortened to two months, it ended up being a relatively successful one for the Rams. Winning their group, they then defeated Clitheroe at the semi-final stage before taking on Church in the final at Acre Bottom on 13 September.

Batting first, Church scored 170-8. Jon Fielding had proved highly economical, his eight overs costing a miserly 16 runs. New recruit that season from Accrington, Kieren Grimshaw, had been chief wicket-taker with 3-36 from his six overs. In reply, the runs did not exactly flow for Rammy and it was a hard grind to get anywhere close to Church's total. For example, it took Daryn Smit 37 balls to reach 12 before being out lbw. With overs dwindling down, despite Grimshaw's 60* and a late thrash from Jon Fielding, 18* off 9 balls, Church ended up President's Cup winners by 3 runs.

At the close of the season, Jon Fielding made the decision to retire as a player. Apart from all his other significant professional commitments elsewhere, Jon had still managed to put in 347 appearances for Rammy. His tremendous record as a bowler had seen him taking 827 wickets (at an average of 14.26), making him the second highest wicket-taker in club history after Fred Duerr.

Bursting on to the 1st XI scene in the early 90s, he had played a major part in the championship-winning year of 1992. His return to the club in 2010 was crucial towards the club winning three competition titles in each of the seasons of 2010 and 2011. His phenomenal feat in capturing over a century of wickets (113) in the championship-winning year of 2010 was the first time this had been achieved in the league since 1939.

Jon's contribution was immense not only as a bowler and motivational captain but also as a more than useful batsman (scoring 2,809 runs at 15.51) and fine fielder (taking 120 catches). A possession Jon was proud to have received in 2016 was a letter from Ian Bell referring to his 'unique achievement in being the only player in the club's long history to have won a Championship medal on three occasions'.

A further letter, dated 02/10/2020 and sent by Secretary, Sheila McQueeney, on behalf of the Committee, stressed how proud everyone at the club was of his many achievements throughout such a distinguished playing career - 'Thank you for everything that you have helped the Club achieve and have a long and happy retirement from playing – your work off the field has only just started!'

Indeed, Trigger's 'work off the field' was destined to commence the very next year - in the light of certain circumstances which would catapult him into the role of Vice-Chairman.

ooooo

What were these 'circumstances'? In short, chairman Rod Hamer had placed certain unacceptable remarks on social media. The fall-out was such that his position as a Rammy Club Cricket spokesperson had soon been declared as untenable by those having responsibility at national level for the standing of the sport of cricket.

It was with much regret that Rod's subsequent successor in the Chairman's role, John Fox, addressed club members in his opening correspondence to them in March 2021: 'It would be hard not to mention the departure of Rod Hamer and the unfortunate circumstances that surrounded it. Whilst we can't condone what was said, we simply cannot erase him from our club's history and we shouldn't forget the positive impact Rod had on the Club or ignore the many successes we had during his tenure – but we have moved on'.

Duly moving on, John then went on to make reference to the term 'Dodransbicentennial' - a term that did not exactly trip off the tongue! Happily, he chose to explain what the word meant - 'Some of you will know this means a 175-year anniversary - I had to look it up!' he humorously confessed. 'Whilst the anniversary was last year, Covid lockdown ruled out any proper celebration. Instead, we would like to use the coming season to hold a number of events to toast the last 175 years but also start to plan for the coming years ahead.

'We are the current custodians of the Club and what it stands for. Since 1845, there is no doubt that this club has been a force for good in the local community. Ramsbottom C.C. is the sum of all the unseen work that goes on behind the scenes of putting out a 1st XI on any given weekend occasion: the parents driving out to Longridge C.C, on a Thursday evening, volunteers clearing up the ground after the November bonfire event, coaches taking the training on a cold winter's night at Woodhey, an All Stars picking up a bat for the first time and the queue at Sandra's on a Sunday morning before junior training. The list is endless and just highlights the many parts of the jigsaw that make up Ramsbottom Cricket Club'.

More than anything, it was this last paragraph of John Fox's letter, in encapsulating what the life-blood of the club would always be about, that motivated the author to wish to make a contribution to the 'number of events' that the club had in mind 'to toast the last 175 years'.

Fourteen: Postscript

DURING 2021, WHICH was to prove to be his final season as pro at the club, Daryn Smit hit 897 runs at 52.8 (including three centuries and five fifties) and took 50 wickets at 14.9. From the entire number of batsmen who had played at least 50 innings in the history of the Lancashire League, Daryn's career average of 76.9 (scoring 4,921 runs) remains second only to the famous West Indian batsman, Everton Weekes, who played in the League for Bacup between 1949 and 1958 and averaged 91.6 (making 9,069 runs).

As an indication of Daryn's modesty, he brought up the point himself during the course of a chat with him that the standard of pro input hadn't been as high during his time as compared to other previous periods in the league's history. Whatever the take on this, it can be stated categorically that Daryn has been the leading pro of his own 'generation'. More than this, although everything in the nature of making comparisons is inevitably hypothetical, it may reasonably be argued he would have more than held his own against others from previous generations. His all-round contribution to the club has been truly immense. In the event, his record, coming second only to the inimitable Everton Weekes, speaks for itself.

ooooo

In 2021, the 1st XI finished 7th out of 12 in 2021 in Division One with 10 W 11 L 1 NR - plus 31 bonus points which amounted to 134 points overall (based on 10 for a win and 3 for a 'no result'). This total fell far short of title-winners Burnley with 189. The Rams had made a poor start to the season before bouncing back strongly in the latter half of it. Apart from Daryn Smit's own massive contribution with the bat, skipper Kieren Grimshaw scored 500 runs at 26.31, Brad Fielding 406 at 20.30 and Jake Clarke 361 at 22.56.

With the ball, apart from Smit's 50, Jake Clarke (who had like Grimshaw joined the club from Accrington) took 25 wickets at 26.84, including a season's best amateur bowling performance of 6-21 in the last match of the season at Clitheroe. Kieren Grimshaw had captured 17 wickets at 23.52 and Josh Dentith 14 at 30.42.

The 2nd XI finished 8th out of 12 in Junior Division One. Their progress over the course of the season had been the opposite of the 1st XI, i.e. starting out well but tailing off towards the end.

At the Presentation Evening on 16 October, Kieren Grimshaw was awarded '1st XI Player of the Year'. Another notable award was that for 2nd XI 'Performance of the Season', going to Alex Olpin (118) and Nick Round (101*) for their partnership of 238 runs made against Norden.

With Daryn Smit moving to Derbyshire C.C. in the capacity of Development Officer, cricket director Andy Dalby stepped in quickly to secure the services of South African, Sen Muthusamy, as pro for 2022. No stranger to Acre Bottom, Sen had been pro in 2018. Although achieving good figures that year, for various reasons he hadn't played the number of matches he would have liked. As Andy Dalby put it himself in his cricket committee update of November 2021, the appointment was made with 'very much a sense of unfinished business'.

ooooo

Major initiatives have developed in more recent times aimed at enabling a wider range of participants to play cricket at the club. This has manifested itself in a variety of ways. For example, the club has both thriving women's and girls' sections now. As is proudly stated on the website: 'Established in 2020, we are able to offer competitive and fun cricket for all ages with L2 and L3 coaches dedicated just to women's and girls' cricket.'

W&G head coach Iain Collier manages the senior teams at the club. Success was achieved when the women's T20 team won the county-wide

Division 2 title in 2020. In 2022, the club will have a team playing 40-over cricket in the top division of the county wide league. As a sign of developing integration, two players Sophie Ullah and Imogen Young broke something of a mould during 2021 by playing in what might previously have been called 'senior men's cricket' teams.

A dedicated Club Committee, chaired by Phil Croft, exists to promote the club's Cricket Academy and ensure the provision of structured coaching for girls and boys from the age of 5 to17. The 'All-Stars Cricket' programme, run by Kelly Newbold, is set to return for 2022, specifically aimed at the 5 to 8 age-range.

In addition, the club has announced the launch of the 'Pathway Development Programme' for boys and girls between the ages of 13 and 17 to add to the foundations already laid within the club's cricket academy. As Chairman John Fox recently stated:

'To help with this, we have seen the return to the playing set-up of Simon Read and Mark Dentith. Both experienced great success at the club as players and are well respected for their cricketing knowledge. Mark will also be taking up the reins as 2nd XI captain, with Chris Wood as manager while Simon will be overseeing the 3rd XI. Meanwhile, Andy Dalby remains as overall Director of Cricket, Kieren Grimshaw 1st XI captain, with Rob Read as manager'.

In addition to outlining the different projects aimed at bringing about broader participation on the playing side, it is worth noting the on-going commitment that ex-players, such as those mentioned above, show towards the club by helping to stimulate the interest of future generations in taking up the game of cricket. Having for so long played a central role in the life of the community, a rich tradition of family involvement, both on and off the field of play, has contributed greatly to the success enjoyed by Ramsbottom C.C. to date. There is every sign that such a spirit will continue into the future.

ooooo

A significant event of interest occurred at the club in recent times, for which the author is grateful to secretary Sheila McQueeney for bringing to his notice. This event came about when the business group

Cinch (new national cricket sponsors from May 2021 onwards), chose the Acre Bottom site to stage a promotional launch. Like so many others before, the company was attracted to the venue very much on account of the majestic setting of the club's iconic green and cream-coloured pavilion. Thus a film crew assembled one summer's week-day to record a bout of play, involving English captain Joe Root together with national women's team cricketer Amy Jones facing up to bowling counterparts Jimmy Anderson (a very welcome visitor in the light of his association with playing in the Lancashire League for Burnley in earlier days) and Kate Cross, with suitable commentary delivered by ex-international players, now T.V. pundits, Phil Tufnell and Graeme Swann. The upshot from this coverage was to emerge in YouTube format, bearing the title: 'Can a village team bowl out England's best batters?'

ooooo

Later on in the year, on a somewhat different tack, another very special occasion took place at the club on the evening of Friday, 19 November, heralded as the '1845 Hall of Fame Inductees: 2021'. With the celebrated cricketing figure Graham Gooch appearing as Guest of Honour, Club Chairman John Fox introduced the occasion as follows:

'We are taking this opportunity to celebrate the club's 175th anniversary by starting up the 1845 Hall of Fame. Tonight we have five former players who we will induct as its first members. This is something that we will continue to do on an annual basis, and I hope you appreciate that selecting the first 'famous' five was never going to be easy due to the number of people who would easily walk into the Hall of Fame due to their past glories. For those who haven't made it this year, your time will come'.

The set of presentations took place across the evening, sequenced as follows:

- Michael Haslam
- Michael Everett
- Ian Bell
- Brian Fielding
- Maurice Haslam.

At the same time as enrolling this first cohort of five players into its newly-founded Hall of Fame, it can be seen from John Fox's above statement that the club is further committed, on an on-going basis, to honouring down the line a vast additional number of other players who have contributed significantly, both on and off the field of play, towards making Ramsbottom the great Cricket Club it is to-day.

As well as taking steps to project the club into the future, it can thus be seen there remains also a healthy interest in celebrating the history and traditions that exemplify the very best that the club has been able to offer over the last 175 years, going back to when the club was founded in 1845.

Appendices

CLUB ROLL OF HONOUR
Lancashire League Champions:
Seasons - 1921, 1925, 1974, 1992, 2010, 2016.
Runners-up - 1911, 1915, 1920, 1935.
Holland Cup Winners - 1960, 1973, 1978, 1993, 1995, 2000, 2005, 2014.
Maden Cup Winners – 1911, 1917.
Worsley Cup Winners:
Seasons - 1939, 1957, 1996, 2001, 2002, 2005, 2009, 2011.
Colne Cup Winners - 1997, 2006, 2010, 2011, 2017.
20/20 Cup Winners – 2010, 2011, 2012, 2019.
Lancashire Junior League Champions:
Seasons - 1910, 1935, 1964, 1966, 1970, 1972, 1973, 2001, 2006, 2007, 2013.
Runners-up - 1986, 1989, 1992, 1993, 2002, 2011, 2016.
2nd XI Knockout Cup:
Seasons - 1972, 1975, 1987, 1993, 1995, 2002, 2003, 2005, 2006, 2007, 2011, 2015, 2019.
Lancashire Under 18s League Champions - 1960, 1982.
Lancashire Under 17s Cup Winners - 2000.
North Manchester League - Runners-up - 1968.
Calverley Cup Winners - 1968. Runners-up - 1974, 1975.
Lancashire League 3rd XI Champions:
Seasons: 1987, 1989, 1995, 1998, 1999, 2000, 2019.

ooooo

500+ RUN SEASONS

Names and Number of Times Achieved + (Season's run tally)

Whitworth, Billy:	11	1929 (579), 1936 (633), 1937 (701), 1938 (739), 1939 (589), 1940 (829), 1948 (694), 1949 (757), 1950 (642), 1955 (504),1956 (512).
Bell, Ian:	10	1984 (626), 1985 (539), 1986 (731), 1987 (554), 1989 (691), 1991 (642), 1993 (758), 1994 (692), 1995 (575), 1996 (593).
Simpson, Jack:	6	1989 (626), 1991 (565), 1993 (599), 1994 (507), 1995 (716),1996 (810).
Ashworth, Stephen:	4	1985 (512), 1987 (540), 1988 (708), 1990 (657).
Leach, Joe:	3	1894 (582), 1895 (538), 1904 (515).
Parton, Thomas:	3	2008 (754), 2013 (670), 2014 (743).
Pearson, Jack:	3	1933 (557), 1934 (691), 1937 (518).
Redfern Jack:	3	1902 (545), 1911 (815), 1913 (565).
Webb, Keith:	3	2003 (508), 2010 (526), 2011 (512).
Bell, Alex:	2	2005 (508), 2010 (510).
Everett, Michael:	2	1978 (551), 1981 (591).
Hayes, Phil:	2	2007 (544), 2008 (629).
Taylor, Brian:	2	1994 (614), 1999 (573).
Bell, David:	1	2010 (644).
Chapman, Arthur:	1	1970 (506).
Daggert, Pete:	1	1982 (501).
Dearden Stephen:	1	1994 (640).
Greenhalgh, Billy:	1	1959 (554).
Grimshaw, Kieren:	1	2021 (500)
Riley, Nicholas:	1	2002 (529).
Rogers, Mick:	1	1984 (531).
Simpson, A:	1	1906 (520).

50+ WICKET SEASONS

Names and Number of Times Achieved + (Season's wicket tally in the league)

Duerr, Fred:	17	1909 (69), 1910 (97), 1911 (101), 1912 (90), 1913 (78),1914 (76), 1915 (87), 1916 (109), 1919 (102), 1920 (94), 1921 (68), 1922 (59) 1923 (82), 1924 (67), 1925 (96), 1926 (55), 1927 (53).
Fielding, Jonathan:	6	1991 (72), 2010 (113), 2011 (106), 2012 (89), 2013 (64), 2018 (65).
Stewart, Terry:	4	1963 (51), 1969 (50), 1973 (51), 1976 (58).
Fenwick, William:	3	1900 (137), 1901 (71), 1902 (80).
Olive, John:	3	1940 (69), 1941 (57), 1942 (63).
Haslam, Michael:	2	2000 (50), 2010 (51).
Longworth, Norman:	2	1937 (50), 1944 (50).
Monkhouse, Steve:	2	1984 (57), 1989 (68).
Price, Mark:	2	1990 (60), 2003 (72).
Brooks, Joe:	1	1893 (59).
Read, Simon:	1	2015 (55).
Riley, Nicholas:	1	1994 (61).
Walker Herbert:	1	1906 (52).
Whitworth, Billy:	1	1935 (50)

ooooo

Interestingly, in terms of 'all-rounder' statistics, it can be seen from the above that the only two amateurs in club history who have achieved both 500+ runs and 50+ wicket seasons are Billy Whitworth (eleven 500+ runs plus one 50+ wicket season) and Nick Riley (one 500+ runs plus one 50+ wicket season).

ooooo

HIGHEST RUN SCORERS (players to have scored 2,000 + in 1st XI League matches)

	Runs	Average
Whitworth, Billy	10,715	27.26
Bell, Ian	9,014	23.91
Leach, Joe	7,468	18.17
Hall, Henry	6,005	14.47
Pearson, Jack	5,814	18.69
Barnes, Tommy	5,509	16.59
Simpson, Jack	5,499	28.79
Redfern, Jack	5,350	25.97
Walker, Herbert	4,649	13.92
Parton, Thomas	4,358	29.65
Ashworth, Peter	4,313	13.15
Taylor, Brian	4,039	19.61
Bell, David	4,018	18.95
Wolstenholme, Albert	3,929	16.04
Webb, Keith	3,879	18.38
Morris, Trevor	3,463	13.96
Greenwood, W	3,459	12.49
Dearden, Stephen	3,452	23.32
Ashworth, Stephen	3,364	26.91
Everett, Michael	3,238	18.29
Bladen, Geoff	3,047	12.34
Hodgson, Derek	3,002	14.43
Ashworth, John	2,979	15.05
Scowsgill, AJ	2,978	13.92
Price, Mark	2,950	15.95
Riley, Nicholas	2,842	14.57
Bell, Alex	2,815	18.40
Fielding, Jonathan	2,789	15.67
Dentith, Mark	2,701	15.35
Marsden, Geoff	2,680	15.23
Chapman, Arthur	2,590	15.60
Horrocks, Jimmy	2,565	12.95

Hall, Stephen	2,507	13.63
Ramsbottom, John	2,481	14.76
Greenhalgh, Billy	2,361	20.01
Chamberlain, Ernest	2,339	12.71
Simpson, A	2,248	10.13
Stewart, Terry	2,203	11.13
Kay, Clifford	2,011	12.34

HIGHEST WICKET TAKERS (players to have taken 110+ in 1st XI League matches).

	Wickets	Average
Duerr, Fred	1,477	10.08
Fielding, Jonathan	823	14.16
Haslam, Michael	611	24.11
Stewart, Terry	595	17.16
Fenwick, William	512	11.68
Olive, John	511	14.78
Whitworth, Billy	390	18.89
Savage, Bill	386	19.07
Fielding, Brian	362	19.61
Longworth, Norman	341	14.91
Read, Simon	337	19.30
Price, Mark	335	17.22
Monkhouse, Harold	325	19.11
Riley, Nicholas	294	23.21
Monkhouse, Steve	259	21.04
Ratcliffe, Stephen	255	19.46
Walker, Herbert	218	16.60
Bradshaw, Fred	210	16.73
Brooks, Joe	203	13.50
Haslam, Maurice	195	21.33
Dearden, Stephen	183	23.01
Moreton, Garfield	164	20.60
Simpson, A.	163	19.34
Barlow, Frank	155	18.28

Pilkington, Alan	140	19.86
Bladen, Geoff	137	20.24
Morris, Alan	115	22.13

HIGHEST NUMBER OF DISMISSALS (players to have achieved 100+ in 1st XI League matches). NB - in the case of wicket-keepers, this is the combined number of catches and stumpings; in relation to out-fielders, purely the number of catches):

	Dismissals	Average per matches played
Isherwood, Jack	421	1.00
Simpson, Jack	402	1.68
Hevingham, Richard	386	1.29
Parton, Thomas	259	1.25
Brooks, Duncan	235	0.82
Walker, Herbert	179	0.46
Waite, Arthur	175	0.77
Whitworth, Billy	164	0.34
Wolstenholme, Albert	155	0.55
Hall, Henry	150	0.28
Leach, Joe	148	0.31
Marcroft, Paul	143	1.13
Duerr, Fred	135	0.33
Read, Simon	121	0.36
Fielding, Jonathan	120	0.35
Stewart, Terry	112	0.29
Ramsbottom, John	111	0.43
Dentith, Mark	110	0.38
Horrocks, Jimmy	110	0.47
Ashworth, Peter	106	0.26
Riley, Nicholas	106	0.36
Barlow, JW	103	0.96
Scowsgill, AJ	103	0.43
Price, Mark	101	0.38

APPEARANCES (players to have made 250+ appearances in the 1st XI)

Hall, Henry	538	Hall, Stephen	308
Haslam, Michael	498	Hevingham, Richard	299
Whitworth, Billy	483	Olive, John	299
Leach, Joe	477	Riley, Nicholas	298
Isherwood, Jack	419	Morris, Trevor	294
Bell, Ian	415	Dentith, Mark	289
Duerr, Fred	415	Brooks, Duncan	288
Ashworth, Peter	410	Bell, David	285
Haslam, Maurice	400	Wolstenholme, Albert	283
Barnes, Tommy	397	Ratcliffe, Stephen	282
Walker, Herbert	390	Hodgson, Derek	264
Stewart, Terry	385	Price, Mark	263
Savage, Bill	379	Ramsbottom, John	260
Fielding, Jonathan	342	Fielding, Brian	259
Pearson, Jack	339	Simpson, A	258
Read, Simon	334	Taylor, Brian	254
Bladen, Geoff	326	Redfern, Jack	251
Greenwood, W	308	(NB – item continued in right-hand column above)	

PROFESSIONALS AT CLUB

1892 to 1894:	Daff Whittaker and N. Jackson
1895:	Daff Whittaker and Fred Hassall
1896:	Ellis Town and A.E. Hatfield
1897:	Ellis Town and Joshua Penny
1898:	Frank Shacklock and A. White
1899:	Ernest Creighton and H. Page
1900 to 1902:	Walter Taylor
1903 to 1905:	Jerry Ellis
1906 to 1907:	Arthur Sladen
1908 to 1913:	Emmott Robinson
1914:	Bert Morgan
1915:	William Benskin
1919:	A. Smith
1920 to 1922:	William Hickmott

1923 to 1924:	James McNamara
1925:	William Hickmott
1926:	Ernest Moss
1927:	L.V. Vaughan
1928:	Hugh Claughton
1929:	Edward Moxham
1930:	Ambrose ('Billy') Williams
1931 to 1932:	Jack Holroyd
1933 to 1939:	Syd Hird
1945:	Reg Santall
1946 to 1948:	Lesley Warburton
1949 to 1950:	Harry Lambert
1951 to 1954:	Gul Mohammad
1955:	Peter Philpott
1956:	Brian Flynn
1957 to 1958:	Eddie Fuller
1959 to 1960:	Peter Philpott
1961 to 1962:	Seymour Nurse
1963:	Ian Chappell
1964:	Seymour Nurse
1965:	Tony Lock
1966:	Keith Stackpole
1967 to 1968:	Peter Kelly
1969 to 1972:	R.G. ('Bapu') Nadkarni
1973:	Clive Rice
1974:	Ray Bright
1975 to 1976:	Wasim Raja
1977:	Trevor Laughlin
1978:	Karson Ghavri
1979:	Greg Hayes
1980:	Karson Ghavri
1981:	Ian Callen
1982:	Ashok De Mel
1983:	Neal Radford
1984:	Murray Bennett

1985:	David Hookes
1986:	Craig Norris
1987	Andrew Zesers/ Ijaz Faqih
1988	Ijaz Faqih
1989:	Brian McMillan
1990:	Steve Monkhouse
1991:	Rudi Bryson
1992 to 1994:	Keith Arthurton
1995 to 1997:	Chris Harris
1998:	Ian Harvey
1999:	Matt Pascoe
2000 to 2001:	Brad Hodge
2002:	Michael Clarke
2003:	Jason Arnberger
2004 to 2005:	Kartik Murali
2006 to 2007:	Sunil Joshi
2008:	Lou Vincent/Shane Harwood
2009:	Brent Parchment
2010:	Francois ('Faf') du Plessis/Alex Doolan/ Ross McMillan
2011:	Shanan Stewart
2012 to 2013:	Pieter Malan
2014 to 2016:	Daryn Smit
2017:	Grant Thomson
2018:	Sen Muthusamy/ Werner Coetsee
2019:	George Linde
2020 to 2021:	Daryn Smit

CLUB CAPTAINS

One of the earliest, most notable of captains was Jack Redfern who led the team during the time Emmott Robinson was pro at the club in the years leading to the outbreak of World War One. Between 1920 and 1923 (including the first championship-winning year of 1921), Jack Isherwood skippered the side. Herbert Walker took over between 1924 and 1926, during which spell Rammy enjoyed their second championship win in 1925.

Arthur Waite captained the side that won the Worsley Cup for the first time in 1939. Geoff Marsden was skipper from 1956 to 1958, during which time the club lifted the Worsley Cup for the second time in 1957. Dally Brooks was captain (1973 to 1974) when Rammy won the championship again in 1974, the club having endured a 49-year wait for the pleasure! Then thereafter -

1975:	Maurice Haslam
1976 to 1981:	Henry Hall
1982 to 1983:	Pete Daggett
1984 to 1985:	Brian Fielding
1986 to 1987:	John Ramsbottom
1988 to 1990:	Jack Simpson
1991:	Maurice Haslam
1992 to 1996:	Jack Simpson
1997 to 1998:	Ian Bell
1999:	Brian Taylor
2000 to 2003:	Mark Price
2004 to 2006:	Richard Hevingham
2007 to 2008:	Simon Read
2009:	Keith Webb
2010 to 2013:	Jon Fielding
2014 to 2015:	Rob Read
2016:	Daryn Smit
2017 to 2019:	Tom Parton
2020 to 2021:	Daryn Smit

ooooo

CLUB'S PLAYER OF YEAR AWARD WINNERS (NB – this highest individual award was introduced from 1961 onwards)

1961	Bill Savage
1962	Derek Hodgson
1963	Terry Stewart
1964	Henry Hall
1965	Trevor Morris
1966	Brian Keating

1967	Richard Wheatcroft/ Duncan Brooks
1968	Geoff Bladen
1969	Terry Stewart
1970	Arthur Chapman
1971	Henry Hall
1972	Michael Galpin
1973	Terry Stewart
1974	John Ashworth
1975	Terry Stewart
1976	Henry Hall
1977	Michael Everett
1978	Maurice Haslam
1979	Ian Bell
1980	John Ramsbottom
1981	Michael Everett
1982	Mark Price
1983	Stephen Ratcliffe
1984	Ian Bell/ Steve Monkhouse
1985	Stephen Ashworth
1986	Ian Bell
1987	Jack Simpson
1988	Stephen Ashworth
1989	Steve Monkhouse
1990	Mark Price
1991	Jon Fielding
1992 to 1993	Jack Simpson
1994	Nick Riley
1995 to 1996	Jack Simpson
1997	Chris Hall
1998	Neil Richardson
1999	Brian Taylor
2000	Michael Haslam
2001	Mark Dentith
2002	Nick Riley
2003	Mark Price

2004	Chris Eardley
2005	Simon Read
2006	David Bell
2007	Michael Haslam
2008	Phil Hayes
2009	Michael Haslam
2010 to 2012	Jon Fielding
2013 to 2014	Tom Parton
2015	Simon Read
2016 to 2017	Jon Fielding
2018	Tom Parton
2019	Jon Fielding
2020	Not awarded due to Covid
2021	Kieren Grimshaw

ooooo

OTHER AWARDS IN ADDITION TO THE WOLSTENHOLME 'PLAYER OF THE YEAR':

As well as honouring the 1st XI player deemed to be 'player of the year'- as shown above - the club has traditionally made a number of other awards, honouring the achievements of players across all different levels of participation in R.C.C. club cricket, including awards made to individual players and also, as in the case of the Danisco Trophy, to individuals making a significant contribution beyond the field of play.

Other awards made on Presentation Evenings - usually occurring in October - include:

Marion Haslam Trophy for 1st XI players' 'Player of the Year'.

John McQueeney Award based on a number of considerations, including sportsmanship.

Coldstream Cup for 1st XI Performance of the Season.

The Stephen Ratcliffe Memorial Trophy for fielding prowess.

Most Valuable Player (MVP) Awards for 1st and 2nd XIs.

Grants Arms Cup for Performance of the Season outside the 1st XI.

Hewitt Cup for Most Improved Player.

Lionel Brocklehurst Cup for 2nd XI 'Player of the Year'.

John Eardley Trophy for 2nd XI all-round performance.
Logan Cup for 3rd XI 'Player of the Year'.
Chris Morris Cup for sportsmanship of the year.
Syd Hird Cup for Under-17 'Player of the Year'.
Danisco Trophy for Club Person of the Year.

ooooo

N.B. – In more recent times, Women's and Junior Presentation Evenings have been introduced, further widening recognition of achievement amongst the whole range of inputs into the cricketing life of the club.

Information about past winners of any or all of these awards can be found on the Lancashire League website by tapping into 'Archive', selecting the respective year and then going to 'Presentation Nights' and viewing 'Ramsbottom'.

About the Author

NIGEL JEPSON LIVES in Ramsbottom and is a keen supporter and member of Ramsbottom Cricket Club.

He first came to the local area in the mid-1990s when taking up post as Headteacher at nearby Haslingden High School. As far as the broader community was concerned, it didn't take long to pick up the vibes regarding the longstanding rivalry between Haslingden and Ramsbottom, much of it existing on a cricketing front as traditional close rivals in the Lancashire League.

Nigel's last UK Head's post was at Kearsley Academy in Bolton from 2010 to 2014. 'Retired', he has though served as interim Headteacher work in Dubai during 2016 and has also carried out teacher training programmes in New Delhi in 2018.

Although having always been keen on team sports, he developed a passion for long distance running which started with the London Marathon in 1982, moving through other events to New York in 2001. More recently, over 2017 to 2019, prior to the Covid pandemic kicking in, he ran four more marathons in Dubai, Belfast, Manchester and Liverpool.

Nigel's list of published work started with fictional writing, including to date:

The Inspector and the Superhead (2000)
Cut and Run (2006)
In a League of His Own (2011)
Speed is of the Essence (2015)

During the last two years, perhaps in some measure as a response to the heightened level of restrictions imposed by Covid, he focussed on writing about the local area in which he lives. This has resulted in the following publications:

Come on you Rams! – The Story of Ramsbottom United Football Club (2020).

Ramsbottom's Revolutionary Doctor – The Life and Times of Peter Murray McDouall (2021).

BV - #0065 - 120522 - C0 - 229/152/16 - PB - 9781914424595 - Gloss Lamination